BERNARDO O'HIGGINS

BERNARDO O'HIGGINS
and the Independence of Chile

Stephen Clissold

FREDERICK A. PRAEGER, Publishers
New York · Washington

BOOKS THAT MATTER

Published in the United States of America in 1969
by Frederick A. Praeger, Inc., Publishers
111 Fourth Avenue, New York, N.Y. 10003
© 1968 in London, England, by Stephen Clissold

Library of Congress Catalog Card Number: 69–11332

PRINTED IN GREAT BRITAIN

Contents

Illustrations

Maps

Foreword

BERNARDO O'HIGGINS belongs to that small band of men who have won a place in history as the makers of Latin American independence. Eclipsed by the genius of the great Liberator, Simón Bolívar, and outshone in strategic brilliance by his friend San Martín, O'Higgins is nevertheless of their company. To him, more than to any other man, Chile owes her independence. Nor is the debt Chile's alone. O'Higgins played his part on the wider American stage, for he also bore arms in the Argentine ranks and devoted himself, and the resources of his country, to the emancipation of Peru.

Yet outside Chile—or at the most, outside Latin America— Bernardo O'Higgins remains little more than a name—and an odd name at that. Behind its curious conjunction of the Iberian and the Hibernian lies the remarkable story of the obscure Irishman who rose in the service of Spain to become Viceroy of Peru. And if the lives of father and son are primarily of importance in the history of Spain and of Latin America, they are also linked in many interesting ways to our own country. The 'English Viceroy', as his enemies maliciously dubbed him, sent his son to be educated in England, and it was here that Bernardo pledged himself to the revolutionary cause and conceived his admiration for liberal institutions. And it was, too, to men from these islands that Bernardo O'Higgins later turned for help in building up the navy which was to play a vital part in the emancipation of the Spanish colonies.

In writing this account of Bernardo O'Higgins' life, I have drawn mainly from the Chilean sources specified in the Bibliographical Note. I should also like to express my thanks to Mr Oswald Hardey Evans and Dr J. Lynch for bibliographical and other suggestions, and to Professor R. A. Humphreys, Dr H. Blakemore and Dr S. Collier for kindly reading the manuscript of this book. The views expressed in it, and whatever errors it may contain, are however my own. I am also grateful to the University of Chile, Santiago, for help in obtaining and permission to reproduce the illustrations.

S.C.

One

An Irishman Enters the Service of Spain

EVER SINCE THE reign of Philip II, Irishmen could be sure of a ready welcome in Spain. It was not only the fervour of their Catholic faith and the ill-treatment they received at the hands of the English which predisposed the Spanish people in their favour; popular belief attributed a common origin to the inhabitants of Hibernia and those of the Iberian Peninsula. Irish soldiers had lent fresh lustre to Spanish arms since the Duke of Berwick had won the Battle of Almansa with their help in 1707, and the three regiments of Irish volunteers—the Irlandia, the Hibernia and the Ultonia—had come to be a valued and most efficient part of the Spanish Army. If they preferred a civilian career, gifted young Irishmen could study at a college specially founded for them in the University of Salamanca. They were free to engage in commerce or even to enter the administration. A royal *cédula* of 1680 provided that they should enjoy the same rights as Spaniards in obtaining official posts to which their merits entitled them, and these privileges were confirmed and extended by a series of subsequent enactments.

By the middle of the eighteenth century, not a few Irishmen had seized the opportunities which Spain offered them with spectacular success. In the 'fifties the post of Secretary of State for Foreign Affairs was held by Richard Wall, an Irishman who had served his adopted country for many years in the Navy, the Army, and the diplomatic service. A decade later, it was an Irish officer, General Alexander O'Reilly, who commanded the loyal troops and suppressed the riots in a rebellious capital. Other Irishmen made their fortunes in commerce and established thriving businesses in Cadiz, engaging in the lucrative South American trade and sending their own representatives to the cities of Peru, Chile, La Plata, Venezuela, Mexico and all parts of Spain's extensive empire.

Connected with one of these Cadiz houses was an Irishman called
Ambrose Higgins. His name first begins to appear in documents
dating from 1757, when he must have been some thirty-seven years
of age. Of his origins and early life we have no information apart
from his own scanty and somewhat contradictory statements and the
accretions of later legend and hearsay.[1] He was probably born in the
year 1720; as to his parentage and place of birth, two different
versions have come down to us. He himself always claimed that he
hailed from Ballinary, in Sligo. In later life, Higgins commissioned
a nephew to go to Dublin and obtain a certified copy of his genealogical tree. This document, which is still preserved in the Dublin
Genealogical office,[2] traces Higgins' alleged descent back through
his parents, Charles and Margaret O'Higgins, and his grandfather
Roger, to John or Shean Duff O'Higgins, 'styled Baron of Ballinary
in the county of Sligo and Kingdom of Ireland, descended from the
Ancient and Illustrious House of O'Neil.' Shean Duff, the document
asserts, had married into the O'Connors, 'the royal family of
Ballintober, *ut audimus*.' Through his maternal grandmother,
Higgins was described as descending from Muredach Mulleathan,
'Sixteenth King of Connaught'. On the strength of this impressive
pedigree, His Most Catholic Majesty in due course authorized
Ambrose Higgins to assume the style of El Barón de Vallenar, or
Baron Ballinary—a somewhat dubious title which we can look for in
vain in the records of Ireland.

Another tradition gives a very different and more modest account
of Ambrose Higgins' origins. It asserts that he was born at Summer-
hill, in Meath, in such poor circumstances that, as a boy, he was
glad to run errands for Lady Bective, the Lady of the Manor, until
being brought to Spain by a kinsman who later became one of the
confessors of Carlos III. Perhaps the truth may lie somewhere
between these two divergent accounts. If we discount the fable of
his family's noble, indeed royal, origin, it is quite possible that
Higgins' parents may have originated in Sligo before coming to
settle in Meath. If they were poor and without prospects, and only

---

[1] For a discussion of this question, see Carlos Vicuña Mackenna: *El orígen de don
Ambrosio O'Higgins y sus primeros años en América* in the *Revista Chilena de Historia y
Geografía*, 1916, Vol XVII, pp. 126–172, and Ricardo Donoso: *El Marqués de Osorno,
don Ambrosio O'Higgins* (1941), pp. 1–10, 46, and 53–4. The version of his poverty-
stricken boyhood was given currency by B. Vicuña Mackenna in his *El Ostracismo del
eneral don Bernardo O'Higgins* (Valparaiso, 1860), pp. 20–21.
[2] Genealogical Office MS. 165, in the National Library of Ireland.

too glad for their children to seek fortune abroad, that was but the common lot of the Irish. Yet there is no need to postulate a youth consumed in grinding poverty and menial tasks. There is evidence that the family was not altogether without resources, and to judge from the man's subsequent attainments—his grasp of subjects so diverse as Greek and engineering, mathematics and geographical science—we suspect that he must have had the benefit of an exceptional education.

The next phase of Ambrose Higgins' life is almost equally obscure. Like other gifted young Irishmen of the day, he may have studied at the college founded for them at the University of Salamanca or at a military academy. George Vancouver, who met him years later during his celebrated voyage round the world, states that 'at an early period of his life he had entered into the English Army; but not obtaining in that service the promotion he had expected, he had embraced more advantageous offers on the Continent.'[1] Juan Mackenna, a fellow countryman and later protégé of the Irishman, maintained with a greater degree or probability that he had begun his career at the modest desk of a bank in Cadiz. We know, at least, from his own statements, that he came to that city in 1751, when he was about thirty-one years old, and lived there for five years, before making the momentous decision to visit America.

This first journey to America seems to have been undertaken chiefly out of a sense of family responsibility. The Higginses were a numerous clan. A younger brother, William, and a later host of nephews, followed Ambrose's example and migrated to Spain. William was intended for the priesthood. By rashly standing surety to a friend who went bankrupt, he lost what money he possessed for his studies, abandoned all thought of entering the Church, and set off to retrieve his fortune in America, where he eventually settled down in Paraguay. Judging his flight from Spain to have been nothing more than an act of youthful imprudence, his elder brother decided to follow him out to America and persuade him to return and resume his vocation. Perhaps Ambrose Higgins was also eager to see what prospects the New World might offer for the advancement of his own career.

In 1756, Higgins left Cadiz for America. He must soon have convinced himself of the futility of trying to induce William to

[1] George Vancouver: *A Voyage of Discovery to the North Pacific Ocean and round the World* (London, 1798), Vol. 3, p. 426.

return, for he found his brother married to a lady of Asunción
and already the father of two children. Since there was clearly
nothing further to be done in the matter, Higgins felt free to turn to
his own affairs. He had business to transact on behalf of the Cadiz
firm of Butler which took him first to Buenos Aires, and thence
across the Andes to Chile and Peru. Here documentary records as to
his activities cease, and legend spreads its colourful tapestry over
the gaps in our knowledge. Tradition has it that the adventurous
Irishman set up his stall outside the palace which he was later to
occupy as Viceroy of Peru. A further picturesque touch adds that
he made friends with a fellow hawker called La Reguera, who later
entered the Church and had risen to become Archbishop of Lima
by the time that Higgins made his state entry into the Peruvian
capital nearly forty years later. All we can say with certainty is that
Higgins remained in Peru for a time to try his fortune in commerce,
perhaps on a modest scale and without much success, for discreet
allusions were later made to these activities in the official address
presented to the new Viceroy.

By the middle of 1760 Ambrose Higgins was back in Spain. He
must have come to the conclusion that prospects were brighter in the
New World than in the Old, for he lost no time in petitioning the
Council of the Indies for naturalization papers which would give
him the right to reside and trade in Spain's overseas possessions.
The Irishman was undoubtedly looking for something more than a
field for fresh markets and rich profits. His own talents were military,
administrative, and political, rather than mercantile. Where could
he find fuller scope for their exercise than in the King of Spain's
vast domains beyond the seas? Carlos III had but recently ascended
the throne, and the cumbrous administrative machinery and decayed
economy of Spain were being galvanized by a series of far-reaching
reforms. The age of 'enlightened despotism' had reached Spain, and
unlimited scope was open to men of progressive views and the
energy to carry them through. No man was more thoroughly
attuned to the spirit of this age, nor more resolved to seize the
opportunities it offered, than this Irishman who had just returned
from the colonies and seen for himself the neglect and sloth in which
they slumbered and their great potentialities for development. But
though certain of his countrymen had obtained high office under the
Crown, Higgins was himself without patrons or influential friends.
The only rung of the official ladder within his immediate grasp

was the exceedingly modest one offered by his friend, John Garland.

Garland was an Irishman who had served first in the Hibernia Regiment and had then been transferred to the corps of military engineers. A year after Higgins' return from America, Garland received orders to report to the Captain-General of Chile. He was authorized to take with him an *ingeniero delineador*, or draughtsman, as his assistant. The post carried with it a rank equivalent to that of Second Lieutenant and a salary of five hundred pesos a year. Modest as the prospects of this appointment were for a man already over forty, Higgins accepted his friend's offer and the two men set sail for America at the beginning of 1763.

The acceptance of this humble office under the Crown did not put a sudden end to Higgins' commercial activities; much subsequent embarrassment might have been spared him had it done so. The expenses of the long and costly journey to Santiago, the capital of Chile, had to be met, and this could best be done by purchasing a consignment of merchandise in Cadiz for resale in America. The last few months before Higgins' departure were spent in collecting these goods and raising the necessary loans with which to pay for them. One promissory note to the value of more than 10,000 pesos was signed jointly by Higgins and another Irish associate called John Power, whose subsequent duplicity in disposing of his share of the goods without contributing a penny towards settling their mutual obligation left Higgins saddled with a burdensome debt for more than thirty years.

Leaving part of his consignment of merchandise in Buenos Aires, Higgins pushed on over the pampa and arrived at Mendoza, at the foot of the Andes, in the middle of June. It was growing late in the season, and the tracks which led over the bleak passes into Chile were already half blocked with snow-drifts which threatened to seal off the Cordillera until the spring sunshine should melt them five or six months later. Mendoza, with its sunny foothills clothed with orchards and vineyards, was a pleasant enough little town in which to linger, but Higgins had no wish to spend the winter months there in idleness. Taking with him three sturdy *chasquis* or porters, he decided to push on. It was a terrible journey. 'Having set out to cross the Cordillera in the winter of 1763,' he wrote of it later, 'I very nearly found myself lost, and I managed to escape with my life only through the special mercy of the Divine Providence and thanks to the valiant porters, one of whom perished.'[1] The experience, far from daunting him, suggested to his practical mind a series of steps which ought to be taken to keep the passes open and to protect the lives of those who had to cross them in winter. The most urgent need seemed to him to be the construction of a chain of stout shelters where travellers could take refuge from the violence of the blizzards. But where other men might have seen this and done no more than grumble at the authorities for neglecting to take such obviously desirable measures, Higgins would not rest until he had elaborated the project and urged it with such persuasive and tenacious conviction that the government finally approved and entrusted him in due course with its realization.

In the meantime, Higgins had his own affairs to see to, and these kept him fully occupied in the Chilean capital whilst awaiting the arrival of his friend Garland who had stayed on in Buenos Aires on similar business. In the middle of December Garland reached Santiago, but it needed all the insistence of the Captain General of Chile before he was on his way to the southern frontier where there was urgent work to be done on the fortifications. The impressionable Garland fell in love with a young lady of the Chilean capital whose father had acquired so considerable a fortune that he had just bought his way into the nobility by purchasing the high-sounding title of Marqués de Quinta Alegre. Doña Rosa was barely twenty-one, but the Irishman was bent on marrying her. The matter, however, was far from simple. It was not enough to win the heart of the girl and the consent of the parents; strict regulations discouraged the intermarriage of officials in the Spanish service and Creole women. The royal permission had to be secured before any such unions could be solemnized. Garland had therefore to rest content with the Captain-General's promise of his good offices in obtaining the required consent, and the reluctant suitor, accompanied by his friend and assistant, set off for the remote and savage solitudes of the Frontier. There the two men threw themselves into their exacting and arduous duties. The months passed, and by the time the king's permission arrived, Doña Rosa had found another husband. The lesson was not lost on Higgins. His friend's fate had shown him that hopes of love and domestic happiness could not be easily reconciled with the stern calls of his career.

[1] *Informe sobre hacer transitable el paso de la Cordillera*, quoted by Donoso, *op. cit.*, pp. 425-8.

Two

The Araucanian Frontier

OF ALL SPAIN'S overseas possessions, the Captaincy-General of
Chile remained not only one of the most remote, but—in spite of its
rich natural resources—one of the most backward and neglected.
Walled off by the mighty chain of the Andes, it was as difficult of
access as an island. A waste of desert separated it in the North from
Peru and the viceregal capital of Lima. To the South, vast stretches
of forest, in whose clearings the warlike Araucanian Indians had
made their homes, blocked the peaceful expansion of agriculture
and interposed their untamed mass between the outposts of Spanish
power. The strongest natural obstacle against the periodic incursions
of the Araucanians was the broad Bío-Bío river. Behind this
bulwark lay Concepción, the provincial capital and the Spaniards'
chief military base, which had nevertheless more than once been
attacked and burnt to the ground by the Indians. One hundred and
thirty leagues south of Concepción, and separated from that city by
the Indian-infested forest, stood the lonely fortress town of Valdivia.
Beyond Valdivia again, the Spaniards had established their further-
most outpost on the island of Chiloé. The settlement of Osorno,
which the conquistadores had founded at a point mid-way between
Valdivia and Chiloé, had been destroyed by the Indians and never
rebuilt. Though these fortresses were thus left without adequate
land communications, both Valdivia and Chiloé could be easily
supplied and reinforced by sea, whilst Concepción had its own
excellent port at Talcahuano, a few miles away.

Ever since the coming of the Spaniards, this southern frontier
had proved a running sore on the body of a young colony, draining
away its life-blood in inconclusive and unremitting warfare. The
defence of the frontier was the constant preoccupation of successive
Captains-General, none of whom had, during over two centuries of
Spanish rule, ever achieved more than a temporary pacification

South America around 1800

or subjection of the Indians. The missionaries had made no more headway than the soldiers, for they had found the Araucanians incurably attached to their traditions of polygamy and plunder, and had totally failed to transform the Frontier into a zone of industrious, peaceful native 'reductions' such as had been established in Paraguay and elsewhere. To the endemic unrest of the Frontier was now added a further preoccupation for the Spanish authorities. Her extraordinarily long and indefensible coastline rendered Chile particularly vulnerable to any hostile foreign power enjoying the command of the sea. In the previous century the Dutch had managed to establish themselves without great difficulty in Valdivia, from which it might have proved almost impossible to dislodge them had they made common cause with the Indians. It was to forestall the danger of another such coup that the Captain-General of Chile was now so anxious to press on with strengthening the fortifications of Valdivia and other Spanish towns in the frontier area.

The town of Valdivia, which then numbered a civil population of about one thousand and a garrison of some two hundred and fifty, lay on the banks of the river of the same name, some sixteen miles from the coast. The plan of fortifications which Garland and Higgins set about drawing up comprised a chain of forts commanding the narrow entrance to the estuary and the anchorage in the bay of Corral. Any vessels forcing a passage up the river would have to run the gauntlet of the Spanish strong-points which, until Admiral Cochrane later carried them by assault, were deemed impregnable from the landward side. The first essential was to complete a thorough survey of the area and to set up brick-kilns, for the work was not started until a quarter of a million bricks had been accumulated. At the same time, light fortifications were thrown up to ward off any surprise attack by the Indians, and the more influential chiefs won over by gifts and flattery, or overawed by a display of force. When the ground had thus been sufficiently prepared, a solemn palaver or 'parliament' was proposed to set the seal on the protestations of peace and friendship which Spaniards and Indians had exchanged.

These 'parliaments' had become a regular and much respected institution on the Frontier, and one which Higgins was later to handle with great skill. The first that he and Garland witnessed was held in December 1764 and was attended by the Captain-General of Chile in person, accompanied by the Bishop of Concepción and a staff of senior officers and dignitaries of state. On the Indian side there came nearly two hundred *caciques* or chiefs, and two thousand four hundred braves. The chief object of such solemn gatherings, Higgins recorded, was 'to propose to them in the name of Our Lord the King how necessary and advantageous it would be to them and to all their people to agree to settle in townships, adopting the Christian and civil mode of life that they saw amongst their Spanish neighbours and the Indian converts. Some of the *caciques* who cherished their liberty and persisted in their customs and in their barbarous ways, showed themselves hostile to this proposal and even to that of accepting missionaries, but the majority agreed and managed to talk the dissentients round, so that all the *caciques* attending the parliament unanimously agreed to settle in the proposed towns, with the result that the President[1] set about the reconnaissance of the country to select suitable sites for the settlements.'

But the results of this 'parliament' were as short-lived as any of the previous attempts to secure a definite pacification of the Frontier. The *caciques* enjoyed the pomp and the palaver of these solemn occasions, and the revelry which followed them, but they had no intention of letting themselves be bound by any of the undertakings given. Five years later, the country was once again the scene of a large-scale Indian rising. Higgins, who at the time was back in the Chilean capital temporarily engaged on his earlier project of constructing shelters in the pass over the Andes, immediately offered his services to the Captain-General and applied for a commission in the field. There was a shortage of good officers, and the Irishman had already proved himself a man of resource and resolution. A commission as Captain of Dragoons was granted him. Thus, at the age of nearly fifty, when other men might well feel beyond the call of active service, Ambrose Higgins embarked upon his military career.

The long and arduous campaign which followed revealed in the new Captain of Dragoons unsuspected aptitudes of an altogether exceptional order. He at once saw the need for raising a body of cavalry able to stand up to the lances and lassoos of the wild Araucanian horsemen. The morale of the Spanish troops was low, and they rarely ventured beyond the safety of their fortified posts.

---

[1] The senior official in Chile combined in his person the offices of Governor, Captain-General of the armed forces, and President of the *Audiencia*, and could thus be referred to by any of these titles.

Higgins advocated the formation of a mounted force trained to fight equally as cavalry or infantry and equipped with light four-pounders. His proposal was accepted and he quickly set about organizing a regiment of a thousand *huasos*—Chilean herdsmen trained to the saddle from infancy—to be known as the Frontier Dragoons. These young soldiers he inspired with his own confidence and offensive spirit so that they were soon able to make sorties against the Araucanian raiders who were laying waste the country on all sides. Higgins wielded his new force with unerring skill. 'So judicious and rapid were his movements,' wrote Juan Mackenna,[1] who had studied the achievements of his career with professional admiration, 'that he succeeded in surprising and attacking separately all the scattered troops of Araucanians either killing or capturing them. These successes gave another aspect to the war. The Spanish troops could leave their forts and sally out into the open, thereby obliging the Araucanians to concentrate all their forces for a general action. After a bloody battle, the Araucanian army abandoned the field to the enemy for the first time during the war.'

Mackenna has left us the following account of the engagement:

Its outcome was the result of the formation in which Don Ambrosio had deployed his regiment. Under cover of a thick wood on the left flank of the Spanish army he led his regiment on as far as he could without revealing their positions. The Spanish army was drawn up in the formation in which it had suffered defeats previously at the hands of the Araucanians; namely, in two lines of infantry, the cavalry being placed on the wings and the artillery in front. The Araucanian forces were composed solely of horsemen armed with lances. Their tactics were to hurl themselves against the line of Spanish bayonets, uttering shrill cries and with their faces covered with their long black hair, quite undeterred by the ravages wrought in their ranks by their adversaries' musket and artillery fire. They were always confident of achieving final victory by throwing back the infantry and putting the cavalry to flight with their long lances which they handled as deftly as their horses.

[1] Letter to Bernardo O'Higgins dated 20 February, 1811, *Archivo O'Higgins*, Vol. 1, p. 90–92. For accounts of his life and friendship with Bernardo O'Higgins *see* Benjamín Vicuña Mackenna: *Vida del General Juan Mackenna* (Santiago, 1902) and Raul Téllez Jánez: *El General Juan Mackenna, héroe del Membrillar* (Santiago, 1952).

When the Araucanians saw that the Spanish army was ready
to receive them, they lost no time in launching an attack with
their accustomed fury, but suffered no little surprise and
confusion on finding themselves suddenly attacked in their
turn by a torrent of cavalry which fell upon their right flank
when they had advanced too far to retire, at the very moment
they received the discharge of the artillery and small arms.
The valiant Araucanians were scattered in headlong flight. In
this battle Don Ambrosio received a head-wound which,
fortunately, was only slight, and his bearing in that engagement
laid the foundation for the respect and consideration in which
he was always thereafter held in the country of Lautaro.

But the war against the Indians was not the sort that could be
conclusively decided by pitched battles. The advantages gained by
the Spaniards, thanks largely to the energy of Higgins and the
efficiency of his new Frontier Dragoons, were followed by further
'parliaments' and alternating spells of pacification and renewed
unrest. The situation was complicated by the alliance which the
Araucanians had concluded with the Pehuenches, a nomadic tribe
living in tents, on the Eastern slopes of the Andes and on the
Argentine pampa. These Indians refused to make peace and for
two years Higgins was engaged in the difficult task of subduing
them. Gradually, through a judicious mingling of severity and
conciliation, the region was pacified. Old forts were re-established
and new ones constructed. The Araucanians were invited to send
envoys to the Chilean capital, where they were received with a show
of respect highly flattering to their proud spirit. The Spanish
settlers began to return to their devastated homesteads, and white
traders hawked their wares again amongst the Indian *rucas*. Over
all these activities, the indefatigable Higgins kept a watchful eye.
He knew that it was from the sale of their cattle and their hand-
woven *ponchos* and blankets that the Araucanians were able to keep
themselves supplied with arms, yet he nevertheless believed that
trade was the mightiest of civilizing agents which would in time
bring quiet and contentment to the region in a way which the
missionaries and soldiers had failed to do. There were some
Spaniards who frankly held that the Araucanian question could
only be solved by the annihilation of the natives by force of arms,
or by fomenting their civil wars. Others thought that a more effec-

tive way was to encourage their natural weakness for indulgence in strong liquors. Higgins was shocked by the cynicism and folly of these views. 'Humanity, the right of nations, and the sovereign justice of the King,' he wrote, 'do not permit us to entertain these atrocities, all the more so when they could only result in turning the country into a desert.'

The arduous years on the Frontier won for Higgins the steadily growing regard of his superiors, and his successive promotion through the grades of lieutenant-colonel, brigadier, *maestre de campo* or Commander-in-chief of the Frontier, to that of Governor of the whole province of Concepción. At the age of sixty-six, the Irishman thus found himself in full control of an area of vital strategic importance, on whose prosperous tranquillity depended that of the whole of Chile. The territory comprised by the province was extensive. It stretched from the confines of the Araucanian lands south of the Bío-Bío to the waters of the other great river, the Maule, which divided it from the province of Santiago. With its fertile soil and equable climate, the potential wealth of the region was immense, but development had been retarded by the unremitting preoccupation with defence. The city of Concepción had more the aspect of a pioneer settlement or military base than that of a provincial capital. Higgins himself, with his friend Garland, had reconnoitred and recommended the site which it now occupied, for it had previously stood some miles away on the coast, where earthquakes, storms, and tidal waves had added their share of devastation to the ravages of the Indians. By the last quarter of the eighteenth century, its population comprised some 700 *vecinos*, or householders, with ten times that number of other Spaniards, Creoles, and Indians. The streets of the town were laid out in the usual geometrical fashion but the houses were modest one-storied affairs of mud and adobe.

Concepción was also the seat of a bishopric, whose incumbent saw in the reforming zeal of the new Governor a challenge to his own authority. In the intervals of attending to weightier matters, the secular and ecclesiastical authorities waged a minor war of precedence and protocol. The Governor of Chile was appealed to, and after much consideration and consultation of advisers, laid down such momentous rulings as to how often, and for how long, each dignitary should honour the other with an official visit, how each should be received, attended, and seated in divine service, and which positions each should occupy in formal processions. Co-operation between the ecclesiastical and civil authorities was essential in that troubled region, for the Governor was anxious to encourage the founding of new mission stations in Indian territory as means of opening regular communication between Valdivia and Chiloé. But despite all his tact and conciliatory gestures, Higgins' relations with the Bishop were never more than outwardly correct. 'God alone knows how much I have suffered,' he later complained to the Court, 'from the opposition I have unjustly encountered from the Right Reverend the Lord Bishop and his followers.'

Once there occurred an incident which caused an enormous sensation throughout the country and all but cost the Bishop his head and the Governor of Concepción his good name. The Bishop decided to undertake a prolonged visitation of his diocese. Fearing that he might be molested by the incorrigible Araucanians, the Governor offered to provide a strong escort, but the Bishop haughtily refused. All went well until reports of the rich baggage-train of clothes, food and Church treasure which the Bishop was carrying with him reached the Indians and aroused their instincts for plunder. At length, a horde of armed savages emerged from the forests and fell upon the Spaniards, seizing first their possessions and finally their persons. The few faithful Indians who accompanied the Bishop, seeing that they were powerless to moderate the fury of their countrymen, hit upon the desperate expedient of suggesting that a *chueca* match—the traditional team-game, like a form of primitive hockey, beloved of the Araucanians—should decide the fate of the prisoners. The sides were formed, the match played, the friendly Indians were beaten, and the Bishop and his followers prepared themselves for martyrdom. Then someone cried out that it should be the best of three games. The teams reformed, the *chueca* sticks swooped and smacked and the friendly Indians proclaimed a victory. We may imagine with what anguished interest the little party of Spaniards followed the fortunes of the third and final game, and with what prayers of thanksgiving they hailed the victory of their friends. The savages who had hugely enjoyed the whole episode and perhaps were secretly more interested in the enjoyment of the booty than in making martyrs, cheerfully kept to the agreement and released their captives. As soon as the news of their adventures spread through Chile, a public outcry arose that the perfidious and impious Araucanians should be taught a lesson which they would never forget. Higgins saw only too clearly what would be the outcome of a punitive expedition; a few hundred Indians swinging from the trees, a few villages burnt, and an embittered, warlike, and vengeful people waging an inconclusive war from the depths of the forests for years to come. So he turned a deaf ear to the clamour for revenge and contented himself with recovering what he could of the Bishop's possessions. But if some pitied the Bishop for his ordeal and others admired him for his fortitude, there were many who murmured that the Governor had been but luke-warm in his rescue-work and strangely indulgent in not punishing the offenders.

Behind this endemic unrest of the Indians and the friction of local rivalries loomed the ever-present danger of attack by some hostile European power. In the autumn of 1779, Higgins received news of the breaking off of diplomatic relations with Great Britain and instructions to take all possible defensive measures. 'I have ordered the immediate removal of all herds of cattle from the coast of Arauco,' he reported to the Viceroy of Peru, 'to prevent our English enemies from being able to provision themselves from them as they have done on previous occasions.' Reinforcements were sent to the garrisons at Valdivia and Chiloé, though Higgins feared that this depletion of the frontier troops might tempt the Indians to take up arms again. But the British attempted no landing, and the danger passed.

A few years later—in February, 1786—fresh alarm was caused by the appearance of a foreign ship off Talcahuano, the port of Concepción. The ship flew the French flag and proved to be on a scientific expedition despatched by the French government under the command of the Comte de la Pérouse. Higgins had always taken the liveliest interest in matters of exploration and geographical enquiry. Now he found himself torn between his desire to meet the Frenchmen and hear about their voyage, and his suspicions that they might find a pretext to spy out the land to further the aggressive designs of the French government. His doubts deepened when La Pérouse made a request for permission to send a party overland to examine the volcano of Antuco—a proposal which he believed his personal enemies had deliberately suggested to them 'in order to turn the resentment of the French against me should I refuse them, or else to charge me subsequently with culpable conduct should I accede to their request.' Higgins therefore politely excused himself

from complying with La Pérouse's desire by alleging the disturbed
state of the Indian territories through which they would have to
pass. And, to counter the belief in the Spaniards' harsh treatment
of the Indians which he thought the French had derived from the
ill-intentioned accounts by English travellers of previous centuries,
Higgins was careful to dilate on the enlightened attitude which the
Laws of the Indies and his own administration had always taken
towards the Araucanians, and the many 'parliaments' which had
been freely held with them. The Irishman's persuasions were not
without effect. 'After an hour's talk with him,' La Pérouse records,
'he won my complete confidence, as he had won that of the Indians.'[1]

When their visit drew to a close, the Frenchman decided to
invite a hundred and fifty of the leading ladies and gentlemen of the
country to a lavish picnic on the sea shore, followed by a dance and a
fireworks display. Higgins, for his part, staged a still more splendid
entertainment for his French guests. He rode down to Talcahuano
and escorted them back to his house in Concepción where the local
notables and their ladies were assembled to meet them. A Franciscan
priest of poetic turn of mind introduced each fresh course by reciting
Spanish verses 'to celebrate the happy union which reigned between
our two nations.' A great ball followed, the ladies adorned in their
most splendid attire and some of the officers, in fancy dress, staging
a ballet. 'Nowhere in the world,' La Pérouse concludes his account,
'could one see a more enchanting entertainment offered by a man
adored throughout the land to foreigners reputed to be the most
gallant nation in Europe.'

Higgins' reception might have been less cordial could he have
foreseen one result of La Pérouse's expedition. The Frenchman's
glowing account of the natural advantages and resources of Chile
did not pass unnoticed in England, and led in 1808 to the British
Government's plan to conquer the country through a naval and
military expedition under the command of General Crauford—an
expedition only diverted at the last moment to Montevideo.
Accounts of important voyages, drawing attention to the economic
and strategic attractions of the little known lands visited, could have
a considerable influence on the formation of national policy.
Higgins himself was most impressed by a copy of Cook's *Voyages*
with which La Pérouse presented him. He read the book with
avidity. Its importance seemed to him so great, as indicating the

---

[1] *Voyage de La Pérouse autour du Monde*, (Paris, 1798), Vol. 2, pp. 78–9.

growing interest taken in the Pacific by foreign powers, and suggesting lines of exploration and development which Spain might profitably follow up for herself, that he drew up a special despatch on the subject which he sent to his patron, the Marqués de Sonora, at the Court. 'I am well aware,' he wrote, 'of the extensive knowledge which Your Excellency has of the world in general, and of New Spain in particular, and I would therefore not venture to obtrude, still less to express an opinion, on this subject from this remote corner, were it not that it is something entirely new and that Cook's narrative may possibly not yet have reached your hands.' Higgins then went on to draw the Minister's attention to the significance of Cook's achievements and the necessity of revising existing maps and charts in their light. He emphasized the desirability of Spain's promoting a similar scientific expedition of her own.

That these urgings did not pass unheeded at Court we may infer from the decision taken some time later to send out a Spanish scientific mission under Captain Malaspina on the lines advocated by Higgins. The Governor of Concepción had shown himself to be the sort of man who not only knew how to hold troublesome Indians in check, but could direct his gaze beyond the Frontier to perceive whatever things were needful for the safety and welfare of His Catholic Majesty's far-flung domains. The Marqués de Sonora died soon after Higgins had penned his despatch, and the Irishman thought it opportune to urge his convictions once more on the Crown. This time his words could have still greater force, for he was now able to sign himself Governor, President and Captain General of Chile—the exalted office to which His Majesty had been pleased to appoint him by a decree of 28 January, 1787.

Three

The Birth of Bernardo

THE DESTINY WHICH brought an unknown Irishman from the humble rank of second lieutenant to the Governor's palace within the space of little more than twenty years may seem to us an eventful and singularly propitious one. But to the sternly ambitious spirit of Ambrose Higgins, labouring amidst the moist forests of the South, the years sometimes seemed to drag by with oppressive monotony and threatened to bring old age upon him before he could achieve the supreme offices to which he aspired. 'Some are destined for advancement,' he complained bitterly to a friend, 'others merely for hard toil.' He feared that the very remoteness of his field of operations from the centres of official authority in Spain and Spanish America might be enough to condemn him to obscurity and he clutched eagerly at any opportunity to leave the Frontier and press his cause in person in Santiago, Lima or Madrid. It is these interludes in his career, together with another episode that contrasts strangely with what we otherwise know of his life and character, which we may now pause to consider.

Ever since he had nearly perished on the snowy heights of the Andes, Higgins had cherished a scheme for the construction of a chain of shelters across the pass. His motives in pressing his views upon the Spanish authorities were not purely humanitarian; there were compelling economic and political arguments as well. For nearly six months in every year, communications linking Chile with Mendoza and Buenos Aires were interrupted. Not only was the despatch of merchandise suspended, but all normal postal communications ceased as well. Vital news such as the outbreak of war or important political changes could only reach Santiago through a lengthy detour via Potosí and Lima. When war was declared between Spain and England in 1762, for instance, the despatches addressed to the authorities in Santiago on this important event were held up in Mendoza for more than four months.

Three years later, Higgins was authorized to leave his duties on the Frontier and come to Santiago to supervise the work of the construction of his *casuchas*. These were stout brick-built structures, something like modern air-raid shelters in appearance. They measured some fourteen foot square, and the vault of the roof sloped sufficiently steeply to allow the snow to slide off. Higgins brought considerable ingenuity, as well as his customary energy and regard for economy, to their construction. A draft of convicts was placed at his disposal to assist the masons, whilst the muleteers, who stood to gain most from the innovation, were induced to bring back loads of material free of charge on their way home from their trips across the mountains. Higgins had proposed that the shelters should be equipped with a few essential utensils and articles of furniture, and kept supplied with fuel and rations. But these were soon rifled by less scrupulous travellers, whom Higgins too readily assumed to be animated by his own spirit of progress and public responsibility.

By the winter of 1766, the work was sufficiently advanced for a postal service to be maintained across the passes without interruption on account of bad weather. But the change of climate and altitude had begun seriously to affect Higgins' health. With the satisfaction of knowing that the back of the task which he had set himself was now broken, he obtained leave to return to Spain in order to re-establish his health. He was also eager to obtain from the Court some recognition of his services and the promise of further advancement.

Back in Spain, Higgins met with a frankly indifferent reception. But he would not let himself be discouraged. If he had no friends or relatives to apply to, Higgins knew of one influential fellow-countryman who might recognize and help to reward his merit. Richard Wall had retired two years before, after a brilliant career in Spanish politics and diplomacy. Wall received him affably, but he could not have bothered to recommend him very warmly at Court, for Higgins never succeeded in obtaining an audience of the Minister for the Indies. To all his petitions for some administrative post in Peru or elsewhere, Higgins met with the reply that he should return to his work as assistant engineer and to his salary of 500 pesos a year. But one advantage he did secure. Before he left Spain, he was commissioned to submit a report on Chile—a task to which he eagerly applied himself, submitting in due course his *Description of the Realm of Chile, its products, commerce, and inhabitants; reflexions on its present state, together with some proposals regarding the reduction of the heathen Indians and the progress of these dominions of His Majesty.*[1]

The *Description of the Realm of Chile* gave Higgins an opportunity of displaying his shrewd insight into the problems of Spanish America and of propounding statesmanlike views on how to deal with them. The memorandum began by describing Chile's rich natural resources in mines and agriculture. He went on to draw attention to the country's slow rate of progress which he held could only be accelerated by encouraging greater numbers of industrious settlers from Europe. He even discreetly hinted that it would be advantageous for Spain to modify her traditional commercial monopoly and permit some freedom of trade—a revolutionary change of policy which the Spanish government adopted eleven years later. But Chile's fundamental need, Higgins urged, was to find a permanent solution to the Indian problem. He suggested that the Frontier should be pushed forward beyond the Bío-Bío to the line of the Toltén river, whence regular communications should be established eastwards, over the Andes, with the province of Buenos Aires, and southwards, by a series of forts, to Valdivia and Chiloé. The Indians should be treated firmly, but with justice and understanding. Their language and customs should be studied by the missionaries in special colleges, and functionaries appointed to act as intermediaries between Indians and white men, as had been done with success in Canada. Mission-stations, the nuclei of future settlements, should be planted too in the remote and still barbarous regions of the Magellan Straits and Tierra del Fuego—a project which had to wait for nearly a hundred years for its fulfilment.

What consideration was given to Higgins' memorandum by official circles in Spain it is not easy to say. Two dramatic events were then absorbing general attention—the British occupation of the Falkland Islands and the expulsion of the Jesuits from all Spanish domains. That Britain might harbour designs against the mainland of Spanish America was commonly suspected, and Higgins ventured beyond the terms of reference of his memorandum to advocate the effective fortification of likely ports on the coast of Patagonia and the

[1] Reproduced in Donoso, *op. cit.*, pp. 430–444.

construction of a line of forts, around which colonies of settlers could develop, across the wild pampa, as far as the Chilean frontier. The memorandum did not speculate on the effect which the expulsion of the Jesuits was likely to have in Chile, but on the map which Higgins prepared to go with his manuscript, the location of each Jesuit mission is carefully indicated. Perhaps he took the opportunity of urging at least verbally on Wall and others a project which he had much at heart. He wished to encourage large-scale Irish immigration and to use the Jesuits' confiscated property in strategically important areas for Irish settlements which would serve as defence posts against possible English aggression and also help in the general development of the country. Had not the American War of Independence attracted the main stream of Irish emigrants northwards, Higgins always maintained that South America would have acquired a large and valuable Irish element in her population.

Nearly five years after his return to Chile Higgins had another opportunity of pressing his claims in person on the Spanish authorities. In 1773, he was given leave to go to Lima to report to the Viceroy in detail on conditions on the Frontier. Higgins was no stranger to the City of the Kings; he had lived there for some time as a modest merchant in the obscure period of his life about which little is known. But now he must have looked at the teeming and splendour-loving city around him with different eyes. The Viceroy Amat ruled over a gigantic territory stretching more than 3,500 miles from Panama to the south of Chile, and some 3,000 miles overland from Lima to Buenos Aires. Under him were ranged seven subordinate commands, each worth a kingdom in itself; Chile, Quito, New Granada, Tierra Firme, and the River Plate provinces of Tucumán, Buenos Aires (soon to be created a separate Viceroyalty) and Paraguay. Over this vast area, sustained by a somewhat creaky administrative machine and a handful of regular troops, brooded the long peace of colonial Spain, shaken only by occasional tremors of Indian unrest and by the first stirrings of something which few men suspected was to grow into a sense of nationhood and a desire for national independence. Seven years after Higgins' visit to Lima, Peru was shattered by the terrible convulsion of Tupac Amaru's Indian rebellion. This was repressed with severity; but reforms followed, old abuses were removed and a more effective administration under the *intendencia* system introduced. For the

spirit of enlightened despotism, with its confident belief in perfecta-
bility by decree, had spread from Spain to her overseas possessions.
It drew together men of sanguine outlook and public spirit, opening
splendid careers to their energies and talents. As he listened to the
grave discourse of the Irishman from Chile, his account of what had
been achieved on the Frontier, his zealous labours, and his plans
and aspirations, the Viceroy Amat recognized in Higgins a man
animated by the new spirit, a man of whom much could still be
expected for the greater glory of the Crown. After three months in
Lima, Higgins returned to his duties with the warmest commenda-
tion of the Viceroy and his promotion to the rank of Lieutenant-
Colonel.

Amat had grown rich through his years as Viceroy, and no small
part of his fortune had been lavished on his mistress, the famous
Perricholi. Higgins could not have failed to observe the splendid
palace which he had built for her amidst the flowering orchards on
the outskirts of Lima, proclaiming the place which she held in the
viceregal affections and in the society of the capital. To keep a
mistress with such ostentation offended neither piety, convention,
nor the royal command; to take a wife would have been a much
more hazardous business. Spanish officials, from Viceroy down-
wards, were strictly forbidden to marry into local families in order
to preserve the administration from all taint of nepotism. Permission to marry could be sought from the Crown and might, in
exceptional circumstances, be granted. But years could elapse
between the submission of a petition and its granting, and in the
meantime, the lady might well grow tired of waiting. Higgins
remembered how the courtship of his friend John Garland had
ended.

Whether Higgins himself had ever thought of marrying we do
not know. If he had had affairs of the heart before devoting himself to
affairs of state we know nothing of them. We see him only in middle
age—a distinguished but hardly an attractive figure, sturdily built,
with strongly marked features, bushy eyebrows, and a high complexion which earned him the nickname of *el camarón*—the shrimp.
He was scarcely a man one might suspect of amorous adventures.
Yet behind the stern exterior, beneath that dedication to duty and
the calculated pursuit of power, there must have lurked some
tenderness of heart to which circumstances denied all but a fleeting
and belated expression. Some four years after his return from Lima,

when the incessant round of military duties claimed him once again, Higgins found himself enamoured of a girl almost forty years younger than himself.

Isabel Riquelme was the daughter of a respectable Creole land-owner whose estate lay near the town of Los Angeles, the military headquarters of the Frontier. The Riquelme family claimed to trace its descent back to the Conquista and beyond, for their crest showed a rich helmet or *rico yelmo* which an ancestor was reputed to have won in combat with the Moors, thereafter taking the name in memory of the deed.[1] Isabel's mother had died shortly after her daughter was born, and the girl had been brought up by her father, Don Simón, and his second wife, Doña Manuela de Vargas. When her beauty first began to touch the elderly Irishman's heart she could not have been more than eighteen; indeed, some accounts say that she was no more than a child of thirteen or fourteen. Isabel Riquelme was small and slender, with jet black hair and expressive, deep blue eyes. The beauty of her oval face and finely moulded features was set off by a complexion whose porcelain delicacy she retained, together with her sweet gentleness of disposition, into old age.

The course which this strange courtship took and the strategy which succeeded in winning the heart of the young Creole girl for the enamoured veteran, we can only conjecture. She may have yielded—as her son claimed later—to the solemn promise that her lover would obtain the King's permission to marry her. It is even said that Higgins had secured the formal consent of her father for the union. But the Irishman showed no signs of jeopardizing his career by hurrying to redeem his pledge, if indeed he had ever seriously intended to do so. The fruit of their brief idyll was born, in all secrecy, in the neighbouring town of Chillán, on 20 August, 1778, the feast of St Bernard, whose name was given to the boy. Bernardo spent his first four years in the care of foster-parents, for his mother was soon to wed a respectable neighbour and kinsman. But her marriage was of short duration; Doña Isabel was left a widow in 1782, after giving birth to a daughter called Rosita.

One day, when Bernardo had grown into a round-faced, four-year old boy with blue eyes, chestnut hair, and a rosy complexion

---

[1] For an account of the history of the Riquelme family, see Luis Roa Urzúa: *Casa Riquelme de la Barrera* in the *Revista Chilena de Historia y Geografía*, Vol. 54, No. 58 p. 389.

which bespoke his father's origin, a small detachment of dragoons rode into Chillán with orders to remove the child. They brought him to an estate belonging to Don Juan Albano, an elderly Portuguese friend of Higgins who had settled near the town of Talca. Albano had a son called Casimiro, some five years older than Bernardo, and the two boys soon became inseparable companions. Albano took his charge to be secretly baptized in the parish church of Talca, and the following document is still preserved in the church archives to bear witness to Bernardo's parentage:

I, Pedro Pablo de la Carrera, priest and vicar of the township and parish of Saint Augustine, Talca, do hereby certify and bear witness, as is required by law, that on the twentieth day of the month of January of the year 1783, in the parish church of this township of Talca, I christened and conditionally baptized an infant named Bernardo O'Higgins, who was born in the Bishopric of La Concepción on the 20th day of August, 1778, being son of the Commander of the Frontier Forces of this Kingdom of Chile, and Colonel in the royal armies of His Majesty, Don Ambrosio O'Higgins, bachelor, and of a lady of quality in that bishopric, also unmarried, whose name is not given here for the sake of her reputation. The said child Bernardo O'Higgins is in the charge of Don Juan Albano Pereira, resident of this township of Talca, who informs me that the child was sent him by his father, the above mentioned Don Ambrosio O'Higgins, to care for his upbringing, education, and doctrine, as is vouched for in his letter which he has written for this purpose, and which is held by the former duly signed, and which also charged him so to arrange matters that the child may at all times be able to prove that he is his son. And I baptized him conditionally, as it was not possible to ascertain whether he had or had not been baptized when he was brought to me, nor who may have been his godparents in order to enquire from them whether he had been properly baptized. Godparents at this conditional christening and baptism were the said Don Juan Albano Pereira who has charge of him, and his wife Doña Bartolina de la Cruz; and so that there may be a record of it I hereby certify these things at the request of the said Juan Albano Pereira in this township of Talca, on 23 January, 1783, and I have copied it in this book so that it may serve as an entry to which I bear witness.

DON PEDRO PABLO DE LA CARRERA.[1]

Though he had thus provided for the boy and ensured that Bernardo's parentage, though now kept secret, should be well attested, Higgins was soon again absorbed by his military and administrative duties and showed no apparent concern for his son. It was only when he was stricken by a sudden fever that he decided to send post-haste for a friend to whom he wished to confide his secret and make arrangements for the boy's future. This was an Irishman called Thomas Dolphin or Delfín, who had established himself in Concepción as a merchant. To him Higgins entrusted the whole story of the brief Indian summer of his heart, and confessed that his conscience bitterly reproached him for the wrong he had done to Doña Isabel. Now that he feared that he might die— and Albano, too, was growing old—he asked Dolphin to promise to bring the boy up. The detailed instructions which he proposed to draw up in his will would lay down how he wished this to be done. But the will seems never to have been made, for Higgins recovered and was soon absorbed afresh in the exacting cares of government. Dolphin was sent to visit Bernardo and report to his father how the boy was shaping. Another friend was let into his secret as well. Juan Martínez de Rozas, the brilliant young lawyer from Mendoza whom Higgins had chosen as his legal advisor or *asesor* in the provincial administration, was shown the boy and informed of his real parentage.

In the autumn of 1788, when Bernardo had reached the age of ten, the calm life of Albano's country house was interrupted by an unaccustomed stir. There arrived a stout, stern-faced gentleman whom the master of the house received with mingled deference and affection. The stranger spoke to the boy in grave and measured terms and gazed down at him with more than casual interest. He was the representative of His Majesty the King, they explained to the child; the newly appointed ruler of the land who was on his way to his palace in the capital. We do not know whether they revealed to him too that the visitor whom he had now seen for the first and last time in his life was also his own father.

---

[1] *Archivo O'Higgins*, Vol. I, p. 1-2.

Four

Governor-General of Chile

SANTIAGO, THE CAPITAL of Chile, was at that time a city of some thirty thousand inhabitants. Though lacking any special distinction of architectural style, it had the advantage of a salubrious climate and a fine natural position in the fertile central valley of Chile. It was backed by the magnificent snow-capped wall of the Andes and washed by the Mapocho river, whose unruly waters the new Governor lost little time in containing by the construction of powerful embankments. Designed on the chess-board pattern usually preferred by the Spaniards, the city was divided into *cuadras* or squares, each originally comprising the house and gardens of the conquistadors who founded it. The central *cuadra* had been left free to form the principal plaza, round which the Governor's palace, the unfinished cathedral and other public buildings were grouped.

Whilst Higgins made a two days' halt on the outskirts of Santiago waiting for the heavy rains to abate, the capital prepared to receive the Governor with the pomp customary on such occasions, but with somewhat mixed feelings. The common people were frankly out to enjoy a splendid spectacle and the festivities for which the *cabildo* had voted the sum of fifteen hundred pesos. But the wealthier classes awaited the coming of the new Governor without enthusiasm and, in some quarters, with real resentment. For all his long and distinguished career on the Frontier, Higgins remained in their eyes a foreigner and an upstart. The *cabildo* had petitioned the Crown to appoint a candidate of its own choice, and felt slighted by the nomination of the Irishman. The wealthy land-owners, many of whom kept houses in the capital and formed the most influential part of society, were too easy-going and set in their privileged ways to share the Governor's passion for reform. And, indeed, there was much that cried out for reform, both in the capital and in the life of the nation as a whole. It was customary for each Governor to mark his advent to power by issuing a special proclamation known as a *bando de buen gobierno* exhorting the citizens to lead an orderly and God-fearing life, and setting forth a number of detailed rules for their observance. As the same regulations figure over and over again in successive *bandos*, we may take it that the citizens were often lax in their observance and stood in need of frequent reminders. They enable us to form a good picture of the existing state of society, its habits, tastes, and aspirations, and the limitations of the human material and institutions which an energetic Governor like Higgins would encounter.

In standards of cleanliness and hygiene, the capital set but an indifferent example to the rest of the country. Higgins' *bando* found it necessary to forbid the inhabitants to let their pigs roam at will through the streets, do their laundry in the *acequias* or public irrigation streams, or throw into the streets the clothes of patients who had perished by infectious diseases. The morals and civic duties of the inhabitants were the subject of still closer solicitude. Men were exhorted to refrain from oaths and blasphemies, from carrying arms, brawling, gambling, indulging in provocative dances or repeating satirical or salacious couplets. Every citizen must do his bounden duty to God and the King, close his shop or office at nine in the evening in winter and ten in summer, and then stay quietly indoors until morning. Erring husbands were ordered to return to their wives, beggars and idlers to join the army or leave the country within three days, and revellers in carnival time warned to keep their pranks within bounds. In the customary observances of Holy Week—and here we can note the good sense of the new Governor, whose piety had little in common with the prevailing bigotry of the day—penitents were no longer permitted to scare the life out of women and children by parading through the streets scourging themselves or staggering under immense crosses.

If the shortcomings of the capital could be reformed by *bando*, the country at large was beset by ills for which it was less easy to prescribe a remedy. Next in importance to the Indian problem, to which Higgins had devoted so many arduous years, was the grave economic crisis through which the country was passing. Though trade between Spain and her possessions was still the preserve of her own subjects, the ancient monopoly first of Seville and then of Cadiz, with the periodic sailing of the *flota* along a set sea-route, had been abolished and trade could now be freely carried on between all major ports. This liberalization of commercial policy, at which Higgins had discreetly hinted twenty years before in his *Description of the Realm of Chile*, had at last come about. Its effects were spectacular and often disconcerting. In the decade before Higgins' governorship, the value of the whole South American trade is said to have increased sevenfold. But in the last year of that period, Chile's imports rose so steeply that they amounted to three times the value of her exports. These imports were largely European goods such as fine clothes and furniture which a poor country could scarcely permit itself the luxury of enjoying. But if the public's appetite for such hitherto almost unobtainable goods seemed insatiable, the bottom of its pocket was soon reached. The glut of goods which resulted caused the bankruptcy of sixty Santiago merchants—a large number in a city of limited mercantile enterprise. The picture of a national economy which consumes and imports more than it produces and exports is sadly familiar today; it was something new, but no less disconcerting, to the Spanish colonies at the end of the eighteenth century.

The Governor's reaction to this grave situation was typical of his vigorous and sanguine character. Whilst others demanded a return to the old restrictions, Higgins was convinced that this increased flow of imports would raise the standard of living of the Chileans by bringing them the refinements of European civilization. The problem was simply how to pay for them by increasing the country's productivity and exports. This the Governor proposed to achieve in a number of ways; by revitalizing old industries such as mining, which had been allowed to stagnate, by creating new sources of wealth such as sugar, rice, tobacco and cotton, by building up a merchant fleet to market these goods, and by founding new towns as fresh centres of commercial expansion. The natural field for these ambitious developments was the north of Chile. Previous Governors, absorbed by the Araucanian problem, had seldom been able to spare much thought for this neglected region. But Higgins, who knew the southern Frontier like the palm of his hand and who could see that, for the moment at least, all was quiet there, felt free to undertake a prolonged tour of inspection of a province of which he had little first-hand knowledge but great hopes.

The Governor set out on his long journey with a suite comprising his *asesor*, an engineer, a chaplain, a number of secretaries and subordinate officials, and an escort of a couple of dozen dragoons.

Progress was slow and exhausting. There were few roads and no inns. For some of the way, the party travelled by a small coasting vessel. The Governor was now nearly seventy but he was as vigorous and resolute as ever and he inspired those around him with his own reforming ardour. Wherever they passed, he overhauled the haphazard machinery of local administration and scanned the countryside for the sites of new towns and the sources of fresh wealth.

In the far north, separating Chile from Peru, stretched hundreds of miles of desert which had not yet begun to yield up its hidden stores of nitrate and copper. Between these waste lands and the fertile central valley of Chile lay an intermediate zone of small valleys and half-sterile hill country ranged by shepherds and by prospectors in search of silver. Mines had been worked there from the earliest times, but methods were antiquated and production had declined. Higgins was convinced that with modern techniques these mines could be made to increase their yields spectacularly. European experts were urgently needed to reorganize them. Baron Nordenflicht, a noted minerologist, had already been contracted by Peru, and Higgins tried to induce him to visit Chile as well, but the great mines of Potosí claimed him fully. The Governor decided that there was nothing for it but to attempt the experiments himself. He commissioned an engineer to construct a special apparatus for this purpose, and some time later we find him writing to his friend and fellow-countryman, Thomas Shee, in Coquimbo; 'I have been trying out various experiments in my house, which though they have not yet corresponded to my hopes, still less to my desires, I am still persevering with.'

Attempts to improve and diversify the country's agriculture met with difficulties of a different order. The wealthy landowners who had long reigned supreme in this neglected province viewed the Governor's coming with distrust. Few of them showed any eagerness for innovations which might well prove highly rewarding. Higgins urged on them the advantages to be expected from growing sugar, which flourished well in Peru and could, if introduced into Chile, save that country the expense of importing it from her northern neighbour. Only one improving landlord was growing sugar on his estates and though he placed a quantity of seedlings at the disposal of the Governor who had them replanted in suitable sites, the other landowners were but luke-warm in following his example. Attempts to stimulate the growth of rice and cotton met with a similarly half-hearted response.

The trouble was partly the prevailing shortage of labour and the antiquated—and in Higgins' view, unjust—system on which it was still largely based. In the early days of the colony, the first Spanish settlers had been given *encomiendas*—grants of Indians, whom they were supposed to protect and instruct in the Christian faith, in return for the use of their labour. Originally some degree of economic compulsion was probably essential if the land was to be cultivated, for the Indians were averse to the drudgery of sustained agricultural work. The system lent itself to many abuses, and attempts had been made earlier on in the century to declare its abolition, for the conditions originally justifying it had changed, and few Indians were now in fact affected by it. But the landowners had bitterly opposed any attempt to interfere with their privileges and the system had been allowed to continue. Higgins was determined to put an end to it once and for all. He made a point of speaking to the Indians still on the *encomiendas* and making a thorough investigation into the conditions under which they lived. He found that their lot was one of virtual slavery, for they were bound to labour in the mines or on farms all the year round with no other return than some coarse cloth for clothing and a diet of dried goat-meat and onions for the support of themselves and their families.

Higgins' indignation at the treatment of these Indians was so great that he thought of calling their masters to account before the law. But he decided instead to limit himself to proclaiming the final abolition of the *encomienda* system, which he did in a decree dated 7 February, 1789. This inevitably deepened the hostility of the landowners who protested bitterly to the Court that they would be ruined. But the Crown endorsed Higgins' action. The Governor was confident that the *encomienda* system had been largely to blame for Chile's backward economy. He also hoped—no doubt too optimistically—that its abolition would encourage the wild Araucanians to live peacefully with the Spanish settlers without fear of enslavement.

Another cause of the backwardness of the North was the inadequacy of the towns. Even La Serena, capital of the province and next in importance to Santiago and Concepción, was little more than an overgrown village. Higgins was determined to promote the growth of towns as centres of commercial expansion and civic progress and during his tour of inspection in the north he founded no less than five new ones. One of these—which was also the slowest to prosper—he christened Vallenar, in memory of his native Ballinary. Another was Los Andes—a town carefully sited one day's march from the summit of the pass which Higgins had done so much to improve, where travellers had hitherto been obliged to camp in the open. These new foundations were tenaciously opposed by the rich landowners who regarded them as a menace to their privileged position and preferred to see mineworkers and labourers grouped in wretched settlements round the comfortable *haciendas* which employed them. Even the small proprietors, who stood to gain from being given free plots on the site of the new towns, often refused to move into them. Some the Governor had to threaten with banishment; others only stirred when he sent a party of men armed with hatchets to pull down their old homes.

Higgins saw the sources of the North's potential wealth in her mines, her agriculture, her new towns—and in the sea. *Congrio* and other excellent fish were plentiful, and would make a valuable addition to the monotonous diet of the poor. Chile needed more merchant ships and cadres of trained sailors in time of war. But the fishermen could not develop their industry because of the selfishness of the landowners who refused to let them use the sea shore on their property, or levied a tax in the form of a proportion of their catch. Higgins sought to end this abuse by declaring that the shore could be freely used by fishermen for a distance of a hundred yards above high water mark. Then, with the help of his friend Delfín, from Concepción, he tried to encourage the formation of regular fishing companies.

Nor was it only the material conditions of the poor which excited the Governor's stern compassion. The parish priests too often neglected their spiritual needs and denied them the consolations of religion. Higgins found that many of the poor were living without having entered into any form of marriage, and that their children were consequently illegitimate, for the parents would not or could not pay the marriage fees demanded by the priest. The Governor wrote to the Bishop of Santiago urging him to remedy this sad state of affairs.

Such reforms and improvements as the Governor was able to achieve were accomplished in the teeth of suspicion and opposition

2*

from the bulk of the Creole aristocracy, whom Higgins found
jealously attached to their privileges, set in their ways, and deplorably lacking in public spirit. He was too prudent a man to clash
openly with them except where this was unavoidable for the success
of his plans of reform; he was generally able to get his way by
cleverly playing off one set of vested interests against another. Yet
the Governor was well aware that the Creoles would never accept
him as one of themselves. His very name seemed to them barbar-
ously unfamiliar; in early documents we find it appearing in the
most fanciful of versions; Higges, Ignes, Ihiggyns, Egis, Hexiz.
Though he inwardly scorned their pretensions and condemned
their selfishness, he was aware that his origins placed him at a
disadvantage and secretly cast about for some way of strengthening
his social position. It was then that an ingenious idea occurred to
him. The Crown had shown him repeated favours and marks of
confidence, but had not hitherto accorded him any rank, beyond the
purely military, commensurate with his present importance. He had
petitioned for the coveted Order of Knighthood of Santiago,
but in vain; perhaps the Crown would be readier to recognize a
title of nobility allegedly inherited from Ireland, his country of
origin. The Governor resolved to entrust his nephew Demetrio
Higgins, who had also entered the Spanish service, with the
delicate task of obtaining proofs of his descent from a noble Irish
house which would allow him to adorn himself with a suitable title
in Chile.

In July 1788, Demetrio succeeded in obtaining from Sir
Chichester Fortescue, Knight Ulster and King-of-Arms of Ireland,
a document tracing his uncle's alleged descent from a certain Shean
Duff O'Higgins, styled Baron Ballinary. Though the authenticity
of this claim was vouched for by a respectable kinsman of the
petitioner and endorsed by no less a person than the Spanish
Ambassador, it is difficult to regard the pedigree as anything more
than a polite fiction, for no record exists of any barony of this name.
Nor may its acquisition have proved a straightforward business,
since Demetrio, for reasons unknown to us, seems to have waited
for nearly seven years before forwarding the documents to the Court
of Spain. But shortly after this a royal *cédula* was issued authorizing
the Governor and Captain-General of Chile to assume the title and
sign himself henceforth Baron of Ballinary, or, in its Spanish form,
El Barón Vallenar. Don Ambrosio O'Higgins—to give him the

name as he now signed it—must have received the news with satisfaction and (if we can suspect so serious a personage of such levity) with his tongue in his cheek. Though mindful always of the dignity of his high office he was singularly devoid of petty vanities. He kept the ostentatious display of rank and authority to the state occasions where it rightfully belonged.

One such occasion occurred not long after the Governor had assumed office. On 14 December, 1788, Carlos III died, and the reign of the monarch whose zealous belief in the principles of enlightened despotism accorded so well with that of Higgins came to an end. The news only reached Santiago the following April, and it was not until seven months later, when the northern tour of inspection was over that the new monarch was ceremoniously proclaimed. The festivities were preceded by the public display of portraits of the new King and Queen which were hung in heavy silver frames above the entrance to the Governor's palace. Three days later, when the public had been given time enough to familiarize itself with the features of the new monarch, the Governor left his palace in state and mounted a dais which had been raised in the *plaza*. He was accompanied by a train of civil dignitaries and the chief citizens of the capital, and he bore the royal standard in his hands. An added novelty was the presence of four Indian chiefs representing the King's Araucanian subjects. After the King-of-Arms had called for silence, Higgins addressed the Indians through an interpreter, after which they knelt down and kissed the royal standard, thereby swearing homage and fealty to the new King, to the admiration of the assembled multitude. The Governor then stepped forward and raised the standard aloft, crying out three times in his sonorous voice: 'For Spain and the Indies! Long live King Carlos IV!' At this, the bells of the city began to peal, a royal salute was fired from the fort of Santa Lucia, and the people began cheering and shouting 'Long live the King!'

The Governor and his train then went in solemn procession through the city and the ceremony was repeated. The streets were lined with militiamen, and the houses on the route had been freshly whitewashed and hung with tapestries and embroidered cloths. Everyone had donned their best clothes, and many rode on richly caparisoned horses. Money was distributed to the poor, and medals to the rich. A strikingly attired lady with a powerful voice recited an ode extolling the virtues of the new monarch.

As night fell, the city was illuminated and the fireworks bursting in many-spangled splendour over the roof-tops were answered by the glow of bonfires on hill-top and mountain-side. On this and succeeding nights, the Governor gave a series of banquets for the nobility, the members of the *cabildo* and the *audiencia*, and the chief military, political and ecclesiastical figures in the country. Never did a people seem more attached to the institution of monarchy nor more fervently loyal to the person of the sovereign. It did not occur even to the ever watchful Governor that the replica of the Wooden Horse of Troy, which was amongst the carnival figures dragged in gaiety through the streets of this stronghold of royalism, could be a symbol of dire prophecy.

Five

England – Friend or Foe?

BY THE BEGINNING of 1792, unmistakable signs of unrest were once more appearing amongst the Indians in the Valdivia area. Now that he had completed his inspection of the north, the Governor decided that he must turn his attention again to the southern Frontier. It was time to hold the solemn 'parliament' customary on the appointment of every new Governor-General. For the meeting-ground, O'Higgins chose the field of Negrete, near the fort of Los Angeles, where several similar assemblies had previously been held.

This was destined to be O'Higgins' last journey to the Frontier, and as befitted his age and the dignity of his office, he made it not on horseback but in a stout carriage drawn by four strong mules. On his arrival in the south, he found the tribes torn with feuds, though their fighting had not yet involved the Spanish settlements. For two months the Governor negotiated patiently with the warring chiefs, trying to induce them to lay down their arms and be reconciled. At the last his persuasions were crowned with success. The 'parliament' was summoned and attended by an array of high officials and some 1,500 soldiers on the Spanish side, whilst the Araucanians mustered 187 *caciques* and nearly 2,500 braves. The proceedings opened with a speech by the Governor couched in the pompous rounded phrases which appealed so greatly to the Indians.[1]

> Chiefs! My ancient and honourable friends! Full of joy and satisfaction that I now meet upon this happy ground of Negrete, as formerly on that of Longuilmo, the great chiefs and principal leaders of the four Butalmapus, into which this valuable country is divided, that stretches from the south of this great river Bío-Bío to the outer parts of the most southern continent, and from the Cordillera to the great ocean; I salute

[1] The English version of O'Higgins' speech is given in Vancouver, *op. cit.*, pp. 446–8.

you all with joy and with the utmost sincerity of my heart. I am ordered by the King, my master, to salute you in His Majesty's name, and to congratulate you on the felicity of this auspicious day which, through my mediation, on account of the love I bear you all, has restored the inestimable blessings of peace to the four Butalmapus.

With the utmost precision and despatch, I have taken care to remove every obstacle that impeded the attainment of this most welcome object. I have also been indefatigable in disposing to peace the minds of those who were restless and prone to revenge or to take great umbrage on little occasions; and I have been unwearied in all the conferences I have had with the several chiefs, since my arrival at the fort of Los Angeles, and in this encampment, during the time that I have waited for the arrival of those more distant leaders, who are now collected with the other members of this assembly. I have patiently and fully examined the complaints of some, and heard the excuses of others, on the distressing subject of your dissensions, your animosities, and your wars, so that nothing now remains for me to learn of all their dire causes. Today, however, the sun shines bright, and I see, with heartfelt joy, that on my once again drawing nigh unto you, a kindly disposition appears in all to terminate the unhappy differences which long, too long, have subsisted between you; and I perceive that you are prepared once more to unite in those sacred bonds of peace, in the full enjoyment of which I left you on my departure for Santiago. I rejoice that you all wish to bury, under the sod of this encampment, all your animosities, heart-burnings, disputes, and differences; and may the present meeting be a commencement of perpetual felicity to all the children of man who reside in the countries that extend from the Bío-Bío to Chiloé.

The orator then recalled the state of Araucania when he first came to them—'desolate and laid waste, and all its inhabitants suffering the dreadful calamities of unceasing furious wars, brought on by their own intemperance and unruly passions; many of whom were obliged to retire, with their women and children, to the mountains and were reduced at last to the necessity of feeding on their faithful dogs that followed them.' The Governor then outlined, in contrast, the conditions of peace and prosperity which prevailed when he left them. He praised the Indians for keeping their pledges to refrain from attacking the Spanish settlements and concluded by assuring them of the King's favour so long as they remained his loyal and law-abiding citizens. The speech made a great impression and must have inspired the Indians to emulation, as no less than eighty-three Araucanian orators took the floor before the 'parliament' was done. By the time they dispersed, the Indians had consented to bury their differences and to live at peace amongst themselves and with their white neighbours. They had also agreed that Spaniards could pass freely through their territory without first obtaining the permission of the *caciques*. This was an important concession, as news had just been brought to O'Higgins that the ruins of Osorno, the town which the Spaniards had established midway between Valdivia and the island of Chiloé and which had been utterly destroyed by the Araucanians in 1600, had been discovered. The Governor resolved to refound it. Its position was of strategic importance for his overland communications, and it stood in a fertile country which could be made to support a large population and so exert a civilizing influence on the savage Araucanians. The refounding and prosperous development of Osorno was to remain a favourite project of O'Higgins until the end of his life. Lastly, the Indians pledged their word that they would render no assistance to any enemies of Spain who might try and establish themselves on American soil. This, too, the Governor regarded as most important, for his imagination was keenly alive to the danger of foreign invasion.

Of the foreign powers whose designs were most to be feared, England and France ranked first. Though the sympathies of the Bourbon dynasty in Spain had been for France, the latter country might now be regarded as the greater menace. Ever since the Revolution had shattered the old order, the contagion of subversive ideas had been coupled with her expansionist aims. The cordial days of La Pérouse's visit were past. When, in 1792, a French frigate, the *Flavia*, came in search of the La Pérouse expedition which was then feared lost, O'Higgins accorded it a very different reception. Though he had orders from Spain to render the Frenchmen assistance, O'Higgins felt it prudent to take the most stringent precautions. He sent troops to patrol the shore and kept an armed boat within gunshot of the ship to prevent landing or any communication with the inhabitants.

Such measures as these were, however, powerless to exclude the spread of 'dangerous ideas' entirely. Medals, watches, snuff-boxes and other knick-knacks bearing symbolic figures representing the triumph of the French and American revolutions found their way into the country despite strict customs regulations forbidding their importation. Books somehow circulated in spite of a still more rigorous scrutiny. Though the *Encyclopaedia* had been banned since 1784, some of O'Higgins' closest friends and associates, such as his *asesor* Juan Martínez de Rozas, were known to be avid readers of works of dangerously liberal sentiments. The watchful eye of the Governor-General ranged the furthest corner of his country for the slightest signs of subversion. When the University of Chile held a debate, in which some of the disputants were rash enough to challenge the idea of the divine right of kings, O'Higgins immediately intervened, sending a sharp note to the rector instructing him to report fully on the affair and give him the names of those who had supported the heretical motion. He even ordered that private correspondence might be intercepted when occasion seemed to require it.

If the danger of the spread of subversive ideas was most serious from the French, the abuse of contraband and the desire to get a foothold on the mainland were probably greater from the side of England. The Spanish doctrine that the South Seas were a Spanish preserve had always been challenged by the English from the time of Drake and the early buccaneers. A royal *cédula* of 1692 had laid it down that any foreign ships, even those of allied nations, should be treated as enemies if they were found without authorization in those waters. Did the rule still stand? 'My archives contain no instructions, either of ancient or recent date,' he wrote in April 1791 to the commander of a Spanish war-ship, 'regarding the navigation of these seas by foreign vessels, nor do I know of any treaty in which their freedom to do so is stipulated.' Practical sense dictated compromise; if foreign vessels were intercepted on the high seas, it was enough for a Spanish commander to enquire their destination and let them proceed. If they were stopped in territorial waters, they should be brought into a Spanish port, as it could be assumed they were bent on unlawful trading. But what if a foreign ship had put into a Spanish port suffering from damage, and her crew prostrated by scurvy? Needlessly harsh measures were repugnant to O'Higgins' humanitarian sentiments, and he was prepared to extend help as far as circumstances allowed. But some-times these privileges might be abused and a dangerous precedent established. When an American frigate in need of repairs put into Juan Fernández, the island of Robinson Crusoe, which was a traditional port of call for buccaneers, he punished the Governor's laxity by dismissal.

The famous incident at Nootka Bay brought matters to a head and threatened to precipitate war between Spain and England. Spain's ultimate recognition of the right of British vessels to fish in the Pacific seemed to O'Higgins a most dangerous concession opening a breach in the Spanish bulwarks against foreign interven-tion. He saw that it might lead to the English attempting to establish friendly relations with natives and found settlements in unpopulated parts of the South American coast or islands. He instructed his naval officers to keep the sharpest look-out against this, and promul-gated a draconian decree of 2 February, 1792, threatening the death penalty against any Spanish subjects entering into unauthorized contact with foreigners:

> The frequency with which English and other foreign ships have been putting into the ports of Peru and the island of Juan Fernández, under the pretext of whaling, leads me to fear that should these expeditions be repeated and the natives grow familiar with the sailors, trading posts would soon follow, to the great harm of these lands...I therefore order and command that no inhabitant of this country should have dealings nor contact with a crew bound for Valparaíso, nor with any other who may put into the same port, under pain of death.[1]

The war against France, in which Spain and England became allies, saw a further break-up of the old Spanish monopoly and a relaxation of these stern measures. By a royal decree of 25 March, 1793, the Spanish authorities were instructed to give whatever assistance might be required by English warships. Thus, when George Vancouver reached Valparaíso two years later, after visiting Nootka Bay and exploring the whole west coast of America, he was able to put into the Chilean port to request help in obtaining medical treatment for his crew and repairs for his ship. O'Higgins sent a cordial message inviting Vancouver and his officers to visit Santiago, and dispatched a couple of Irish dragoons to act as guides

[1] Donoso, *op. cit.*, p. 257.

and interpreters to them. In his *Voyage of Discovery* Vancouver has left us an interesting account of his visit to the Governor-General and his impressions of O'Higgins' life and character.[1]

O'Higgins was fond of comparing the physical structure of a country to the anatomy of the human body; the heart being the capital, and its roads being the arteries which carried the life-blood to its extremities. Of these arteries, the most important for Chile was the road connecting Santiago with its chief port, Valparaíso. Though it had been in use since the earliest days of the colony, this road was nothing but a rough track, exceedingly dangerous to life and limb when crossing the three ridges which lay between the capital and the coast. The desirability of improving so important a highway was self-evident, and the Governor determined to undertake it. But here again, as in so many of his most needful reforms, he found himself opposed by resentful and suspicious landowners who imagined that the new road would somehow be a threat to their independence and spoil the amenities of their estates. In the teeth of this opposition and of considerable technical difficulties, O'Higgins persevered with his plans, and by the time Vancouver set foot in Chile, the new road was nearing completion. It was a great achievement, though the work was somewhat rough and ready, as might be expected from the general backwardness of the country and the primitive resources at the Governor's disposal. Vancouver has left us the following description of the work in progress:

> There were about fifty men at work with common pick and shovels; and to supply the place of wheel-barrows for the removal of earth from the higher to the lower side of the road, the hide of an ox was spread on the ground, and when as much earth was thrown on it as would require the strength of two men to remove, the corners of the hide were drawn together by them, and in that state dragged to the depressed side of the road, and emptied where requisite, to preserve a gentle slope in the breadth; or else discharged over the brink and sent down the side of the hill...The lower side or brink had neither bank or earth, nor rail of wood, as a fence; nor did we understand that any form of protection was designed to be made, the want of which gave it a very unfinished naked appearance and...it appeared to be dangerous in a high degree.

[1] Vancouver, *op. cit.*, pp. 412–9.

In spite of the hazards of this unfinished highway, Vancouver and his party safely reached Santiago where they received a 'polite and cordial reception from Don Ambrosio.' They were brought straight to the palace where the Governor greeted them warmly and in fluent English, which astonished them 'when we were informed by his Excellency that he had now been resident in New Spain twenty-four years, during which time very few opportunities had occurred to him for speaking English. We now learned from Don Ambrosio himself that he was a native or Ireland, from whence he had been upwards of forty years, that at an early period of his life he had entered into the English army; but not obtaining in that service the promotion he had expected, he had embraced more advantageous offers on the continent.'

The English officers were entertained to dinner at which 'all sort of ceremony was laid aside.' They found the Governor very interested to hear the details of their exploration of the north-west coast of America. He also recounted 'with great indignation' an episode which occurred when England and Spain were at war and when Sir Edward Hughes was sent out to the East Indies via Cape Horn with secret instructions to attack Spanish colonies in the Pacific coast, beginning with Concepción, where Higgins was then Governor. The Irishman added that it was only because he reinforced the garrisons and improved fortifications that the British did not carry out such an attack.

When Vancouver and his party retired to rest in the palace, they found their beds 'tolerably good, but we could not help being much disgusted at the insufferable uncleanliness of our apartments; the floors of which were covered with filth and dirt.' When they asked for brooms to be brought, they were told 'such things were not in common use in Santiago; the only alleviation we could obtain was that of water to sprinkle the dust, which was so thick in the officers' apartment that it would rather have required a shovel than a brush for its removal.'

The following Sunday morning, the Governor-General held a levée, which Vancouver and his party were invited to attend. 'The room, which is spacious, was neatly, but not extravagantly furnished; the ante-chamber was large in proportion, and the entrance to each was from the ground, through large folding doors. In the ante-chamber were the portraits of the several presidents of Chile, from the first establishment of the Spanish authority in this part of the country to the present Governor, whose portrait was one of the number. The inside walls of these rooms were covered with glazed tiles, resembling those from Holland, for about eight or ten feet from the floor, which had a good effect, and was a great relief to the dead white plaster of the remaining part up to the ceiling. At the upper end of the audience room was a small stage raised a few feet from the floor, upon which was placed the chair of state, ornamented with a canopy of red damask, and decorated with the portraits of their Catholic Majesties, which were placed on either side of the chair.' Vancouver was embarrassed by the threadbare appearance of his party, amidst so many gorgeous uniforms, but the Governor soon put them at their ease by recounting to everyone how many trials and dangers they had successfully passed in their important mission. The levée was followed by another—more ceremonious still—in the Bishop's palace, after which they returned to lunch with Don Ambrosio at about two in the afternoon. This meal was 'served on a plain deal ill-constructed table, by no means corresponding with the magnificence of the dinner service which was entirely composed of silver.'

Vancouver and his brother officers returned to their ship well pleased with their reception at the hands of the Governor. 'His Excellency's character,' he records, 'not only in respect of his great attention and urbanity to strangers, but of his parental care and constant solicitude for the general happiness and comfort of all the people who lived under the government, were the constant topics of our conversation.' O'Higgins, for his part, was probably no less pleased with their visit, for he liked to converse with well-informed and intelligent travellers, specially when they could bring him news of the scientific and geographical discoveries in which he took a lively interest. Though they were Protestant and English, temporarily allied with Spain but her traditional and still potential rivals, whilst he was an ardent Catholic, the Governor was singularly free from prejudice. As a zealous believer in enlightened despotism, he admired the public spirit, the political and administrative abilities, and the progressive outlook of the British. His enemies were later to taunt him with the epithet of 'the English Viceroy' and to spread slanderous reports of how he was planning to betray the southern outposts of Chile to the English. The contrary, we know, was the truth; for the Governor was adamant in all matters concerning the defence of his territory.

O'Higgins was soon to give a singular proof of confidence in England and its institutions. During his years as Governor of Concepción and then of all Chile, his natural son Bernardo had grown to adolescence. Although his father, in the interests of a dedicated career, had dared to see him but once and kept his very existence a secret from all but his most intimate friends, he had devoted much thought to the question of his upbringing. His constant fear was that he might die before his son had been well placed in life. But how to reconcile his obligations as a father with those of a high official, and ensure a good education for the boy without prematurely revealing the circumstances of his birth? O'Higgins first sought to solve the problem by sending Bernardo to the college at Chillán which had been founded to educate the sons of Araucanian chiefs, and where a few white boys were also accepted. So Bernardo Riquelme (for he kept his mother's name) grew up to have young Araucanians as his playmates, and to learn their language and take pride in the heroes of their race. But tongues began to wag, and the secret of the boy's origin was rumoured abroad. His mother, too, was now the subject of fresh scandal. The young widow had never remarried, but had formed an attachment to a neighbouring *hacendado*, Manuel Ignacio Puga, and had born him a daughter, Nievecita, in 1790.[1] It was these cirumstances which led, later in the same year, to the arrival in Chillán of an emissary from the Viceroy to remove Bernardo from school and take him in all secrecy to Talcahuano, where O'Higgins' Irish friend Delfín was waiting to put him aboard a ship bound for Peru. A few weeks later, Bernardo found himself wearing the black suit and cocked hat of the pupils of the Royal College of San Carlos,—an institution founded by the Jesuits for the education of sons of high Spanish officials. How the boy took to this sudden change and the more spacious life of the viceregal capital we do not know. Once more, the unseen hand of his father was outstretched to guide him to new destinies. After four years in Lima, he was removed from school by Don Ignacio Blake, another Irish friend and old business associate of O'Higgins, and put on board a ship for Spain. Thence he had instructions to proceed to

[1] Manuel Balbontín Moreno and Gustavo Opazo Maturana: *Cinco Mujeres en la vida de Bernardo O'Higgins* (Santiago, 1964) p. 87. Nieves was brought up mainly by her father and never became so intimate with Bernardo as did his other half-sister, Rosita. She married an Irishman, John Agustine Borne, who served in the Chilean navy and was killed in 1819.

England, where he was to complete his education. He must have arrived in London at the age of sixteen or seventeen, sometime in 1794 or 1795—the year in which a royal decree elevated his father to the supreme office of Viceroy of Peru.

Six

London and Lima

WE KNOW LITTLE of how Bernardo spent his first years in England except that he probably felt strange and lonely, and suffered from being kept short of money. His father had appointed as his guardian Don Nicolás de la Cruz, a son-in-law of the kindly Juan Albano, in whose country house Bernardo had spent much of his boyhood. Don Nicolás had left Chile to settle in Cadiz, where he had amassed a considerable fortune by trade. He was a cultured man, and spent much of his time travelling in Italy, adding to his library and art collections, and in translating a history of Chile. But he seems to have taken only the most perfunctory interest in his charge, whom he soon shipped off to England. Bernardo found himself without friends in a strange land.[1] The allowance of £300 a year which his father is reported to have made him should have been more than enough for his needs, but little seems to have got beyond his guardian's agents in London. Fragments of letters and bills have survived amongst Bernardo's correspondence recording the sordid wrangles which took place on this score with Spencer and Perkins, the rather dubious firm of clockmakers who were supposed to be looking after him financially.

Soon after his arrival in London, Bernardo went to Richmond, where he lodged in the house of a Mr Eeles and began to receive tuition in English, French, geography, history, music, drawing, and other subjects. Here he seems to have been happy enough, and soon formed a tender attachment to his host's daughter, Charlotte. Long

[1] In his *Memoria de Bernardo O'Higgins* (Santiago, 1844), Casimiro Albano declares that whilst O'Higgins was in England, 'the English aristocracy, so singular in the world for the simplicity of its manners, admitted him into its circle', and that he was even presented to the King and the Royal Family, 'where we may infer that at this time he participated in the highest circle of English society.' This appears to be a flattering invention of Bernardo's boyhood friend, and is extremely unlikely from the evidence of such documents as survive.

after he had left England, when many turbulent years of war and revolution lay between, Bernardo still remembered Charlotte Eeles with affection and sent a friend to enquire after her family and bring back her picture. Bernardo had developed into a sensitive, warm-hearted boy, passionately devoted to a mother from whom he had been long and reluctantly parted. For his father—that august and forbidding personage whom he had seen but once and who remained coldly aloof to his son's proffered affection—he cherished sentiments of respectful veneration, tinged with an unspoken resentment which was later to find an explosive outlet elsewhere. Now, as he grew to manhood in a strange land, scarcely knowing his parents or the name to which he had a right, undecided as to where his loyalties lay, and uncertain as to the career he should follow, he took up his pen and haltingly begged counsel of his father;[1]

My dearest father and benefactor [he wrote on 28 February, 1799] I pray Your Excellency will excuse my using this term so freely, for I do not rightly know whether I may address you thus or not; but if I must choose between the two expressions, I will follow the inclinations of nature (having no other guide), for had I different instructions I would obey them. Although I have written to Your Excellency on several occasions, fortune has never favoured me with any reply, being seemingly hostile to me in this; but I still trust that she will at length relent and grant my desires. Your Excellency must not think that I presume to complain, for in the first place this would be taking a liberty to which I have no right. I know that it is to Your Excellency that I owe what education I have so far received. I am now twenty-one years old, and I have not yet embarked on any career, nor do I see any likelihood of doing so. I wish to join some naval academy if I can manage it, to learn the career to which I feel myself most attracted, and so hope that, as I have already written in previous letters which I trust Your Excellency received, you will decide about it as seems fit and proper, seeing that I feel myself well suited to it, and that a career of arms can bring advancement and

---

[1] The first historian to examine Bernardo O'Higgins' private papers was Benjamín Vicuña Mackenna. They included an exercise book containing the drafts of the letters which Bernardo had written to his father when in England. The exercise book was bequeathed by Vicuña Mackenna to the Biblioteca Nacional in Santiago from where it has since disappeared. The extracts used by Vicuña Mackenna are reproduced in Vol. I of the *Archivo O'Higgins*.

honour with it at present, which is certainly what I would like
and feel I have some aptitude for, so that I eagerly await Your
Excellency's orders to obey and undertake as you dispose, confident that my duty and intention is only to please you. I will
give Your Excellency a brief account of the moderate progress
which I am making here in my studies which are English, French
geography, history ancient and modern, etc., music, drawing,
and the exercise of arms, in the last two of which I can say without boasting that I am tolerably proficient, and I should very
much like to send Your Excellency some of my paintings,
specially the miniatures, did not present circumstances prevent it.

Bernardo Riquelme.'[1]

If the distant Viceroy could not or would not offer the love and
counsel of which his son stood in need, there were others nearer at
hand ready to mould the young man's impressionable nature and
warm him with the flame of their own inspiration. One of these was
a South American with an adventurous, romantic past and a burning
faith in his country's revolutionary future. His name was Francisco
Miranda. In the intervals of scheming to enlist the help of England
to further his plans for the emancipation of his native Venezuela, he
earned his living as a teacher of mathematics. In Bernardo, Miranda
found a pupil of no particular aptitude for his science but of fine
malleable stuff for his revolutionary ideals. Miranda's passionate
denunciation of the evils and injustice of Spanish rule and his belief
in the rights of her overseas possessions to independence and nationhood fell on his young pupil's ears with the force of a revelation.
Here was a generous and noble cause to which a man might fittingly
devote his life. Bernardo thought of his Araucanian playmates and
the tales of their heroes who had died fighting to preserve the liberty
of their race against the Conquistadors. He thought of how his
mother's honour had been sacrificed to a career in the service of the
Spanish Crown. He looked around at the people amongst whom he
was now living and saw how proud and prosperous they were with
their parliament and their constitutional liberties. He began to forget
his own miseries and perplexities in the noble dream of his people's
independence.

Miranda had hoped to use Bernardo as a courier who would take
back to his countrymen a promise of British assistance should they

---

[1] *Archivo O'Higgins,* Vol. i, pp. 6–7.

attempt a rising against Spain.[1] But the British government was
cautious and would not commit itself. So Miranda had no summons
to revolutionary action to entrust to his young convert, but instead,
after testing him carefully for a year and a half, and being convinced
of his absolute trustworthiness, he summed up his beliefs, the lessons
of his experience, and his advice for future action, in a sort of political testament for the younger man. Bernardo had no idea when or
how the opportunity would come of striking a blow for the revolutionary cause, but he treasured Miranda's document with the
greatest care—if found by the Spanish authorities it might have cost
him his life—and after copying it onto thin paper he kept it sewn
up in the lining of his clothes. The document ran as follows:

ADVICE OF AN OLD SOUTH AMERICAN TO A YOUNG COMPATRIOT
ABOUT TO RETURN TO HIS COUNTRY FROM ENGLAND.

My young friend,
The warm interest which I entertain for your happiness
prompts me to offer you some words of advice before you
enter the great world in whose waves I have been tossed for so
many years. You know the story of my life, and can judge
whether my advice deserves to be listened to.

The frankness with which I have opened my heart to you is
proof of how highly I esteem your honour and your discretion,
and the proffering of this advice is evidence enough of the high
opinion which I have formed of your good sense, for nothing is
more foolish and at times more dangerous that to give advice to
a fool.

When you leave England, never forget for an instant that
outside this country and the United States there is not another
land where you can risk speaking a word of politics except to an
intimate friend.

Choose your friend therefore with the greatest care, for
should you prove mistaken you are lost. On several occasions
I have mentioned the names of various South Americans in
whom you could have confidence, should you happen to come
across them, which is unlikely as you live in different parts of
the continent.

Having but slight acquaintance with the land where you

---

[1] *Archivo de Miranda*, (Caracas, 1938) Vol. XV, pp. 169 and 351.

reside, I cannot give you my opinion on the education, qualities, and character of your compatriots, but to judge from their greater remoteness from the Old World, I should esteem them correspondingly ignorant and bigoted. In my long connection with South America, you are the only Chilean whom I have met; I have therefore no means of judging your country save from what has been published of its history and which shows it in a favourable light.

From the facts revealed in this history, I would expect much of your countrymen, specially those from the South, where, unless I am mistaken, you are thinking of settling down. Their wars against their neighbours must have made them familiar with handling arms, whilst the proximity to a free people must have brought to their minds the idea of liberty and independence.

Returning to the question of your close friends, I would have you mistrust every man who has passed the age of forty, unless you know him to be an assiduous reader of those books which have been banned by the Inquisition. Other men are too set in their prejudices for there to be any hope of their conversion, and it may even be dangerous to attempt it.

Youth is the age of ardent and noble feelings. Amongst the young people of your acquaintance you will be sure to find those who are ready to listen and be easily convinced. But, at the same time, youth is the age of indiscretions and rash deeds. You will thus have as much to fear from these defects in young men as from the timidity and prejudices of the old.

It is also a mistake to imagine that every man with a tonsured head is necessarily a blind slave, a bigoted fanatic, and a declared enemy of the rights of man. I know by experience that amongst this class are to be found some of the most enlightened and liberal men of America, but it is very difficult to get to know them. They know what the Inquisition is, and that their every word and act is weighed in its balance, and that however much indulgence may be shown to an irregular life, there can be none whatsoever for a liberal opinion.

Always bear in mind the difference which exists between the character of the Spaniards and that of the Americans. The ignorance, pride, and fanaticism of the Spaniards are invincible. They will look down on you for having been born in America and detest you for having been educated in England. So keep them at arms length. The Americans, candid and sociable, will be eager to hear of your trials and adventures, and you will easily be able to form some idea of their intelligence by the sort of questions they put to you. You must pardon their profound ignorance and consequent immaturity and judge their character by the degree of attention which they pay to what you tell them and how intelligently they evaluate it, and bestow your confidence accordingly.

Never permit despondency or doubt to invade your mind, for once this happens you will be incapable of doing any service to your country. Rather fortify your mind with the conviction that not a single day will go by, after your return to your country, without something occurring to shock you by the folly and wickedness of mankind and lead you to despair of ever overcoming the obstacles to which they give rise. This I have always striven to impress upon your mind and I would desire you to be always aware of it.

You love your country; nourish this sentiment constantly; strengthen it by all possible means, for only through its force and persistence will you be able to achieve any good.

With regard to the probable destiny of your country, you already know my ideas, and even if they were unknown to you, this would be no place to discuss them.

Read this paper through every day of your voyage and then destroy it. Do not forget the Inquisition, nor its spies, its dungeons, and its tortures.

Francisco Miranda.[1]

Whilst Bernardo was struggling between filial submission and the call of a revolutionary crusade, Don Ambrosio O'Higgins was immersed in his viceregal duties. Only the faintest whisper of the gathering storm penetrated past the guard of halberdiers, resplendent in their blue uniforms with facings of gold lace, their silken stockings and velvet shoes, to reach him as he toiled at his desk or

---

[1] There are several versions extant of this document, two of them given in Vol. 1 of the *Archivo O'Higgins* (pp. 19–25), with amendments added in the *Primer Apendice* to the *Archivo* (1962), p. 2–4. The text, presumably written by Miranda in Spanish, has survived in the English rendering made by Bernardo's secretary Thomas, and was first re-translated into Spanish by Benjamín Vicuña Mackenna for his life of O'Higgins.

sat in state, beneath a canopy of crimson velvet and the sombre portraits of his predecessors in office, to receive the compliments and petitions of his entourage in the Hall of the Viceroys. The Viceroy of Peru was still the most important functionary in the new world, though New Granada and Buenos Aires had now been created separate viceroyalties, whilst the Captaincy-General of Chile, through the intrigues of his enemy the Marqués de Avilés, who had succeeded him there and was to replace him later as Viceroy, had been rendered administratively independent. The Viceroy ruled over more than a million people, nearly one quarter of whom were of mixed Indian blood and over one half of pure Indian descent. This was but a small population for so vast an area, and lack of manpower meant that many of its natural resources lay virtually untapped. The wealth and splendour of the country were concentrated in the colourful, luxury-loving city of between fifty and sixty thousand inhabitants of which the viceregal palace was the social and political centre.

At the apex of the social pyramid stood the dignitaries and officials of the viceregal court, the heads of the ecclesiastical hierarchy, the senior officers of the army, and a handful of privileged landowners, many of whom bore hereditary titles. Then came a small class of modest merchants and tradesmen, followed by an intermediate caste of mixed blood—the great population of *mestizos*, mulattos, *zambos*, and others, largely engaged as attendants and domestic servants. Negro slaves accounted for nearly one sixth of the population of Lima. The Indians, of whom not more than a few thousand lived in the capital, formed the base of the pyramid and supplied the labour for agriculture and mines throughout the country. All sections of the population showed a love of luxurious living, idleness, and gambling very alien to the austere spirit of the new Viceroy who strove to moderate these vices by the promulgation of an appropriate *bando de buen gobierno*. In this he was zealously seconded by the Archbishop, with whom he was rumoured to have been intimate in the early days of his career, when both were impecunious and unknown. Certainly they were like-minded men, animated by the same ideals of order and moderation.

In front of the long façade of the Viceroy's palace, and the adjoining residence of the Archbishop, with its green glazed balconies, stretched the great plaza and the teeming life of the market. Here the Indians flocked to sell their wares; joints of freshly slaughtered beef, mutton and goat's flesh; *charqui*, *cecina*, and other meats, smoked or dried in the sun, from the interior; fish in plenty from the neighbouring coast—crayfish and anchovies, *congrio*, *pejerreyes*, *corvina*, and salted cod; gaily coloured heaps of beans, guavas, *paltas*, maize, yams, casava, bananas and *chirimoyas*. The flower-stalls made banks of richer, more luxuriant colour, amongst which hovered the ladies of Lima, elegant in their classic attire of *saya* and *manto*, and intent on their purchases and their gossip. As the day wore on, the fierce sunshine would disperse the morning mist, and signal the *fresquero* to ply his trade of iced pine-apple water, lemonade, or almond milk, whilst the water-carriers led their mules to the great fountain in the centre of the square and filled their casks from its cool streams. Then, at about half past nine in the morning, the cathedral bell would announce the elevation of the Host. In an instant, the pulsing life of the market-square was stilled. Many dropped to their knees, the men doffed their hats and not a whisper, not a footstep was heard, until the third tolling of the bell, when all the bustle and noise would break forth once more.

The Church was the chief institution which held together this variegated and unruly life of Peru. It was customary, amongst all classes, to attend church at least once a day. Sumptuous ritual and processions were the delight of the populace, and feast days were so numerous that, together with Sundays, they amounted to almost half the entire year. Much of the nation's wealth was drained off to support ecclesiastical endowments and benefices. Lima alone boasted twenty-two monasteries and fourteen convents, in addition to its numerous churches. Many of the clergy were worldly and turbulent, greedy of possessions and temporal power, and given to quarrels amongst themselves, especially over the election of their superiors. They still held a monopoly of teaching posts and con-trolled the censorship of books and the press, for foreign news-papers were banned by viceregal degree and fines were imposed on any caught possessing them. But, within the last hundred years, the University of Lima had added to its traditional disciplines of theo-logy, Latin, and law, the new study of medicine, in which the dominant figure was Hipólito Unánue, the geographer, scientist, and editor of the learned review *Mercurio Peruano*, who soon became one of the closest friends of the new Viceroy.

To the penetrating gaze of Don Ambrosio O'Higgins, the weak-nesses of this pleasure- and tradition-loving society were all too evident. The Viceroy was now nearing eighty. His old zeal for order, progress, and reform still burned within him, but he was aware of the immensity of the tasks before him, the strains and stresses which were pressing upon Spain's overseas possessions, and the few years which were all that could remain to him for the accomplishment of his designs. Nor could he forget the tasks which he had set about in Chile and which still demanded his personal attention. Foremost amongst these was the resettlement of the town and fertile region of Osorno, which he believed could one day be made to support a population of half a million. The report from his nephew Thomas, whom he had sent to see how the infant colony was faring, was soberly encouraging. 'It is now no longer ruins which cover the ancient city of Osorno,' wrote Thomas O'Higgins, 'but a hundred houses built by the ninety-three settlers and the seven married soldiers who compose this colony.'[1]

The Viceroy resolved to speed the development of the settlement by appointing as its Governor another young Irishman, Juan Mackenna, who had entered the Spanish service. With him he despatched a number of other Irish settlers, mostly artisans, and some foreign seamen taken off captured whaling-vessels, who he hoped would settle down as carpenters, smiths, and other craftsmen. But most of these proved idle, took to drink, and had to be sent away. More serious for the progress of the colony was the secret hostility of the Governor-General of Chile. The Viceroy wrote in confidence to Mackenna to warn him against the machinations of 'the mean and treacherous Marqués de Avilés', who was sending all sorts of malicious reports to Spain about the 'English' colony established in the South. 'May God deliver you, my friend,' he went on, 'from such men—hypocrites disguised with false devotion and piety...Let your conduct be ruled by the most faithful loyalty to the King, and the most beneficent and friendly dealings with his subjects, seeking to protect and deal justly by the poor and wretched Indians, even at the risk of offending his Spanish subjects, the farmers of Valdivia...A feeling of charity and benevolence towards the Indians, and my efforts to protect these benighted and primitive owners of the land in some part of their rights to the fields which they possess, raised up against me, at the time when I was governor of the Frontier, a whole swarm of enemies, but God and the King have always strengthened me against them.'[2]

[1] Donoso, *op. cit.*, p. 365   [2] *Ibid*, p. 370.

But despite these dangers and setbacks, Osorno steadily prospered. By May 1800, the Viceroy could report to the Crown that the agricultural resources of Osorno were sufficient to keep Valdivia supplied if blockaded by hostile forces, and that communications between Osorno and Chiloé had been opened up, so that the island could be reached by reinforcements overland. He planned to build a modest house there for himself, where he could spend his last years in retirement, and when the King crowned his services with the bestowal of a title of nobility, the style he assumed was that of Marqués de Osorno.

But there could be no thought yet of peace and retirement. So much cried out to be done in the Viceroy's wide domains; roads to be built, industries to be started and resources to be tapped, abuses to be righted and the whole administrative machine to be overhauled. Don Ambrosio would have liked to see a new highway linking Lima with Cuzco, the old Inca capital in the Peruvian uplands. But this was too vast a labour even for his fierce energies, and instead he concentrated on rebuilding the road linking the capital with its port, Callao, which was ceremoniously opened at the beginning of 1799. To improve communications in this land of mountain, plateau, and desert was of the utmost importance; could not the camel be introduced into this country of llamas to help solve the problem? But these and many other projected reforms had to be abandoned in favour of more pressing matters. The political climate had changed too in Madrid. The enlightened zeal of Carlos III and his ministers had given place to the corrupt and reactionary régime of Carlos IV and his favourite Godoy. The very men who had so faithfully served the Crown in its enlightened endeavours at reform now themselves seemed suspect. The Court lived in the blindest fear of revolutionary contagion, and distrusted all change which was not a reversion to the narrowest conservatism.

O'Higgins had not been more than a few months in office before Spain and England were once more at war. Defence became again an overriding preoccupation. But how could the long exposed coastline of Peru be defended against a powerful naval power when all he could muster was a single frigate and a few improvised smaller war-ships? To his constant demands for more ships Spain turned a deaf ear. O'Higgins had always seen the root of the danger in the concession granted to the English to carry out whaling in the South Seas, and he wrote to Godoy urging him to take the opportunity of

war to make an end of the agreement. 'If this should be attained,'
he pleaded, 'I am sure that it would be of greater benefit to the
security of the state than any other of the measures which have been
discussed, on account of the dangerous, indeed fatal, consequences
arising from foreign vessels continuing to frequent her ports.'[1] As
long as such vessels were allowed to approach the Spanish possessions, there would remain the menace of smuggling and the spread
of undesirable contact with foreign men and ideas. The Viceroy
issued a proclamation declaring that anyone caught smuggling,
whether Spanish subjects or foreigners, would be strung up on the
shore on the scene of their crime 'without mercy or remission.' In
expectation of an attack on Callao and Lima, he hurriedly strengthened their defences, placed the army on a war footing, and called
out the militia.

But no attack was launched. English designs against Spanish
America might, it seemed, take another and more insidious form.
For months, Madrid had been kept informed of the intrigues of
Miranda and other conspirators to enlist British support for their
plans to foment a revolt in Spain's overseas domains and bring about
their eventual secession. The government warned the Viceroy in a
secret despatch to be on the look-out for any signs of the conspiracy
in his territory. O'Higgins sent his reply in July of 1800 assuring the
government that he would redouble his vigilance, and that the people
under his administration remained orderly and loyal. Then one of
Miranda's fellow conspirators turned king's evidence and betrayed
the full details of the plot to Madrid, together with copies of
Miranda's memoranda to the British government and a list of all
those who had been involved. Amongst the names of the conspirators was that of Bernardo Riquelme, natural son of Don
Ambrosio O'Higgins, Marqués de Osorno and his Catholic Majesty's
Viceroy of Peru.

---

[1] *Ibid*, p. 359.

3

Seven

The Viceroy Disowns His Son

BY THE TIME the Spanish authorities had gained possession of all the details relating to Miranda's conspiracy, Bernardo was no longer in England. For months past, as a result of the indifference of his guardian or of the rapacity of the latter's London agents, shortage of funds had been making his existence increasingly difficult. Only the help of a few friends and a modest subscription of a couple of guineas a month raised by kind-hearted merchants kept his head above water. From his father he heard never a word; in two and a half years his guardian had written to him only once. 'I am at a loss to account for it,' he wrote to Don Nicolás de la Cruz in despair. 'My parent must have disowned me, or something of the like, as otherwise you surely cannot have forgotten and abandoned me in this way. My plight is such that instead of learning and making progress in the various subjects to which I have applied myself I am beginning to forget them for lack of guidance, and seeing myself treated in this way by those I considered my best friends fills me with worry and wretchedness.'[1] It was only when Bernardo was seriously thinking of accepting the help of some friends who offered to give him a free passage to Trinidad or Philadelphia, whence he would try and make his way to South America—'for however hard I might find things there, they could never be worse than they are here'—that Don Nicolás was finally stirred into giving some sign of life. Most probably he hoped to get him off his hands once and for all by finding him an opening in the Spanish Army. Towards the end of April, 1799, Bernardo was at last able to set sail from Falmouth. As England and Spain were again at war, he went first to Lisbon and travelled on from there to join his guardian in Cadiz.

Since the beginning of the century, Cadiz had steadily supplanted Seville as Spain's main entrepôt of trade with her American

---

[1] *Archivo*, Vol. I, p. 7–8.

possessions. Amongst the richest Cadiz merchants could now be numbered Don Nicolás de la Cruz, whose wealth later enabled him to purchase the title of the Conde del Maule, after the great river of that name near his Chilean home. Don Nicolás possessed a fine and spacious house, embellished with many objects of art which he had brought back from his travels in Italy. In a modest room in this mansion, he somewhat reluctantly allowed his ward to reside. Bernardo, who combined a warm and sensitive nature with a passion for deeds of valour, had hoped to enlist in the army only to find that career closed to him on account of his irregular birth. He therefore resigned himself to offering to work—in much the same way as his father had done more than half a century before—in a Cadiz firm, and he entered his guardian's business as an unpaid clerk.

It was a miserable and humiliating life, for which Bernardo felt himself ill suited. 'My blood boils with envy when I see so many young men setting off for the wars,' he complained to his father, 'destined for a rapid career which will bring them either an honourable post in the service of their country or else a glorious death. It seems that an adverse fate has condemned me to live in this obscure corner, a prey to every imaginable misfortune and necessity, without the chance of embarking upon a career, unknown to all the world, with no art nor skill in flattery, which is one of the first requisites in these lands.'[1] Bernardo was now a young man of twenty-one, of slightly less than medium height, but broad-shouldered and deep-chested. He had thick, curly chestnut hair, his father's high complexion, and rather small blue eyes which he had a habit of continually screwing up in a restless, puzzled way, as a result of an irritation of the eyelids from which he had suffered as a boy. His expression was good-natured, frank, almost naïve; robust rather than particularly intelligent, but redeemed from coarseness by the fine moulding of the mouth and chin, which suggested a certain artistic sensibility and recalled the delicate features of his mother. In Don Nicolás' opulent but unfriendly mansion, in which he occupied a status little higher than that of a servant, Bernardo felt himself more lonely and forsaken than ever. 'To see all my countrymen getting letters from their parents fills me with envy,' he wrote to his father, 'whilst I, poor wretch, have none.' His father's silence remained unbroken, and the war with England meant not only that he was prevented from leaving Spain, but also that the eagerly awaited letters from

[1] *Ibid*, p. 18.

his mother, to whom he continued to pour out his heart, failed to reach him.

Bernardo had to wait nearly one year before an opportunity was given him of trying to break through the British blockade and reach South America. But luck was against him, for the convoy was captured by a squadron under the command of Rear-Admiral Duckworth after a short engagement in which the Spaniards, in the words of Duckworth's report, 'displayed a gallantry in commencing an action with such a superior force as might be truly termed temerity.' The booty was a rich one, for it included a valuable cargo of quicksilver and a number of important passengers, amongst them the Archbishop of Buenos Aires. 'We are assured,' commented the *Naval Chronicle*, 'that Admiral Duckworth's share of the prize money will amount to £75,000 and that of his Captains £25,000 each.'[1] For Bernardo, the fate of the Spanish convoy meant the loss of his few humble possessions, and the frustration of his hopes for returning home to Chile, as we can see from his own artless account of his adventures:

Cadiz, 18 April, 1800

My dearest and most beloved father,

I hope that this letter will find you enjoying all the good health and happiness that your son desires for you.

It is with sorrow and regret that I write to tell you of the latest misfortunes which have overtaken me. I have already written to you of my plans to return to Chile, and of how I had taken my passage aboard a merchant frigate, the *Confianza*, bound for Buenos Aires. After waiting for more than three months for her to sail, we weighed anchor on 3 April, in convoy with His Majesty's frigates, *Carmen* and *Florentina* for Buenos Aires and Lima, and *La Sabina* for the Canaries, as well as the *Divina Providencia, Madre de Dios,* and the brigantine *Barcelonés* for Lima; the *Confianza, Bartonera, Tártaro Joven, María Josefa,* and the schooner *Jesus Nazareno* of the Philippines Company and a sloop for Buenos Aires called the *Caraqueña,* and four smaller ships for Vera Cruz.

At seven in the morning, when I was fast asleep, they roused me with the news that sails had been sighted astern. I had scarcely got half dressed when a cannon ball was fired over the

[1] *Naval Chronicle*, 1800, Vol. 3, pp. 407–8.

main mast without doing much damage, which made us think that they must be English, so we put on more sail, but this did not help us either, for in less than ten minutes an English frigate and two seventy-fours bore down upon us, and in view of the great danger we stood in from being exposed to the continuous fire which they opened upon us from the frigate and the two ships, we made ready to heave to, to find out for sure whether they were English or Spanish. The forty-six frigate thereupon came up to windward and the two seventy-fours to starboard, a pistol's shot away, and in the dark we could not make out any flag or show our own. The English frigate hailed us in their language, and I took the megaphone to answer them. They warned us to surrender or else they would sink us, and such-like threats, whilst they kept sending shots over us from time to time. Not a single one of our sailors showed himself on the quarterdeck; they had all taken refuge below. The Captain and myself with the megaphone were the only ones to show our faces. Since we were on the point of being boarded by the frigate and the two other ships, we surrendered. When the English admiral sent a heavily armed boat to take possession of our ship, and convey all the prisoners on board his own, I was kept at his beck and call to act as interpreter. At dawn the following day, the said ships and the English frigate were only a musket's shot from the Spanish frigates *Carmen* and *Florentina*, and opened fire on them and took them after a sharp engagement, killing one officer and mortally wounding another, the chief pilot also being killed and some twenty others dead and wounded. After that, they seized the convoy, excepting the *Tártaro* and *María Josefa*, merchant ships bound for Buenos Aires, and the two brigantines for Vera Cruz, which managed to get away, whilst the frigate *La Sabina*, which was carrying troops for the Canaries, was fortunate enough to put into Cadiz, although one of the seventy-fours gave chase to her. After a few days' sail, they took us to Gibraltar. I was stripped of all I had with me. I cannot tell you what I went through; for three days on end I did not have a scrap to eat and I had to sleep on the bare floor for a week, all because I did not have a single *real* with me on board, as I have not received a farthing since leaving London.

From Gibraltar I went on foot to Algeciras, half fainting

with hunger, heat and exhaustion, where I had the good fortune to meet with Captain Tomás O'Higgins, who had also been made a prisoner on board the frigate *Florentina*, where he was a passenger. He was also short of money but gave me a peso. Then, as best I could, I took a passage on board a ship bound for Cadiz, offering to pay on arrival. The next day after setting sail, we were again given chase by the English. A war-ship bore down upon us in full sail, but we were the faster and had the good fortune to reach the protection of the castle of San Pedro, where, at night-fall, we weighed anchor and slipped out under cover of darkness into Cadiz Bay. So I am lodging once again in the house of Don Nicolás de la Cruz, whom I most deeply regret troubling. Now I simply do not know which way to turn. My misfortunes have quite dashed my hopes of seeing my father, my mother, and my country again. I fear I shall die without ever seeing again what I so long for. But still I must not give up hope. May God grant my wish, and may He give Your Excellency health and happiness. May God preserve your precious life. Farewell, my dearest father, until heaven grant me my desire to embrace you; until then, I shall not know any pleasure or happiness. With heartfelt longing to see you, your loving and dutiful son,

Bernardo Riquelme.[1]

Don Nicolás de la Cruz could have spared little sympathy for his ward's misfortunes, and Bernardo felt himself even more of an unwanted guest in his house. 'It breaks my heart to find myself a prisoner in this unhappy Europe,' he wrote to his father, 'without any means of escape or any friend to help me. All the time I have been in Spain, I have never known what it was to feel the touch of a *real* in my pocket; but at least I shall have the satisfaction of knowing that I have bothered nobody for as much as a pin, but have rather put up with every conceivable embarrassment, even latterly to the point of not venturing from my room for lack of common necessities, as a result, as I have already written to you, of my falling prisoner and losing the few clothes and trifles which I brought from England, both for myself and my mother, and I am only left with the little I stand up in with no other resources except for what I can expect

---

[1] *Archivo*, Vol. I, pp. 10–12.

from your generosity. So until then, there is nothing for it but for me to have patience.'[1]

But further trials were still to come. An epidemic of yellow fever swept over Cadiz and sent Don Nicolás and his household to seek safety in Sanlúcar de Barrameda. Captain Tomás O'Higgins, who had helped Bernardo after their capture by the English, fell a mortal victim and Bernardo himself sickened and was soon so gravely ill that the doctors gave him up for lost. The last sacraments were hurriedly administered and his guardian hastened to procure him a coffin. Bernardo had barely strength enough to ask for quinine—a drug whose efficacy had long been known in America, but of which doctors in Europe were still sceptical—and after he had taken a dose began to mend. An old Irishman called Philip Hoche, who had been a friend of his father's long ago, tended his convalescence. At length, in December 1800, he was able to report to his father his complete return to health and the less gratifying news that he was back once again under the roof of Don Nicolás, in still more wretched plight:

I am still living in the house of Don Nicolás, in conditions which cannot but drag a man down to the depths of human wretchedness and misery, without a single friend to turn to for help and advice, whilst the very thought of staying on in this house is enough to kill me. During the two years which I have been under his roof, I have not exchanged a single word with its owner, nor have I once unburdened myself of everything which is on my mind or asked or received a single *real* from him, even when I set out for Buenos Aires. With regard to my clothes, I bought six shirts when I embarked, which cost me seven duros, and a pair of trousers. When I returned from Gibraltar, without anything beyond what I was wearing, as everything else had been taken by the English, he did not buy or give me a stitch of clothing; so that I have been forced to keep to my room as I simply am not fit to appear in company, and with his consent I have sold my piano which I happened to have left in Europe when I embarked, and with some of the proceeds I paid off the debts incurred during my illness. The remainder, which amounted to a hundred pesos, I handed over to Don Nicolás, who wishes to use them to offset past expenses,

[1] *Ibid*, pp. 12–13.

and thus to deprive me of those few coins and leave me without even an overcoat for these winter months. Lack of resources has forced me to interrupt my studies for fear of public ridicule.[1]

Bernardo's hopes of arousing some spark of sympathy in his father's breast were soon to be brutally shattered. The more desperate his plight became, the more absolute, so it seemed, were the incomprehension and hostility of his unnatural parent. Now, when fate appeared most adverse and he stood in greatest need of human sympathy, the cruelest blow of all was struck. One day at the beginning of March, 1801, Don Nicolás summoned his ward to his presence and with due solemnity informed him that the Viceroy was gravely displeased with the conduct of his son, whom he accused of filial ingratitude and an inability to embark on any career, and that his guardian was instructed to expel him from his house.

Bernardo was dumbfounded. He felt overwhelmed with the enormity, the fantastic injustice of these charges. How could he, whose only wish had been to receive some recognition, some sign of affection from his father, who had written to him constantly and earnestly begged his guidance—how could he be branded as undutiful? How could he, who had so longed to find an honourable way of earning his living, be denounced as incapable of following any career? In his grief and indignation at these accusations, the real but undisclosed reason for the Viceroy's displeasure altogether escaped him. Bernardo's admiration for Miranda and his creed was more than the passing enthusiasm of an adolescent, for he had brought introductions to a small group of like-minded revolutionaries in Cadiz and was still in close touch with them. That obedience to a father whose life had been devoted to the service of the Spanish Crown and membership of a movement vowed to its destruction were altogether incompatible never seems to have occurred to him. Was it not equally right and natural to love and obey one's father, as to love one's country and desire its freedom? So at least it seemed to Bernardo, who never stopped to ask himself whether the emotion he felt for his father was indeed love, nor what the freedom of his Chilean fatherland would involve for the Viceroy and everything he stood for. Bernardo's nature was naïve and guileless in the extreme, as incapable of understanding the mind of another as he was of

[1] *Ibid*, pp. 14–15.

analysing the contradictory impulses which swayed his own. Without pausing for a moment's reflection, he took up his pen and wrote a desperate letter of protest and vindication:

Cadiz, 8 January 1801.

My dear Father and my only protector,

I have just learnt from Don Nicolás that Your Excellency remains in good health, for which I thank God. At the same time he read out to me a letter from Your Excellency (the date of which I do not know) informing me that since I was incapable of following any career and ungrateful for the favours shown me, he should forthwith despatch me and expel me from his house. I cannot tell, Sir, what crime I have committed to deserve such a punishment, nor how you can accuse me of ingratitude (the vice which I most abhor) since all my life I have done my utmost to please Your Excellency, and now that I see this hope frustrated and my Father and protector angered I am all confusion. A knife-thrust were easier to bear. I cannot think why I do not fall down dead of shame to hear such words. I have never been afraid of death or poverty; but this has taken the heart quite out of me and made me feel the worst and most wretched of mortals. I do not know who has been so wicked of heart as to destroy me in the opinion of Your Excellency, who are my father and protector. I call him to account before God's mercy-seat—as I do not know him in this world.

Don Nicolás tells me that he does not know what has aroused Your Excellency's anger against me as he has always reported well of me to you and has justly written of my conduct and honourable behaviour in his house. If in the past, being misinformed by the London agents, two miserly watchmakers who were swindling me, he wrote that I had been spending too much money, he later realized what sort of men those agents were and changed his views, for they have not yet given any account of how they spent the money received, and have not even sent a receipt or acknowledgement for the last 3,000 pesos and for the last two years that I have been here they do not so much as answer any of the letters sent to them. For my part, I have received no more than a guinea a month to cover all my minor expenses, according to Don Nicolás' instructions,

3*

and there have been times when I have been forced to go without any food at all. Thanks to Don Diego Duff and Don Bernabé Murphy, I might have got a job in the former's office. But since Don Nicolás recalled me to Spain to put me in the army, I did not accept his offer.

I trust Your Excellency will form a more favourable opinion of my conduct from the good reports which Don Nicolás has sent Your Excellency on all these matters, and also on account of the two years I have stayed here without troubling or requesting any money from Don Nicolás, nor spending anything except for my laundry and shoes since the time—on my arrival here— that he told me he had orders from Your Excellency not to advance me anything. I am my own barber and hairdresser; I do my own sewing and mending, and in fact, for the last year, I have not wasted a single farthing, not for lack of friends willing to lend me money, for there are various Irish houses here who offered me some, but because I did not wish it to be said that I was acting improperly, for I know that the slightest negligence on my part would immediately reach Your Excellency's ears, and for this reason I have suffered, and still suffer, the torments of martyrdom in this house, scorned and treated like the meanest servant, with no more clothes than the modest suit which I have been wearing for the last four years, without even an overcoat in this cold winter weather, though only just recovering from a severe illness in which I nearly lost my life.

Your Excellency will understand that I have had reason enough to try and leave this country, if only to save Your Excellency's own honour, for here you can keep few secrets from anyone, though I have not breathed a word or opened my heart to a living soul apart from my own father; but even one's closest friends abuse friendship. I think I have said enough of that matter; I only trust that it will reach you in time to cause Your Excellency to form a different judgment as to my conduct, which has always been modest, respectful and full of gratitude for the benefits received at your hands, as also as to the conduct of whoever has persuaded you of the contrary.

I have ventured, Sir, to write to you too frankly; but I have done so trusting in the nobility of soul, ready to pardon and protect the wretched, which I hope will make Your Excellency forget all the shortcomings, past and present, of your poor

Bernardo, who, having no means of showing or offering his affection, constantly prays God to reward my father and benefactor for his generosity in supporting and educating me to the age in which I can earn my own living. Such goodness deserves praise in this world and a just reward in the next.

Sir, I will not trouble you further. May God still prolong your precious life for many years. Your Excellency's most humble and grateful son,

Bernardo Riquelme.[1]

This *cri de cœur* never reached the ears of Bernardo's father. Before the courier brought his letter to Lima, Don Ambrosio O'Higgins, Baron Ballinary and Marqués de Osorno, Viceroy of Peru, had passed beyond the honours and the troubles of this world.

[1] *Ibid*, pp. 15–18.

Eight

The Eve of Revolt

THE DAWN OF the nineteenth century, which found Bernardo frustrated and aggrieved in Cadiz and his father at the peak of viceregal power in Peru, held little apparent promise of change in the leisurely traditional-loving life of colonial Chile. Miranda was right when he judged that its greater remoteness from Europe would tend to breed ignorance and bigotry, and Don Ambrosio had experienced for himself how the best of reforms could be frustrated by unimaginative selfishness. But if the landed gentry who formed the dominant social group in that country lacked refinement and sophistication, and preferred ease to enterprise, they were on the whole sober, sociable people, who often treated the ignorant *inquilinos* on their estates with benevolence, and conducted their affairs with due regard to order and established precedent. From the hour when they would be roused by a knock on their bedroom door and the greeting '*Deo gratia*', to which they would reply with a sleepy 'for ever and ever amen', parents would rule their numerous household with a patriarchal authority and according to an accepted routine which varied little with the passage of the years or the part of the country in which they might reside. The management of the estate and the pleasures of an open air life, with frequent picnics and evening *tertulias*, enlivened with music, dancing, and not a little gossip, diversified an otherwise rather monotonous existence. Further interests were provided by the duties of the recently formed militia, which were not taken very seriously but were valued for the opportunity they offered of acquiring rank and of displaying uniforms, or by the few winter months passed in a town house where the men could play the limited part permitted them in public affairs.

Such a society could hardly be described as promising revolutionary material or smouldering with the desire for national indepen-

76

dence. Both aristocracy and people were attached in a vague way to the institution of monarchy, and felt loyal to the Crown which had often sought to protect their rights against local injustice. But to the peninsular Spaniards who had settled in Chile as officials or merchants the Creoles harboured a deep and sometimes vehement antipathy. They felt divided from them by differences of temperament and environment, and were jealous of the plums of office which fell to them. The Creoles were acquiring a taste for running their own affairs. The institution of the *cabildo* or municipal council had offered them a traditional field of public service, which could be later developed into a valuable instrument in the coming struggle for national independence.

The structure of Spanish colonial life thus stood, to all appearances, as solid and foursquare as ever. But, of recent years, certain props had been kicked away and strains and stresses set up. In 1767, the Crown had seen fit to expel the Jesuits, who were not only the most enterprising pioneers in Chilean agriculture, industry and education, but the most fervent royalists and the most subtle conciliators between antagonistic Spaniards and Creoles. Then had followed the upheaval of the French revolution and the dissemination of disruptive radical ideas. The Chilean landowning classes were themselves too conservative and conscious of how much they stood to lose to be greatly affected by this subversive influence. The 'dangerous books' of the Encyclopaedists, Montesquieu, and others found their way to Chile—Ambrosio O'Higgins' own friends and advisers were amongst their readers—and in the 'seventies an abortive plot was even hatched by a French adventurer and a visionary writer of Utopian constitutions in favour of a Chilean republic. The affair was too fantastic to be taken seriously and the authorities succeeded in hushing it up, the chief conspirator ending his life in a Cadiz dungeon, as Miranda himself was to do twenty-six years later.

More attractive to the Creole aristocracy was the appeal of the American revolution, which the Spanish government had so unwisely done its best to encourage. American ships engaged in contraband, and American merchants found their way to Chile anxious not only to discover a market for their wares but to convert others to their belief in the virtues and benefits of national independence. The order and prosperity which their northern republic enjoyed was the most eloquent of arguments. The ministers of

Carlos III and zealous administrators of the type of Ambrosio O'Higgins had believed that the same benefits could be brought to a country by the reforms and innovations prescribed by the creed of enlightened despotism. If there was unrest in Spain's overseas possessions, hostility between Creoles and Spaniards, or even luke-warmness in their loyalty to the Crown, they attributed it all to the neglect and injustices which the colonies had suffered in the past. All, they believed, could be remedied by vigorous and enlightened legislation; more roads and schools, new industries, a juster, more efficient administration. But these things also meant heavier taxes, more centralized and authoritarian control to overcome local inertia or hostility. Instead of a grateful and enthusiastic response, the policy of reform excited, all too often, distrust, resentment and active opposition. Far from reconciling the Creoles to the position which they occupied under the Spanish Crown, the well-meant endeavours of these conscientious and devoted men paradoxically fed the flames of nascent nationalism. No more than the first warn-ing flicker of danger was as yet apparent; it was only to be fanned into a blaze by the wind of world events. For the moment—the spring of 1802, with France and Britain in an uneasy truce—all seemed quiet.

To Bernardo, indeed, it must have seemed a blessed time. His personal fortunes had taken a sudden and dramatic turn for the better. The father who had striven to keep his existence a shameful secret and had finished by disowning him altogether, had relented on his death-bed. In his will he had left him a valuable estate in the south of Chile. By a stroke of the pen, Bernardo thus found his life transformed. It is true that the stigma of his illegitimate birth could not be altogether removed, but at least he was resolved to assume his father's illustrious name and take his place amongst the rich and powerful of his native Chile. He was free to return home, no longer an outcast without family or country, and be reunited with the mother whom he adored and whom he could now comfortably provide for. It was with high hopes and a mind tempered and enriched, but no longer embittered, by his experience of Europe that Bernardo O'Higgins landed from the frigate *Aurora* in Valparaíso, after a stormy passage round the Cape Horn, in the September of 1802.

There were many tiresome formalities to be fulfilled before Bernardo was able to enter upon his inheritance. To get probate for the late Viceroy's will was a lengthy business, as matters were held up until the completion of the customary *juicio de residencia*, or posthumous enquiry into the record of every high Spanish official, whose goods and property remained under seal until the investigating judges had formally approved his conduct of affairs. The *residencia* took place in Lima, and to try and expedite matters, Bernardo hurried to Santiago where Don Tomás O'Higgins, nephew of the Viceroy and namesake of the luckless officer who had died of yellow fever in Cadiz, offered him the hospitality of his house. Tomás was five years older than Bernardo. He had entered the Irish Regiment in the Spanish army at the age of seventeen and Don Ambrosio had petitioned the Crown that he should be transferred to the Frontier Dragoons of Chile since 'I am now drawing towards the end of my life, and am in a foreign country, without any relative near me, after so many years' absence from my own family and country.'[1] The old man had come to regard Tomás almost as his adopted son and had sent him on a number of confidential missions of inspection to different parts of Chile before appointing him Captain of his own viceregal guard. On his death, Don Ambrosio had left him a large part of his possessions.

In Tomás O'Higgins' hospitable Santiago house Bernardo stayed whilst he wrote off to Lima urging the trustees to expedite the probate; then he hurried off to the south of Chile to join his mother. Rosita, his half-sister, had grown into a buxom girl, very like her brother in looks. The two became deeply attached to each other. But Bernardo's chief affection remained, as always, and until the end of her life, for his mother. The family was at last happily reunited, and soon there came news from the trustees in Lima authorizing the manager of the Las Canteras estate, which Don Ambrosio had left to his son, to hand over, on due security, a certain number of cattle which Bernardo could sell to pay off the debts incurred through his voyage to Chile and to meet his most pressing current expenses until the final settlement was made. Fortune had indeed begun to smile on them.

But there was still one dark cloud which, both for his mother's and his own sake, Bernardo would have given much to dispel. That was the stain of his illegitimacy. Could not the wrong which had been done Doña Isabel be repaired, even at this late hour? Bernardo sought out the friends who had been in the confidence of the late

[1] Note dated 11 November, 1794, quoted by Donoso, *op. cit.*, p. 413.

Viceroy—Tomás O'Higgins, Delfín, Juan Martínez de Rozas, whom Don Ambrosio had chosen as his *asesor* when Governor of Concepción. From them he obtained affidavits relating to the circumstances of his birth, which he presented to the courts at Lima with his petition for legitimacy. Then, resolving to press his suit in person, he left for Peru and stayed for two months in the City of the Kings.

From Tomás Delfín, Bernardo also learnt many things concerning the last years of his father's life and of his death-bed decision to become reconciled with his natural son. At the end of January, 1801, the Viceroy suffered a grave haemorrhage and felt his last hours approaching. He sent for Delfín and asked for his help in drawing up his will. Delfín suggested that a lawyer, whose prudence could be vouched for, should be called in. But to this the old man obstinately refused to agree. The secret would leak out; people would talk; it would soon be all over Lima that he had a natural son. Perhaps it would even be known that this son was one of Miranda's fellow conspirators. No; these shameful things should only be revealed when the Viceroy was in his tomb. O'Higgins declared that he was still strong enough to draw up the will himself. Then he sent Delfín off to Chile, but not before the latter had pleaded long and earnestly with him to pardon a son whose misdemeanours could be nothing more than the impulsive indiscretions of youth and the consequences of the lack of parental control and affection under which he had grown up. How could the father so mercilessly condemn a son for whose irregular birth and furtive upbringing he was alone to blame? The dying man was left to the reproaches of his conscience. On the 14 March, four days before he died, he dictated his will, revealing the secret he had so long striven to maintain and making what amends he could to the son he had disowned.

And did Bernardo, for his part, now comprehend more clearly what had lain behind the seemingly unjust resentment of his father? From these friends, and from Juan Mackenna, with whom he was later to become intimate, Bernardo must have heard the story of his father's final fall from favour and dismissal. Appearances had been prudently preserved. 'In so much as the Marqués de Osorno, Lieutenant-General of my royal armies, is suffering from ill health and is now advanced in years, serving now in his fifth year as Viceroy, Governor and Captain-General of the Kingdom of Peru,' began

the royal *cédula* of 14 July, 1800, decreeing his removal from office
and his replacement by his hated rival, the Marqués de Avilés, who
had not ceased to intrigue against him at court. Even before the
official despatches reached Lima, O'Higgins had learnt of the ramifications of Miranda's conspiracy and could foresee what the consequences of his son's complicity would inevitably be on his own
position.[1]

After Bernardo had spent two months in Lima and stood in silence
at his father's tomb, the probate formalities were happily concluded.
An old school friend from his days at the San Carlos College, the
Marqués de Torre Tagle, and another of the Viceroy's Irish nephews,
Don Demetrio O'Higgins, had smoothed the way for him and made
his stay in the Peruvian capital a pleasant one. But one thing neither
they nor Bernardo's other friends could achieve for him; his legitimacy suit was not granted. Bernardo O'Higgins was free to return
to Chile and take possession of his inheritance, but it was not to be
under the proud title of the second Baron Ballinary and Marqués de
Osorno. How hardly, we wonder, did he take this disappointment?
For himself, in all probability, this meant but little. His personal
tastes were simple and unassuming, and he had never harboured
social ambitions. But for his mother's sake, as a belated righting of
the wrongs done her, he would have welcomed the honours denied
him. Had the decision gone in his favour, we cannot but speculate
on the future course his life might have taken. Would a man who had
inherited such honours and titles from the Crown have been so eager
to destroy the source from which they emanated? Would a marquis
have fought so passionately to establish a Republic?

For the next year or two, Bernardo was able to throw himself into
the work which he liked best and for which he felt himself to be most
fitted. As he wrote to a friend, once it became clear that this peaceful
life would soon be exchanged for that of soldier and rebel: 'I might
have become a good farmer and a useful citizen, and if it had been
my lot to be born in Great Britain or Ireland, I would have lived and
died on my estates. But fate wished that I should first see the light
of day in Chile, and I cannot forget what I owe to my country.'[2]

Las Canteras was a large and fertile tract of farm-land, lying in

---

[1] The dismissal of the Viceroy was decided upon, once the Court had been informed
of the details of Miranda's conspiracy, by a decree dated 19 June 1800. Donoso, *op. cit.*,
p. 408.
[2] *Archivo*, Vol. 1, p. 64.

the heart of the Frontier zone a league from Los Angeles, its chief military base. Don Ambrosio had purchased it, in whole or in part, from the Indians, but his incessant administrative duties had never left him the time to develop it. Bernardo now turned to this task with enthusiasm. The estate already supported three thousand head of cattle. Bernardo decided that the soil was also suitable for vineyards, and in the course of two years planted no less than 100,000 young vines. In addition, he built new farm buildings and a roomy house to be the home of his mother, his half-sister, and his uncle Manuel Riquelme, who helped him run the estate. The implements he required for the farm he imported wherever possible from England.

Bernardo's position as a well-to-do landowner carried with it social and political responsibilities which he eagerly took up, and which soon brought him into conflict with Don Luis de Alava, the arrogant, narrow-minded and ambitious Governor of Concepción whose personality symbolized for Bernardo all those odious features of Spanish rule which he most abhorred. The antipathy was mutual. Alava was not ignorant of the young man's English sympathies, nor of the contact and correspondence which he maintained with likeminded friends whom the Governor more than suspected of harbouring subversive designs. He kept a watchful eye on Bernardo, summoning him from time to time to Concepción on the pretext of helping with the interrogation of captured English sailors 'on account of the knowledge which he possesses,' the Governor ironically explained, 'of that nation which I suspect will attack us before long.' Another clash followed over the rights of the *cabildo* of Chillán, to which Bernardo had recently been elected, and which the highhanded actions of the Governor were infringing. Alava openly threatened to have Bernardo arrested and shipped off to Lima, but desisted through fear of increasing his already considerable local unpopularity. He contented himself instead with ordering the destruction of all the herds belonging to the owner of Las Canteras on the island of Quiriquina, on the pretext that they might be used to provision enemy ships.

The distrust of the Spanish authorities, however mean and misguided it may have seemed to the master of Las Canteras, was by no means without foundation. Ever since Drake's daring challenge to Spain's monopoly of the South Seas, the attractions and advantages of securing a foothold on Chilean soil had been present to adventurous minds. The glowing descriptions given by La Pérouse, whom Ambrosio O'Higgins had perhaps too generously welcomed, of the natural fertility of Chile and its great potentialities had revived men's appetites and proved a powerful factor in the British government's approval, in the autumn of 1806, of a plan for an expeditionary force to be sent to that country under the command of Brigadier-General Robert Crauford. The instructions issued to the Commander-in-Chief provided for the invasion and complete subjection of the southern province, the Catholic religion to be respected and Spaniards to be replaced by Creoles in the administration. The instructions complacently assumed that the invaders would be welcomed as liberators by the Creole population, impressed with the contrast between 'the oppressive dominion of Spain and the benign and protecting government of His Majesty.'[1] The expedition was diverted at the last moment, with most unhappy results, to the Argentine where it met with an opposition as vigorous as that which it would have encountered, in all probability, had it followed its original destination to Chile.

Bernardo, who thus escaped being faced with a clash of loyalties between his pro-English sympathies and his Chilean patriotism, remained of course totally ignorant of these plans. He was never tired of holding forth, in the *tertulias* where political talk was mingled with the pleasures of social intercourse, of the merits of the British constitution and the liberties enjoyed by her people from the time of the Magna Carta, which document he even translated for the edification of his friends. The latter were mostly young and ardent spirits like himself, but there was one amongst them whose greater experience of public affairs and brilliant intellectual gifts invested with special authority. This man was Juan Martínez de Rozas, to whom Bernardo felt at once drawn not only by the liberalism of his ideas but through the friendship which had once united him to his father in the days when he served Don Ambrosio in the governship of Concepción. Rozas was now in his late forties, and was allied by marriage with the Urrutia Mendiburu family, one of the wealthiest in the South. He had worked for a time as *asesor* to Alava, but the latter distrusted his influential connections and dangerously liberal ideas and he had been forced to resign. His subtle intelligence, political dexterity and mastery of intrigue made

---

[1] Instructions to Brig.-General Robert Crauford, 30 October, 1806. (Public Record Office, War Office Records, 1/161.)

him a dangerous enemy of the régime. He was now brooding over his grievances and biding his time to return to public life on his own terms.

The moment came in 1808—a year fateful in the lives of Rozas and Bernardo O'Higgins, and in the destinies of Spain and her overseas possessions. The immediate local cause was the death in February of the Governor of Chile, Muñoz de Guzmán. The right to nominate a temporary successor was normally vested in the *audiencia*, the choice falling on the *regente*, the senior member designated for this purpose. But in Chile, the constant threat from the Araucanians had meant that a soldier should be the Governor of the country. The army therefore resented the choice of a civilian *regente* and held that the prize should go to a high-ranking officer. But to which? The Governor of Concepción, invariably a soldier, had frequently succeeded to the highest office. Alava therefore anticipated this honour for himself. But he counted without the astuteness of his former *asesor* who determined to deny him the office by supporting the claims of a rival candidate, García Carrasco who, though something of a nonentity, was in fact Alava's senior. By shrewdly manipulating the votes of the officers' corps Rozas succeeded in securing the election of Carrasco. Alava was compelled to renounce his pretensions, and, as a reward, Rozas was appointed *asesor* to the new Governor of Chile. He left Concepción for Santiago, to the great satisfaction of his friends who had no doubt that he would now be the real power in the land. García Carrasco was a rather colourless man of about sixty, without wealth, influential connections, special abilities or dangerous vices. His chief interest outside soldiering seemed to be cock-fighting. Though affable and not uncultured—he was even a dabbler in 'dangerous books', one of which the Inquisition had once confiscated from him—he remained a convinced royalist at heart. In normal times, he would probably have held office with reasonable competence, if without distinction. But, as the crafty Rozas well knew and determined to turn to account, he was the man least fitted to guide the country through a period of exceptionally acute political crisis.

This crisis had been forced upon Spain's overseas dominions by the series of dramatic events which were now befalling the mother country. In March, the Madrid populace revolted, overthrew Godoy the favourite, and forced Carlos IV to abdicate in favour of his son Ferdinand. Napoleon, however, determined to intervene in this dispute for his own purposes. On the pretext of offering his mediation, he forced Carlos to withdraw his abdication and then to hand over the Crown to Napoleon's own brother, Joseph. The Spanish people not unnaturally refused to accept such a humiliating and cynical bargain and took up arms rather than accept the French King.

These developments confronted the colonies with a genuine dilemma, and at the same time offered them an unprecedented opportunity for indulging their newly acquired taste for running their own affairs. For which monarch should they declare; for Ferdinand or Joseph? Joseph, supported by French arms, was the effective power — but could the authorities recognize such an obvious alien usurper? Ferdinand, on the other hand, though the legitimate prince, was a prisoner. Rozas, O'Higgins, and the small band of radical thinkers, plainly saw that by recognizing the theoretical sovereignty of the captive king, they would in fact be able to have things very much their own way. Moreover, they would enjoy the enormous tactical advantage of being able to take the first steps towards independence under cover of an unimpeachable display of legality and loyalty, to which the convinced royalists, no less than the great mass of the undecided, could wholeheartedly subscribe.

In the capital, the astute Rozas bent all his efforts to persuading the new Governor to recognize Ferdinand. García Carrasco felt more and more uneasy. He had already let himself be talked into authorizing the *cabildo* to increase its strength by the inclusion of twelve new members, thereby broadening its representative character and increasing its strength *vis-à-vis* the chief royalist organ, the *audiencia*. Rozas now hinted that if he were unwise enough to recognize a foreign upstart as king, the *cabildo* and the patriotic officers would join forces to depose him. Such arguments finally won the day, but not before García Carrasco had decided that it would be safer in future to dispense with the services of his embarrassing adviser. Moreover, both Governor and his asesor had aroused public indignation by their obvious complicity in a piece of corruption by which the customs had been scandalously defrauded. By the end of 1808, Rozas deemed it prudent to resign his post, retire to Concepción, and to watch events from there.

These now followed thick and fast. Whilst García Carrasco was clumsily trying to steer a middle course, recognizing Ferdinand but outlawing prominent Chileans suspected of harbouring disloyal

designs, news came that the patriots of Buenos Aires had overthrown the Viceroy there and set up a *junta de gobierno*. This greatly
encouraged Rozas, O'Higgins and their circle, and their like-minded
associates in Santiago, where the main drama was now being played
out. The *cabildo* felt itself sufficiently strong to demand the resignation of García Carrasco and his replacement by a still more docile
figurehead. This they found in the person of the aged Conde de la
Conquista, a worthy and wealthy merchant who had bought a title of
nobility and now found himself, at the age of eighty-three, still less
able than his predecessor to confront an increasingly difficult
situation. A violent struggle took place to win a permanent ascendency over his vacillating and senile mind; the royalists—European
Spaniards, prelates of the Church, and *audiencia* officials on the one
side, pitted against *cabildo*, and Creole lawyers and landowners.
Whilst the battle raged, news came from Spain that a Council of
Regency had been established which demanded an oath of loyalty
to Ferdinand from the colonies. Repulsing attempts to evade the
issue, the royalists succeeded in getting this oath sworn. But their
victory was short-lived. After desperate vacillations, the old Conde
ceded to the demands of the extremists who demanded the calling
of a *cabildo abierto*—a sort of enlarged municipal council, on which
all the principal citizens were represented. This body, by some four
hundred votes, resolved on the replacement of the aged governor by
a *junta*. Though the latter was anything but revolutionary, and
merely represented the wish of the Creoles to have a greater say in
governing themselves,[1] the date of its inception—18 September,
1810—has been generally taken to mark the beginning of Chilean
independence.

---

[1] The very moderate nature of Creole aspirations at this time is apparent from the
text of the announcement issued on 18 September, 1810, by the *Cabildo* of 'the most
noble and loyal city of Santiago': see *Anales de la Revolución* (ed. Luis Valencia Avaria,
Santiago, 1951, Vol. 1, pp. 3–5).

Nine

The Rise of the Carreras

THE MOMENTOUS EVENTS which we have just outlined occurred in the capital, or far beyond the frontiers, of Chile. Concepción was no more than a provincial backwater, to which the astute Rozas could retire as matters suited him. Alava had been eliminated from the scene by a ruse of Rozas, who spread alarming reports of the imminent arrival of a rebel army and frightened him into taking a ship to Callao. Such talk was as yet no more than the merest bluff. Rozas himself shrank from the prospect of armed conflict, and hoped always to hit upon some legal formula, some cunning manipulation of the political cards, which would avoid the arbitrament of war. Bernardo, less subtle and far less intellectually gifted, at least saw clearly in this; the great issue whether Chile, and the other Spanish colonies, would ever gain their national freedom could only be decided by arms. Whatever government might be in power, Spain would temporize as long as the French threat prevented effective action. But as soon as her hands were free, she would try to compel her rebellious colonies to surrender the concessions and compromises which necessity had thrust upon her. The Creoles must expect this to happen and be armed and prepared. There was little time to lose.

But how best could they be armed and prepared? O'Higgins was only too painfully conscious of his own inexperience. Apart from a few conventional lessons in England, he had received no military training whatsoever; he knew nothing of strategy, nor even of tactics. He felt the need of someone to whom he could turn for guidance. Perhaps it was the lack of a father's care in his youth which made him strangely susceptible, all through his life, to the ascendency of men of stronger personality and keener intellect. In England it had been Miranda; later it was to be San Martín. Where could he now find a military mentor? His thoughts turned first to his cousin, Tomás. But though he was fond of him and knew him to be an experienced soldier, Bernardo feared that he was too strongly attached to the Crown to have much sympathy for the new ideas. Instead, he decided to approach another Irishman, who had also enjoyed the protection of his father but whom he believed to be more inclined to the cause he had at heart. This was Mackenna, the former Governor of Osorno.

On 5 January, 1811, Bernardo O'Higgins took up his pen to compose a long letter[1]—he chose to write it in English—to his new confidant, frankly setting forth his aspirations and his fears, and asking for advice as to how best to begin preparing for the struggle which he foresaw. 'I trust you will not think me a coward when I confess that I cannot bear the thought of ending my days in some obscure dungeon,' he wrote, 'without being able to raise a hand to help liberate my country—which is the aim which I most cherish ever since my talks with General Miranda.' The district of La Laja, of which his estate of Las Canteras formed a part, supported a population of some 34,000 souls. This he calculated would be enough to furnish two good cavalry regiments, one of which could be composed mainly of his own tenants, whilst the inhabitants of the town of Los Angeles could form the nucleus of the infantry militia. That was as far as he could see at present.

It was two months before Bernardo received Mackenna's reply, but it came at last—a bulky memorandum which he set about studying with care.[2] After surveying the international situation and the effects which either a French or a British victory in Europe would have on the prospects for South American emancipation, the Irishman gave it as his opinion that the struggle against Spain was bound to be long and bloody. Then followed some concrete advice in reply to the younger man's queries. Bernardo should first find a good sergeant of dragoons who would teach him the use of carbine, sword and lance, and the basic movements of small infantry and cavalry units. He was to train on horseback, with sabre and lance. Only then, when thoroughly proficient, could he set about instructing his men with the help of the sergeant. When experienced in the command of a company, an officer should teach him how to handle a troop. The regiment from which he could learn most was that of the Frontier Dragoons, formed by Don Ambrosio O'Higgins.

[1] *Archivo*, Vol. 1, pp. 61–69.   [2] *Ibid*, pp. 70–104.

Once more the memory of his own father, never far from his mind, and now invoked to help overthrow the cause of Spain to which the Viceroy had devoted his life! Those whose friendship Bernardo most valued, and whom he looked upon as his comrades in the gathering storm—Tomás O'Higgins, Rozas, Mackenna— were the same men who had enjoyed the protection and friendship of his remarkable parent. Mackenna, specially, professed a boundless admiration for him. 'If you study the life of your father,' he declared, 'you will find in it military lessons which are the most useful and relevant to your present situation, and if you always keep his brilliant example before your eyes, you will never stray from the path of honour, and should you not succeed in winning great distinction, at least you will never do anything you need be ashamed of.' The Irishman warmed to his theme. Don Ambrosio, he believed, had military gifts of the first order. 'In my opinion, your venerated father possessed these qualities more than any other man of the century in which he lived, with the exception of Frederick the Great. He had a clarity of intelligence which simplified the most complicated and difficult problems, and an understanding for whose power of perception nothing was too small. The life of your father, faithfully related, would present one of the finest moral lessons in the history of humanity. I know of none other better calculated to impress on youthful minds the inestimable value of inflexible honesty, indefatigable work, and immovable firmness.' After recalling his rise from humble origins, without friends, money, or favour, to the greatest office in South America, Mackenna concluded: 'when I think about the extraordinary life of your father, the study of which has been of more service to me than anything else, I have often stopped to ask myself whether he could ever have really existed, or whether it was not all a dream. No one can grasp the miraculous nature of your father's career without knowing by experience the Court of Spain, its depravation, its favouritism, and the antipathy of the Spaniards for foreigners. Although your father was Irish—of which I feel proud—he was generally dubbed by the Spaniards "The English Viceroy"—a nickname which more than once brought him to the verge of ruin.'

Whilst Bernardo was exchanging letters with his new mentor and preparing himself for the approaching clash of arms, the junta in Santiago, to which Rozas had returned as the dominating figure, was taking measure after measure which could only make a final rupture

with Spain inevitable. The structure of the old colonial administration was steadily demolished. The *audiencia*, so long the bastion of
royalist power and sentiment, was dissolved with scarcely a protest.
The momentous decision was taken (February 1811) to end Spain's
traditional economic monopoly and throw open the country to
foreign trade with other nations. This was resolved both for ideologi-
cal and for practical reasons, since trade with Spain had dried up
as a result of the war in Europe. But though radicals like O'Higgins
hailed it as a great step forward, the measure aroused the resentment both of the Chilean traders who had done well out of the
legitimate trade with Spain, and also of the less scrupulous who
looked to make quicker fortunes from smuggling. Another highly
controversial move was the attempt to take over church patronage
from the Crown, and thus to gain a hold over that stronghold of
conservative sentiment. All these provocative steps led to an
attempted coup against the junta by a royalist officer who was
caught and summarily executed. As a further act of defiance against
Spain and a sign of solidarity with the revolutionaries of Buenos
Aires, the junta despatched a small expeditionary force to the
Argentine to help to repel the threat of an expeditionary force from
Spain.

This action of Rozas, a native of Mendoza and thus something of
an Argentine at heart, met with some strong opposition in Chile,
not only from those who were royalist in sympathy but amongst the
more radical group as well. Was it not the height of rashness to
denude the country of troops when Chile might itself at any moment
have to repel an invasion from Peru? The country was still woefully
unprepared to offer any effective military resistance. Mackenna had
prepared a plan for the junta advocating the thorough training and
equipment of a permanent force of just over one thousand men
which would serve as the nucleus for a militia of 25,000. He had also
urged that a school for the training of future officers should be
immediately set up, the fortifications of the chief ports strengthened,
and a stock of supplies and weapons built up. Rozas, still trusting to
his skill in political manipulation to weather the storm, made little
effort to carry out even this simple plan. Half-hearted attempts were
made to remedy the almost total lack of arms by purchases from
Buenos Aires and foreign traders, and by starting an armament
factory in Chile. For the rest, Rozas contented himself with forming
a new army on paper, placing persons in command whom he judged

personally loyal to himself, and wherever possible, connected to him by family ties. Even the owner of Las Canteras had to suffer the indignity of seeing the regiment which he had personally raised from amongst his own *inquilinos* entrusted to a brother-in-law of Rozas. But Bernardo soon forgave the slight in his enthusiasm on learning that Rozas had at last taken an important political step which he had long urged upon him; the summoning of a national congress, to broaden the basis of popular consent on which the somewhat arbitrarily composed junta at present rested.

The wisdom of calling a congress at this critical stage of the country's fortunes had been earnestly discussed by Bernardo and Mackenna. Ardent in his youthful faith in democratic institutions, the younger man had written to his friend: 'My personal conviction is that the first Congress in Chile is bound to display the most puerile ignorance and be guilty of all sorts of stupidity. Such consequences must inevitably follow from our present situation, lacking as we do any sort of knowledge and experience. But we have to begin some time, and the sooner the better.'[1] The Irishman was more sceptical. One might just as well expect a blind man to distinguish colours as for the Chilean people suddenly to acquire the art of legislating, he replied. It was all very well to say that when his sight is restored, the blind man can learn to see colours, and that the people of Chile will learn to govern themselves. 'But who,' he concluded, 'is the man who will teach them—and if one is found— will they indeed listen to him?'

The future was soon to give the answer and to provide some justification for these misgivings. The first dispute concerned the way the Congress was to be constituted. Santiago province had a population of well over 300,000, Concepción, its rival, only a fraction of that number. But not content with counting Rozas, the real power in the junta, in their ranks, the spokesmen of the South insisted on equal representation with the capital. O'Higgins, who had hurried up to Santiago to offer his sword to repel the attempted royalist coup, took his seat with the other delegates from the South. When the Congress was opened on 4 July, 1811, Rozas solemnly delivered up his mandate to the assembly. The struggle to elect a new junta was bitter and confused, for the contest between extremists and moderates was complicated by the issue between Santiago and Concepción. Congress finally elected a junta of

[1] *Ibid*, p. 68.

moderates. An attempt to forestall it by a military coup was abandoned at the last moment for reasons we shall see.

The wrangles of Congress were interrupted by an unexpected and embarrassing event. A message was received from Valparaíso announcing that Captain Fleming, of HMS *Standard*, had arrived with a commission from the Council of Regency in Spain to take back with him the Chilean deputies for the proposed *cortes generales*, together with a substantial contribution in Chilean funds to assist Spain in her struggle against the French. Here was a searching challenge to probe the sincerity of the Creoles' protestations of loyalty to the captive King Ferdinand. Congress prevaricated, and Captain Fleming renewed his demand in unambiguous terms. None favoured the sending of delegates, but some of the moderates were prepared to compromise by sending money to Spain. Bernardo denounced this suggestion violently and even threatened that he and his comrades would use force, if need be, to prevent the funds from leaving Chile, as every peso would be wanted for the great tasks which lay ahead. His eloquence carried the day, and Congress sent a refusal to Captain Fleming on both counts. But this was the only victory which the extremists could claim. When Congress elected its new junta of moderates, Bernardo O'Higgins and eleven others ostentatiously resigned in protest. This was Bernardo's last intervention in public affairs for two months, for he was forced to keep to his bed with a violent attack of articular rheumatism. By the time he recovered, the political scene had entirely changed, and a new figure was dominating the stage.

HMS *Standard*, which had conveyed Captain Fleming and his unwelcome demands, also brought a passenger who was soon to exert a still more dramatic effect on the fortunes of the Chilean revolution. This was a young Creole officer, resplendent in the uniform of the Galician Hussars, called José Miguel Carrera. His family was one of the few which could still trace an unbroken line of descent from the Conquistadors. Don Ignacio, its present head, had been elected to the junta. Fair-minded, staid and respected, he represented the best qualities of the Creole aristocracy. But his four children—three sons and one daughter—were made of more inflammable stuff, in which the pristine passions and energies of the race seemed to have been dangerously transmitted and compressed, ready to burst into flame at the spark of some political clash. All had been turbulent in their youth. José Miguel, the most ungovernable, fell foul of the law before he was twenty and was shipped off first to Peru, thence to Spain, where the European wars gave him a chance to display a dare-devil courage in the army. The news from Chile fired him with dreams of wildest ambition. With his father a member of the first junta, what could not he and his brothers become? He saw himself and the members of his family filling the posts of honour and power in the new Chile, as Napoleon had placed his kith and kin on the thrones of Europe. The most brilliant role of all, he believed with the sublime confidence of his twenty-six years, was reserved for himself.

The return of the young firebrand from Spain was eagerly awaited by Doña Javiera, his sister, and his two brothers, Juan José and Luis. Javiera was a young woman of imperious character, even more fanatically attached to the cult of the family than her brothers. She had done her utmost to arouse José Miguel's ambitions as a means of saving him from the consequences of his youthful escapades, and her domineering, vengeful nature found satisfaction in goading him on to ever wilder pretensions. Luis, the youngest brother, was hot-tempered, high-spirited and impulsive, devoted to his sister and to José Miguel. Juan José, conscious of his seniority, was sometimes sullenly resentful of his more brilliant brother's pretensions, but his own manifest inferiority of gifts and personality always compelled his eventual submission.

If the Carrera family was formidable by virtue of the fanatical ties which bound its members together and the vehemence of its ambitions, there were others whose immense ramifications rendered them more powerful still. Of these, none was more influential than the Larraíns, whose proliferating branches and clannish spirit had won them the nickname of the 'Eight Hundred'. Like the Carreras, they had embraced the cause of independence and their first taste of power had whetted their appetite. They had formed an alliance with Rozas and his following in the South against the more numerous moderate party. Juan Mackenna had married into the family, and O'Higgins—though his personal convictions and irregular birth gave him no special love for any section of the aristocracy—found his friends and supporters chiefly amongst the powerful Larraín clan for the greater part of his public career.

The Carreras began by making common cause with the Eight Hundred. José Miguel's first action, on disembarking in Valparaíso, was to call on Mackenna who was then Governor of that port.

Mackenna's wife and the young Hussar had been childhood playmates, and the Irishman greeted the newcomer with some cordiality,
little suspecting how soon differences of temperament and outlook
would estrange them. He learned from Carrera the latest news of
events in Spain, and explained to him in turn the course things were
taking in Chile. Juan José and Luis were conspiring with the
Larraíns to stage a coup against the moderates in the new junta and
to replace them by extremists. José Miguel hurried on to the
capital to persuade his brothers to postpone the coup until he had
had time to familiarize himself with the situation and to play a
leading part in it himself.

On 1 September—forty-one days after landing in Chile—José
Miguel felt himself sufficiently master of events to deliver the blow
his brothers had planned. With the help of Juan José's grenadiers
and Luis' artillery, he surrounded the building where Congress and
junta were in session, and forced through the resignation of the
latter body and its replacement by a new junta of extremists, which
included both Rozas and Mackenna. It was, in short, a complete
victory for the Eight Hundred; but it had been won at the price of
setting the dangerous precedent of applying force to overthrow the
civil authorities. Nor did it bring any corresponding advantages to
José Miguel and his family, who indignantly rejected the inferior
offices offered them. The Carreras were left smarting with resentment that they should have been used as the cat's-paw for the
benefit of the Eight Hundred. Matters were not improved by the
head of the clan, Friar Joaquín Larraín, who boasted in José
Miguel's hearing that the coup had brought them all they aspired
to. 'All the Presidents are now our own people,' he complacently
declared, 'the President of Congress, the President of the Junta,
even the President of the High Court.' This was more than José
Miguel could stand. 'And who,' he remarked darkly, 'is the President
of the Bayonets?'

This was a disturbing reminder that force was still the decisive
factor—both in the struggle against Spain and for supremacy
within the patriot ranks. But the extremists now controlling the
junta did little more than their luke-warm predecessors to prepare
the country for the inevitable ordeal by arms. They did not even
take the measures necessary for their own security. Mackenna relied
perhaps too much on the friendly assurances he had received from
José Miguel, Rozas on his mastery of political intrigue. Bernardo

O'Higgins, still weak from his recent sickness, resumed his seat in Congress and devoted his energies to securing the passage of an unlikely and most unwarlike bill; nothing less than a measure putting an end to the insanitary but cherished custom of burial beneath church floors, and the establishment instead of cemeteries outside the city walls. This was a reform which his father, in the days of his governorship, had fought for in vain against the prevailing bigotry. It was a deep source of satisfaction to his son to feel that his first act as a legislator should be to continue the work begun by his father. Even in the thick of his struggle against Spain, Bernardo always preserved the conviction that he was somehow furthering the aims which Don Ambrosio had striven for.

With this modest triumph behind him, Bernardo obtained leave of Congress to return home to complete his convalescence and devote some time to the management of his estates. But on the morning of his departure he was detained by startling news. After holding office for a mere six weeks, the new junta had itself been overthrown by a fresh coup of the Carreras and the supremacy of the Eight Hundred brought to an end. Congress was hurriedly recalled, and, in the midst of considerable turmoil, a new junta elected; José Miguel Carrera for Santiago, Rozas for Concepción, and a Dr Marín for the North of Chile. But Rozas was away in Concepción, and Carrera pressed Bernardo to act as his deputy. O'Higgins at first refused. He disapproved of a change which was so blatantly the outcome of military force, and the work of the capital at that. But Carrera was full of specious arguments, of appeals to his patriotism and to his friendship for Rozas. Bernardo finally agreed, on the condition that the arrangement was endorsed by the constituents of Concepción.

Scarcely had he taken this decision when Bernardo was astonished to learn that Carrera, without so much as a word to his two colleagues on the junta, had ordered the arrest of Juan Mackenna and other prominent leaders of the Eight Hundred, whom the new dictator now regarded as his most dangerous rivals. The pretext was the alleged discovery of a plot against the Carreras. O'Higgins protested angrily and demanded that José Miguel should give an account of his actions to Congress. Quite unabashed, Carrera consented. In the stormy scene which followed, he taunted Congress itself with being implicated in the conspiracy. 'There are murderers here, even within these four walls', he exclaimed. Within a few hours,

Congress itself had ceased to exist. The President of the Bayonets had once more thrown his troops into action and demonstrated where real power was to be found. This was the third armed coup which José Miguel Carrera had carried out within little more than ten weeks of setting foot on his native shore. He could now feel himself the master of the capital, if not yet of the whole of Chile.

In face of such high-handed action which he was powerless to prevent, O'Higgins' only course was to resign. What is less easy to understand is why he did not first denounce the flagrant illegality of the new dictatorship instead of pleading the still precarious state of his health and the need to attend to his private affairs. Naïve and inexperienced as he was in political intrigue, he may himself have fallen to some degree beneath the spell of the dazzling Carrera and been easily persuaded by his fair words. By nature frank and unsuspecting, he was reluctant to believe that anyone professing patriotic sentiments could really be actuated by ambition. He was soon destined to give further proof of his gullibility.

Though the master of Santiago, Carrera had still to reckon with the bulk of the country's armed forces mustered on the southern Frontier. He had good reason to expect that it would prove hostile. He had intercepted a letter to the President of the Congress from the provincial junta in Concepción, who were still ignorant of the latest events in Santiago, denouncing Carrera's forced change of junta as illegal and offering to put troops at the disposal of Congress. If that had been the response of the South to Carrera's cavalier treatment of the junta, how would they regard his still more summary dissolution of Congress? Concepción commanded the bulk of the country's military resources. To overcome them, José Miguel needed time to muster his own followers and raise his own troops in central Chile. He set out to temporize and to pacify Rozas.

Carrera therefore approached O'Higgins once more, playing on his patriotism with great astuteness and appealing to him to use his good offices to reach an agreement with Rozas on his behalf and thus avoid the fratricidal bloodshed which would imperil the whole cause of the incipient revolution. Couched in such terms as these, O'Higgins could not resist the request and hurred off to confer, as Carrera's plenipotentiary, with the junta of the South. A draft agreement which Bernardo hoped would satisfy both sides was soon worked out. The central government of Chile was to consist of a junta of three persons, each representing one of the three main regions of Chile, and the defunct Congress was to be replaced by a smaller consultative senate acting as a check on the junta's arbitrary power. Carrera sent his plenipotentiary messages of congratulation and encouragement but showed not the slightest signs of any action to ratify the agreement. On the contrary, he went so far as to co-opt two other persons representing powerful Santiago families onto his junta, and at the same time pushed on with his military preparations. His father marched south to Talca with an armed force; by the beginning of March, 1812, Juan José followed him with a division of more than one thousand. It looked, as the dictator intended it to look, as if serious hostilities were intended.

Bernardo realized at last that he had been cynically exploited by Carrera who had no serious intention of implementing his recommendations. Impulsively abandoning his endeavours as a peacemaker, he put himself at the head of his armed *inquilinos* and placed his sword at the disposal of Rozas. The Commander-in-Chief of the southern armies, though resplendent in the trappings of a Brigadier, was not cast for a military role. His powers were beginning to fail and he wished to avoid bloodshed at any cost. O'Higgins, more bellicose by nature and now smarting under a sense of personal affront, urged that he should be authorized to lead a detachment over the river Maule, fall upon Carrera's troops whom he was confident of routing, and push on to Santiago. But Rozas, still hoping to find a peaceful way out, preferred to negotiate. The leaders of the two factions met in a fairly cordial but inconclusive interview. Negotiations dragged on, and the autumn rains set in, causing discomfort and demoralization amongst both of the hostile camps. At length, a limited agreement was reached, each leader consenting to disband his forces, but no decision being taken on the fundamental question of the political organization of the country. Rozas found that he had been outwitted by the younger man, and his military superiority frittered away. He returned discredited to Concepción, and was shortly afterwards removed from office by a pro-Carrera coup and banished to the Argentine, where he died soon afterwards.

Bernardo, disillusioned by his first taste of public affairs, returned to Las Canteras resolved to withdraw from public life and devote himself to his estate. Instead of marching boldly towards full independence, he saw the country weakened with internal dissensions and in the power of a despotic and irresponsible family. He

4

thought seriously of migrating with his mother and sister to the Argentine where he had friends and where the prospects for the revolution seemed brighter. But his schemes were interrupted by the arrival of momentous news. On the 27 March, 1813, an expeditionary force sent by the Viceroy of Peru to enforce obedience landed in the south of Chile. In the face of this tremendous challenge old feuds must be healed and new resolves taken. The hour which he had long foreseen and now secretly welcomed had struck at last.

Ten

The First Round

IF SANTIAGO HAD led the way in taking the political steps towards Chilean independence, the initiative passed to the South once matters were put to the test of war. As in the centuries of colonial history, the military importance of Concepción province remained fundamental. But now the strategic position was reversed. Instead of serving as a base for action against the Indian lands beyond the Bío-Bío, Concepción had become the spring-board for the conquest, in favour of Rebels or Royalists, of central Chile. Whoever held the South could draw on the formidable Araucanians as allies in their northward advance. Moreover, through controlling the port of Talcahuano, supplies and reinforcements could be received by sea, and more important still, an expedition could be sent up the coast, outflanking any hostile forces which lay between, and land at Valparaíso to march on the capital. If this tactical advantage was neglected by both sides it was due to the prevailing shortage of ships and a general failure to realize the decisive role of sea-power when deployed against a long, exposed coast.

The main theatre of operations was the long thin stretch of country between Santiago and the Araucanian forest-land of the South, in particular the sixty leagues which lay between the rivers Bío-Bío and Maule. This elongated parallelogram, of which the Andes and the Pacific Ocean formed the longest sides, was crossed by low ranges of hills, running from the Andes to the coast, and by a number of rivers, the command of whose banks and fords formed the constant tactical objectives of the opposing generals. Though heavy rains would sometimes bog down the armies, their manoeuvrability was generally great, thanks to the immense herds of horses on which, at least in the early stages of the war, they could freely draw.

The troops on both sides were splendid natural horsemen, and

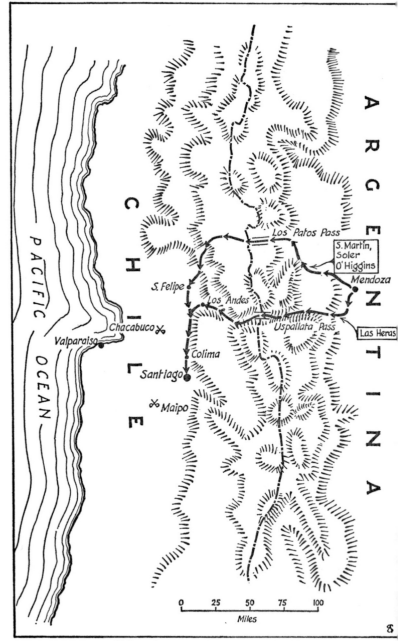

Chile: the campaigns in the South

the whole population of the frontier province was warlike and accustomed to bearing arms.

But in conventional military training and discipline both armies were deplorably weak. Antonio Quintanilla, one of the most competent of the Royalist officers, admitted in his memoirs that 'if either side had possessed merely two companies capable of manoeuvring and retaining formation during an action, they would have been sufficient to decide the outcome of the war in their favour.'[1] Operations were carried out in an essentially amateur way, but were none the less ferocious for that. There was no question of professional armies trying to outmanoeuvre each other by scientific rules. There were very few pitched battles, no orderly movements, no real generalship, no grand strategic conceptions, and very little idea of tactics. Both sides suffered from a serious lack of trained officers and the numbers engaged in active operations were very small. At the outbreak of hostilities, the forces maintained on the Bío-Bío Frontier represented the strongest concentration of military power anywhere in the Spanish colonies. Whilst Lima could hardly muster more than a thousand men, the Frontier boasted a regular force of some four hundred dragoons, six hundred infantrymen, and a hundred gunners.

The armies had little to distinguish them in arms, uniforms, equipment, or fighting spirit. It was not a question of Spanish against Chilean forces, for each was composed almost entirely of Creoles. No Spanish regular troops whatsoever took part in the war until a much later stage. It was essentially a civil war of Chileans against Chileans. Most Spaniards, but by no means all, were to be found fighting on the Royalist side. The rank and file would choose their flag according to the lead given by their local landowner. They would frequently change sides, or simply go home if discontented with their officers, lack of pay, or the general conditions of the campaign. Many officers were almost as unreliable, and their allegiance was less to a cause than to the persons of some *caudillo*.

The Royalists had the initial advantage of knowing clearly why they were fighting—for the King, and the established order. Many citizens of solid worth were to be found in their ranks. The 'Patriots' had no clear idea of their objective—or else contradictory ideas. They fought because they had an antipathy to the Spaniards and

[1] Antonio de Quintanilla: *Apuntes sobre la guerra de Chile*, published in *Colección de historiadores y de documentos relativos a la independencia de Chile*, Vol. IV, pp. 204–236.

wanted to govern themselves—but not necessarily to be totally independent. Only a very few, of which O'Higgins was one, were bent on winning complete national independence and the establishment of a republic. Amongst the ranks of the Patriots were to be found not a few adventurers, careerists, even criminals. Many had joined the rebel cause out of personal loyalty to their idol Carrera, and were often ready to make terms with the Royalists, and in some cases to pass over to them, in order to serve their *caudillo's* personal advancement.

An incident of this sort had already occurred in one of the keypoints of Chile and greatly facilitated the Viceroy's plans to restore Spanish domination. The fortress of Valdivia had first thrown in its lot with the Santiago junta, but had then passed under the control of a group of officers who declared themselves for Carrera and then for the King. Together with the island of Chiloé, whose inhabitants remained staunchly loyal to the Crown throughout the war, Valdivia could raise 1,500 soldiers, of which nine hundred were troops of the line. Abascal, the energetic Viceroy of Peru, resolved to make this the nucleus of his expeditionary force, and he now felt himself strong enough to send a peremptory note addressed to 'the three individuals who have seized the government of Chile' summoning them to place themselves forthwith under the orders of the rightful authorities, and threatening drastic measures if they refused. He then gathered together a supply of arms, uniforms, and other equipment, together with some fifty veterans who were to train and command the new army, and shipped them off to Chiloé and Valdivia under the command of Pareja, an officer whose experience had been chiefly in the Navy rather than with land forces. The expedition made a surprise landing near Talcahuano and forced the surrender of that port. Concepción capitulated soon afterwards, protesting, somewhat ingenuously, that 'it had never renounced its loyalty to the Spanish Crown.' Most of the local garrison passed over to the Royalists, thus bringing their numbers up to about three thousand. The army then pushed on northwards to Chillán, collecting some two thousand half-armed and rather useless militiamen on the way, and receiving a rousing welcome from the Franciscan fathers who were the life and soul of the Royalist cause in that city.

As soon as he had received word of the invasion, O'Higgins hastily put himself at the head of a hundred *inquilinos* armed with lances and set off for Concepción. On the way, he learned of the capitulation of the city and was ordered to dissolve his unit, since nothing could be achieved against such overwhelming odds. It was doubtful indeed whether his detachment could even manage to withdraw to the north without being captured or destroyed by the enemy. O'Higgins therefore disbanded his men and set off across country, with only a couple of companions, for the river Maule. This he reached after some days' hard riding, and continued to Talca, where the patriot forces were reported to be mustering. A few hours later he was joined by José Miguel Carrera, who had now assumed the rank of Commander-in-Chief, after delegating his political powers to a junta representing the most powerful sections of the Santiago aristocracy. News of the Royalist invasion had dissolved old differences in a common resolve to resist the enemy.

There was no time to lose. Whilst the regular troops were mustering, it was necessary to act quickly to secure the allegiance of the militia which, left leaderless, would otherwise be incorporated into the Royalist army. Santiago province alone contained some nine thousand militiamen. Though without great military value at the moment, they represented the raw material for the armies of the future.

Bernardo O'Higgins asked for permission to lead a small detachment back across the Maule to fall on the enemy's advance-guard in Linares, and clear the district of enemy so that the militia could be secured for the Patriots. With a handful of horsemen he forded the river under cover of darkness, and made his way through the mist to the outskirts of the town, where he learned that the dragoons were mustering in the plaza. Disposing his little band so as to create the maximum of surprise and confusion, O'Higgins rode into the plaza with great clatter, took the soldiers off their guard and easily secured them. The prisoners were then sent back under a strong escort to Talca, where most of them voluntarily joined Carrera's army. The district was temporarily cleared of the enemy and the militia could be called out and sent over the Maule to reinforce the Patriots with another two hundred men. If we except the brief skirmish when the Royalists landed near Talcahuano, the engagement at Linares may be taken as the opening operation of the war and cheered the Patriots with the example of what could be achieved under resolute and courageous leadership.

Carrera's main preoccupation, meanwhile, was how best to dispose his growing, but inexperienced, forces along the Maule to await the enemy offensive. Here he turned for advice to a recently acquired friend and counsellor, an American citizen called Joel R. Poinsett, who had been sent to Santiago with the rank of Consul,[1] to stake out an early claim on Chile's growing foreign trade. Poinsett's appointment was welcomed by the Patriots, who saw in it the presage of political recognition from abroad. The Consul, as he was generally called, was an intelligent and versatile man in his early thirties, who took up their cause with enthusiasm and soon acquired considerable ascendency over Carrera. As a youth, he had shown a passion for military life and had entered Woolwich against the wish of his parents. Now he had a splendid opportunity to indulge his tastes, and in the prevailing ignorance around him, he found his strategic ideas attentively listened to. Poinsett was in favour of entrenching the advance guard, under O'Higgins, in a hill south of the Maule, the rest of the army being to the north of the river. This salient, he declared, would be sufficient to deny the enemy the passage of the river. In the event, their position would have soon become untenable, since it was too far from the ford to enable them to command it (and there were, in any case, others) and they would then find themselves cut off by the river from the main army. Luckily, the danger was averted just in time by the arrival of the only officer in the Patriot army with any experience and tactical sense. Mackenna, whose presence was judged essential, had been released from arrest and had hurried to make common cause with the Carreras in the emergency.

The Patriot army was drawn up in three divisions, each under the command of one of the Carrera brothers. The first, under Luis, took up positions along the line of the Maule; the second, under Juan José, between the Maule and Talca; whilst the third was centred on Talca itself under the Commander-in-Chief. The advance guard still remained south of the river under O'Higgins, but a sudden illness prevented him from taking part in the next engagement. This was an attempt to surprise the advance positions

[1] G. Feliu Cruz: *El Consul Poinsett y las Campañas de la Patria Vieja* in *Revista Chilena de historia y geografía*, 1924, Vol. 49, pp. 345–360. For a biography of Poinsett see J. F. Rippy: *Joel Roberts Poinsett — Versatile American.* Typical of the uncomplimentary view taken of the Consul by the English is Maria Graham's remark that 'a person named Poinsett, acting as American Consul, was then with the Carreras and appears to have taken an active part in all affairs, even to interfering in the military business of the time; but his ignorance, if not his cowardice, seems to have been of singular disservice to those young men.' (*Journal of a residence in Chile during the year* 1822, London, 1824, p. 206).

of the enemy with a column, six hundred strong, under the command of a militia colonel, Juan de Dios Puga, who knew the difficult terrain. Puga, failing to find the enemy in the positions expected, came upon an encampment in the village of Yerbas Buenas. The camp-fires, in the misty darkness, were taken for those of the advance guard; in reality, Puga had stumbled without knowing it upon the main body of the Royalist army. The Patriots fell upon the enemy with good heart, creating indescribable confusion. They overran the artillery, and then realized that they must be up against a greatly superior enemy. Groups of Royalists began firing at each other in the darkness; neither side heard nor obeyed orders, and only the watchwords of 'For the King'—'Viva la Patria' distinguished the combatants. At the first light of dawn, the Patriots tried to break off the engagement and withdraw, taking with them numerous prisoners and captured material. But just when it seemed that they could count on a hard-won victory, the fortunes of battle changed. The horses they had left behind before launching their attack had disappeared during the night, and a detachment of enemy cavalry, which had not been involved in the fighting, fell upon the weary footsoldiers, creating great havoc and causing them to abandon the spoil. The Royalist officers too succeeded in rallying the disordered units in the camp and followed close on the heels of the enemy. The Patriot withdrawal soon became a rout. Only a handful of the six hundred ever regained their base.

The effect of this set-back was disastrous and altogether out of proportion to the actual losses suffered. Carrera, despite the tenacious opposition of Mackenna, who realized that to abandon the line of the Maule would be to sacrifice the greatest natural barrier between the enemy and Santiago, decided on a general retreat. The officers were the first to run for their lives, and a shameful, panic-stricken rout set in which was arrested only by the arrival of reinforcements. The Royalist commander, though his troops had been shaken and mauled, was not slow to follow up his advantage. He ordered a general advance to the Maule. But on arriving at the banks of that river, the troops from Chiloé refused to venture further. Neither threats nor exhortations moved them. Their morale had been badly shaken by the night attack, and they went in superstitious dread of fresh surprises. Pareja was forced to change his plans and to winter south of the river. His army began to crumble, the militia deserting *en masse* and making off home, and even a few

4*

of the regulars passing over to the Patriots. Pareja himself fell ill
with pneumonia and decided to spend the winter in Chillán.

As the Royalist army withdrew, the Patriots reinforced and
recovered from their panic, surged forward, recrossed the river, and
closed in on the enemy baggage-train. Pareja decided to turn
and face them. He was now seriously ill and could do no more than
encourage his men from a litter, whilst Sanchez, an able Royalist
officer, took over the command. Sanchez had lost his cavalry, but
chose positions where the artillery could play effectively on the
enemy who attempted, with misguided valour, to carry them by
assault. The Patriots suffered heavy losses, and the Royalists,
exhausted and famished, managed to withdraw to the relative
safety of Chillán.

Carrera had now to decide whether to attempt an immediate
assault on Chillán, or whether to bypass the city and cut it off from
its base and from reinforcements from Peru by occupying Concepción and Talcahuano. His advisers were at variance. The first
course was advocated by Mackenna, the second by the Consul, who
wanted to secure the freeing of ten New England whalers held in
that harbour. There is little doubt that the Commander-in-Chief
did well to follow Poinsett's advice. The army lacked artillery and
its morale was low; it was in no state to attempt an assault on Chillán.
Concepción and Talcahuano were easily occupied, and the Patriots
were rewarded by the capture of valuable stores of rifles, artillery,
and other equipment. They were also just in time to seize a ship
arriving from Peru with a group of senior officers, further supplies
and funds on board. Thus strengthened, the army moved back to
lay formal siege to Chillán.

O'Higgins, meanwhile, had been sent to raise what troops he
could in the region round his own estate of Las Canteras. Starting
with a band of thirty, he made for Los Angeles, and broke into the
fort where he surprised the Colonel engrossed in a game of cards
with the parish priest, and the dragoons resting in the guard-room
round the brazier. His courage and enthusiasm were infectious.
Within a few hours, Los Angeles with its garrison had declared
itself for the Patriots. Neighbouring towns and villages followed
suit, and before many days were past, the band of thirty had
swollen to fourteen hundred. With this considerable force, he
hastened back to join the rest of the army now encamped round
Chillán.

O'Higgins remembered the town well from his schooldays. But its normal population of 4,000 had now swollen to more than twice that number through the influx of eighteen hundred Royalist troops and several thousand refugees who had fled from the countryside to escape pillage and bloodshed at the hands of roving bands. The town stood on a slight eminence and its natural advantages had been strengthened by the construction of well-chosen works. The Royalist troops were well ensconced behind the stout walls of the Franciscan monastery. From this shelter they could defy both the threats of the besiegers and the violent rains and winds which were converting the fields into a muddy swamp. Shivering in their improvised tents and short of fuel and rations, the Patriot army rapidly deteriorated in morale and numbers. Every day desertions grew more frequent. After a month's siege, with little to show for it, O'Higgins and Mackenna persuaded Carrera to force a decision before their forces melted away completely.

During the night of 2 August, Mackenna sent troops to occupy a small hill in front of the main positions and placed on it a battery of cannon defended by an earthwork and some five hundred infantry under O'Higgins. Shortly after dawn, the Royalists perceived it and sent out a column to dislodge it. A fierce engagement ensued. A Patriot force, four hundred strong, fortified by a stiff brandy ration and encouraged by the example of their colonels, Lius Carrera and Mackenna, forded the river on the left flank of the city, whilst a cavalry column of similar strength advanced on the right wing to cut off the enemy's retreat. Almost surrounded, the Royalists withdrew into the suburbs with the Patriots at their heels. O'Higgins, in the forefront of the fray, pressed on towards the centre of the city in fierce house-to-house fighting. But his men, intoxicated by alcohol and the prospects of pillage, lost all discipline and were soon forced back in a fierce counter-attack. Carrera saw that they had not yet penetrated the entrenchments in the heart of the town and gave the order to retire. A cannon-ball struck the powder magazine of the batteries brought up by Mackenna during the previous night. A sheet of flame, followed by a dense pall of smoke, was the signal for the Royalists to shift their attack to that point, and only the darkness of night put an end to the savage conflict. The Royalists withdrew to the city and the Patriots to their camp, having lost some two hundred killed, and a similar number of wounded.

The next day the fighting was resumed with still greater ferocity, deepened confusion, and heavier losses. The battle was often a three-sided one, groups of householders banding together to protect themselves against Royalists and Patriots alike. Loot and rape became more attractive objectives than the destruction of the enemy. Neither side could claim a clear military gain and when a consignment of ammunition which Carrera had been expecting from Concepción fell into the hands of the Royalists, the Commander-in-Chief saw no alternative to raising the siege. The Royalists, for their part, were too exhausted to do more than send out an occasional guerrilla band.

Their failure to capture Chillán swung the fortunes of war against the Patriots. The population of the South, which had at first embraced their cause with enthusiasm, now tended to side with the Royalists. The fault was largely Carrera's. Irritated by any challenge to his authority and wishing to ingratiate himself with his troops, he had often given them a free hand to loot and murder and had taken bloody reprisals against families known, or merely believed, to be in secret league with the enemy. These excesses, together with his obvious ineptitude as a general, had turned opinion against the cause. 'It is certain that the province is all up in arms against us,' he admitted in a letter to his friend Poinsett, whose absence had removed a restraining influence over the Commander-in-Chief. Every day brought fresh evidence of this unwelcome truth. The area round Los Angeles, which O'Higgins had raised for the Patriots a few months before, now declared itself again for the Royalists. O'Higgins himself, at the head of three hundred mounted men, suffered a reverse and narrowly escaped capture. Though he managed to avenge this set-back and defeat the guerrillas a few days later, it was not until October that the Frontier was again cleared of the enemy and their forces compelled to retire to Chillán. But before withdrawing, the Royalists took care to carry out a systematic destruction of the whole estate of Las Canteras, burning its house and farm-buildings to the ground, uprooting the vines, carrying off the cattle. Doña Isabel and Rosita, who had taken refuge in Los Angeles, were sent to Chillán and kept as hostages until exchanged for the family of Colonel Sanchez.

South of the Bío-Bío river, too, the Royalists were quietly consolidating their position. They had formed an alliance with the Araucanian chiefs and maintained communications through their territory with the garrisons at Valdivia and Chiloé. They also captured the port and harbour of Arauco, and so possessed good bases for receiving supplies and reinforcements from Lima.

On 16 October, the Patriots were surprised whilst about to cross the river Itata by the ford of El Roble. Carrera only escaped thanks to the speed of his horse, and O'Higgins was wounded in the leg. Bandaging it rapidly, he had himself carried into the front line where he lay under fire and in great pain, encouraging his men with his indomitable example. His troops finally rallied and managed to counter-attack. It was a minor engagement, but reports of it spread through the country and caused people to contrast the courageous bearing of O'Higgins with the incompetence, or worse, of the Commander-in-Chief. For months past, general dissatisfaction with Carrera's leadership had been growing. People had at first been prepared to put up with his high-handed political actions for the confidence which they felt—and which Carrera and his brothers sedulously fostered—in his military genius. But events had shown that the dashing hussar was no organizer of armies, no strategist, no general. The pretentious style of his official communiqués had for some time delayed a realization of the truth. The raising of the siege of Chillán was explained away first as 'a measure dictated by humanitarian considerations' and then as 'necessitated by the rigour of the season.' The clash at El Roble was glorified into a great Patriot triumph, with a highly coloured account of the enemy throwing down their weapons before the victorious Patriots. But it gradually became known that Carrera's forces had suffered losses four times as heavy as those of the enemy, and had only been saved by the valour of O'Higgins and a few devoted officers, whilst the Commander-in-Chief had ingloriously fled.

The junta had long retained its faith in Carrera's generalship and had tried to defend him against the mounting tide of popular criticism. Slowly it became convinced that there could be no effective military leadership, any more than there could be stable government, so long as the arrogant young despot held power. Carrera must go, if the Patriot cause was to be saved. But how? Who was to get rid of him, and who was to replace him? His brothers Luis and Juan José openly threatened to turn out the junta by force if it raised a hand against him. He still enjoyed great popularity amongst the rank and file of the army, and many of the officers were his devoted adherents.

The junta did not know the answers to these questions but

decided, as a first step, to move south to Talca so as to be nearer the scene of operations. Still half believing Carrera's account of the 'victory' of El Roble, it thought that Sanchez might now agree to a truce on terms favourable to the Patriots. But the Royalist leader, well informed of the pitiable state of the enemy army and the tension between its Commander-in-Chief and the junta, haughtily rejected their overtures. The junta then made a formal demand of Carrera that he should lay down his command. He replied with a violent denunciation of the junta, which he blamed for the failure of the campaign. He even thought to secure their persons by force, but was prevented from doing so by the presence of the Royalist forces which lay between Talca and his own headquarters in Concepción.

O'Higgins, like the bulk of the officer corps, was opposed to any change of command. 'I am of the opinion that representations should immediately be made to the government,' he wrote to Concepción from the field in the middle of November, 'that it is essential to make no changes in the present command by the removal of an officer whose services are so very useful and necessary for the expulsion of the enemy.'[1] Some ten days later he urged the same view directly on the junta. He was still clearly under the spell of the legend of the Carreras' military genius, and — in spite of the unfortunate experience which he had himself suffered at José Miguel's hands — retained an equally ingenuous confidence in his disinterested political intentions. He reminded the junta that the Carreras had promised to convene a congress once the war was over, and he added: 'Should they be so unwise as to forget these solemn promises, which can hardly be expected, I pledge my sacred word that I will do everything within my modest powers to make them honour such a solemn pledge. Your Excellencies may be assured that this is the opinion of many honourable men in the army, that once the independence of the country has been achieved, they will make any sacrifice to secure its civil liberty.'[2]

This reply would certainly have increased the perplexities of the junta, had the latter not been confirmed in its original resolve by the arrival of Mackenna, who had left the front to urge in person the absolute necessity for a change of command if complete disaster was to be avoided. Mackenna painted a very different, and no doubt too optimistic picture. By no means all the officers in the army, he

[1] *Archivo*, Vol. I, p. 284.   [2] *Ibid*, p. 315.

asserted, were personally attached to Carrera; most of them would willingly accept O'Higgins in his place; even José Miguel himself would raise no objections to handing over to O'Higgins who in every way was a fit person for high command. On the strength of these persuasions, the junta finally took the step of issuing a decree removing José Miguel Carrera from his command, and nominating Bernardo O'Higgins as his successor.

Mackenna was wrong. The Government's decree was received with anger and scorn in Concepción. Carrera trampled it under foot and threw its bearers into prison. The Bishop preached disobedience to an officer corps only too ready to follow that advice. O'Higgins hurried to Concepción full of perplexity. Not only did he think the army would not recognize himself as its new Commander-in-Chief; he had frankly no desire to take over the post, for which he felt he had neither aptitude nor training. But from Talca, his friend Mackenna kept urging him to accept. 'Courage; save your country!' he exhorted him. 'Should you refuse to accept the command to which you are called by the will of the army and the choice of the government, the whole province will be lost and you will be eternally responsible to God and to your country for its ruin.'[1] O'Higgins was always susceptible to this sort of patriotic blackmail, but he still remained a prey to doubt and indecision. In his perplexity, he took the characteristic resolve to consult Carrera himself as to what he ought to do. Comradeship-in-arms had restored a degree of cordiality between the two men and O'Higgins believed that his own nomination would probably be less odious to the proud hussar than that of another. After earnest discussions together, they agreed that he should go to Talca to inform the junta personally of his reluctance to assume the command, but that if they insisted, he would consent.

Three days' hard riding across country to escape enemy patrols brought O'Higgins to Talca. The junta met to hear his views. He told them that since 'circumstances had made a soldier of him, and he had taken up arms to defend his country as an ordinary guerrilla leader in a moment of danger, he lacked the necessary training required by a senior officer commanding armies,' and that he there-fore did not dare to assume supreme responsibility. The junta replied that their decision was irrevocable; Carrera would never be reinstated in his command; O'Higgins was the obvious choice, for

[1] *Ibid*, p. 310–312.

his proved bravery and prestige in the army; on him depended 'the fortune or misfortune of a million Chileans.'

In the face of such insistence, Bernardo reluctantly agreed and took the oath as Commander-in-Chief to defend his country against all enemies, internal or foreign. Juan José was replaced by Spano, an efficient Spanish officer who had espoused the Chilean cause, as Commander of the Grenadiers. As Bernardo was preparing to hurry back to Concepción, the junta received a message from Carrera saying that he 'received with particular pleasure and satisfaction the news of the choice and appointment of so worthy a person as Colonel O'Higgins,' but added somewhat enigmatically that, to avoid difficulties, he would postpone laying down his command until O'Higgins reached Concepción.[1]

O'Higgins and the junta received this communication with differing reactions. The junta feared that Carrera might refuse to hand over his command and be capable of any act, even of going over to the Royalists, to preserve his power or avenge his fancied wrongs. O'Higgins, ever sanguine and unsuspecting, accepted José Miguel's assurances at their face value. He returned to Concepción with all speed and formally took over his duties as Commander-in-Chief of the Patriot armies on 2 February, 1814.

[1] *Ibid*, p. 321.

Ambrosio O'Higgins

Isabel Riquelme

Juan Mackenna

José Miguel Carrera

Eleven

Towards a Truce

SELDOM CAN AN inexperienced general have taken command of an army in a more deplorable state. For the last four months the Patriot forces had been virtually inactive, and their ranks had wasted away through daily desertions. There remained some 1,800 men, poorly armed and with little ammunition left, clothed in rags and subsisting on short rations. Their morale was low and they had only a handful of officers with any authority or experience. The once plentiful reserves of horses had disappeared and what artillery remained had to be manhandled over the rough tracks. 'The army was so destitute of weapons that the yokes of the oxen were taken and used as clubs,' wrote an English friend in after years. 'O'Higgins caused a large wooden cannon to be made and bound it round with hide, but it burst after the fourth discharge.'[1]

No wonder that the prospect daunted even O'Higgins' boundless optimism. 'Pity me, my friend,' he wrote to his boyhood playmate Casimiro Albano, 'in having to grapple with the greatest difficulties and dangers besetting the post to which the government and public opinion have called me. You know the lamentable conditions of our forces. I dare not call it an army, as I can see nothing, absolutely nothing, in its equipment or morale which justifies that name. Nevertheless, it is a duty imposed by the danger which besets our country, and which one who has pledged his last breath in defence of her liberty and independence cannot refuse.'[2]

The Royalist army, though greatly reduced in numbers and no better off than the Patriots in uniforms, arms, and equipment, was in good heart. It was still concentrated in Chillán, and could count on the friendly disposition of the surrounding countryside. Reports sent to the Viceroy made him confident that it would be enough to send some five hundred reinforcements and fresh supplies for the

[1] Maria Graham: *op. cit.*, p. 24n.   [2] *Archivo*, Vol. I, p. 322.

whole country to rise and welcome a Royalist restoration. He therefore made great efforts to prepare a new Chilean expedition which
was ready to set sail from Callao at the beginning of January 1814.
He placed it under the command of Brigadier Gaínza, an officer
who had had an honourable career in the Spanish army and who
was both level-headed and fair-minded, though lacking in energy
and real military flair. He was accompanied by his legal *asesor*
Rodríguez Aldea and some two hundred troops. His orders were to
land in Arauco, reoccupy Concepción, and demand the total
capitulation of the rebels.

The news of Gaínza's landing reached O'Higgins only four days
after he had taken over his new command. His forces were not only
in deplorable condition but weakly placed strategically. One part
was under his direct command in Concepción, another under
Mackenna further north. His best plan would have been to evacuate
Concepción, now threatened by the new Royalist expedition, and
march north to join Mackenna, with whom he could then hope to
hold a line on the rivers Ñuble or Maule. A note with this advice
was sent him from the junta. But the new Commander-in-Chief
hesitated, tempted by the idea of trying first to reoccupy the
Frontier and make a fresh assault on Chillán before the two Royalist
forces could effect a junction—a hopeless plan in view of the
wretched state of his troops. In his perplexity, he turned to consult
José Miguel Carrera.

Carrera, at this stage, seems to have felt but little personal animosity against O'Higgins. He looked down upon him for his naïveté and
his irregular birth, and regarded him as a puppet through whom he
would still continue to exercise real power over the army. But the
least exercise of initiative or independent judgment on the part of his
successor was bound to arouse his irritation, and this in turn to
deepen into intense resentment. José Miguel saw slights in the most
innocuous of actions. When O'Higgins issued a proclamation to the
troops, the ex-Commander-in-Chief denounced it as wounding the
honour of himself and his brothers. When O'Higgins promoted
some of his officers and pardoned the Royalists of Concepción whom
Carrera had thrown into prison, Carrera branded it as an act of
treachery against his own authority. With malicious gibes and
raillery, he set about undermining the prestige of the new general.
A stream of desertions followed. Juan José put himself at the head
of a contingent and set off for Santiago with the declared intention

of overthrowing the government. Only O'Higgins appeared to remain blind to the dissolution of his forces and wrote off to the junta, with his usual readiness to attribute his own sentiments to others; 'There is now nothing but unity and fraternity, and the desire to get to grips with the enemy.'[1] The junta had nominated José Miguel Chilean representative in the Argentine and after some days he left Concepción with his brother Luis. But no one, except the guileless Bernardo, believed that the ex-Dictator had the slightest intention of letting himself be eliminated so easily from the scene.

But fate had a trick to play which temporarily checked any subversive plans which the Carreras might have been harbouring. Shortly after leaving Concepción, the two brothers were surprised and captured by a Royalist patrol. They were brought before Gaínza, who ordered that the important prisoners should be held in strict confinement. When the news became known in the Patriot camp, it was believed that O'Higgins and the junta had connived at the coup with the Royalists, in order to be rid of their formidable rival.

The position of Mackenna's army at Membrillar had, in the meantime, became precarious. Talca, which lay between him and Santiago, had fallen to the enemy. His officers pressed him to make a hurried retreat so as to place his forces between Talca and the capital. This would have meant the abandonment of O'Higgins' divisions, and their probable destruction at the hands of Gaínza. A council of war was held and the decision taken to wait one more week for O'Higgins to join them. 'Unless you bring up your division at once, everything may be lost,' Mackenna wrote to O'Higgins. 'You, my dear friend, are responsible to your country for your present inactivity and for not pressing on with your division...only come, for God's sake, and all will be well.'[2]

The news that Talca had fallen put an end to O'Higgins' hesitations. Abandoning his idea of attacking Chillán, he set out towards Mackenna's positions. His army—if it could be called such—travelled at a snail's pace. He had neither pack animals nor mounts for his men. The troops dragged their own guns and ammunition, and carried their saddles slung over their shoulders in the hope of catching stray horses. They seemed more like a train of pilgrims or fugitives than an army, and their plight provoked the derision of the Royalists. But despite their ragged appearance and their depleted

[1] *Ibid*, Vol. 2, p. 61.   [2] *Ibid*, p. 111.

ranks, a more determined morale was already apparent. The faint-
hearted had deserted and, with few exceptions, the officers who
had followed Carrera into the war as to some irresponsible adventure, had left with their *caudillo*. The men who remained were in
grim earnest.

Gaínza was not sure whether the objective of this ragged host was
Chillán or Membrillar. He therefore sent on a strong advance guard
to occupy the heights called El Quilo, from where they could keep
him informed which of the two routes O'Higgins' forces would
take, and harass them accordingly. As soon as O'Higgins caught
sight of the enemy, and without waiting to ascertain their strength,
he launched a vigorous attack. The Royalist advance-guard held
out for some time, expecting that Gaínza would send up reinforcements. But the general, fearing that this was a feint, and that he
would be attacked in the flank, or by Mackenna in the rear, did not
dare to move. The advance-guard was dispersed, and the Patriots
captured and entrenched themselves in their very strong positions.
It was fortunate that O'Higgins did not then attempt to push on to
join Mackenna; he would infallibly have come upon the main
Royalist army and been overpowered. Gaínza, not daring to
attack the strong positions at El Quilo, turned against Mackenna's
army at Membrillar, which was also strongly entrenched. The
engagement was an ill-conceived affair, as the Royalist commander
did not wait to bring up his artillery, and after some ferocious hand-
to-hand fighting, his men retired at nightfall, leaving behind a
number of wounded and quantities of equipment. Mackenna, who
had been wounded in the neck, thought their withdrawal a tactical
ruse. He did not realize the extent of his victory and missed the
opportunity of capturing much valuable war material. He was
hourly expecting to be joined by O'Higgins.

But the Commander-in-Chief, who alternated between periods of
wavering and moments of impetuous decision, was slow to leave his
positions, though the sound of distant gunfire reached him.
Mackenna sent him message after message, urging him to make
haste. 'In God's name, let me know what has happened to you and
your divisions...I implore you in the name of God and the Fatherland to hurry on to join forces with me...These delays will be the
ruin of us.'[1] For greater security, the two friends corresponded in
English, confident that if their despatches fell into enemy hands,

[1] *Ibid*, p. 123.

they would not be easily understood. Finally, on 23 March, both armies joined forces. They together comprised 1,500 infantry-men, 200 gunners, and 18 guns, and some hundreds of mounted militiamen. A council of war was held, and it was decided to march on with all speed to attempt to bar Gaínza's way to Santiago.

The Royalist and Patriot armies now began to race, in a parallel advance, to secure the fords over the Maule. By 3 April, both had reached the river. The Patriots found that the enemy already had detachments on the far bank and searched for an undefended ford, over which they managed to cross in safety. They now enjoyed a slight superiority of numbers, as Gaínza's army had been reduced by desertions and some losses in crossing the river. O'Higgins and Mackenna were convinced that a major clash could not long be delayed. They took up positions behind the thick walls of the *hacienda* of Quechereguas, placing sharp-shooters on the walls and improvising parapets from bags of *charqui*. Gaínza reconnoitred these positions and came to the conclusion that they were too strong to be carried by assault. He lacked the necessary supplies and equip-ment for a siege and he dared not risk by-passing the enemy and pushing on to the capital. The only alternative seemed to be to take up winter quarters in Chillán or Talca.

Both sides, in truth, had reached a state of exhaustion. Neither felt strong enough to force the campaign through to a successful outcome. The Patriots saw no prospect of recovering the province of Concepción, and the centre of Chile had been drained of resources and reinforcements. The demands of war and the interruption of normal trade with Peru were causing great economic distress throughout the country. News from Europe showed that Spain had been practically cleared of the French, and the restoration of Ferdinand VII seemed imminent. In other parts of Spanish America the independence movement had been suffering grave set-backs.

In the interests of a more energetic prosecution of the war, the junta had been replaced by a Director Supremo, the moderate and respected Francisco de la Lastra. He had previously served as the Governor of Valparaíso, where he had made the acquaintance of Captain James Hillyar, commanding the *Phoebe* and the *Cherub*, which had been sent to chase the United States' commerce-raiding *Essex* and to keep an eye on British interests on the Chilean

coast.[1] Hillyar had also been entrusted with another and more confidential mission of which the Patriots now considered taking
advantage. Whilst passing through Peru, he had offered his services
to the Viceroy as a mediator with the dissidents in Chile, for Britain
was reluctant to see her Spanish ally's efforts against the French
distracted by difficulties with her own colonies. Abascal wrote to
Gaínza commending Hillyar, whose offer he described as made 'out
of the pure goodness of a heart full of love for humanity.' The
conditions under which a truce could be made were laid down in an
accompanying document.

These conditions, Lastra and his friends learned when they invited
Hillyar to open discussions with them in Santiago, included the
recognition of King Ferdinand and a restoration of the old colonial
administration. To the first condition most Chileans—even those
who only intended to play for time—would have agreed; but the
second was unacceptable. The Creoles had, in the last few years,
acquired too keen a taste for autonomy. The need was now to find
some formula which would reconcile Spanish sovereignty with home
rule. Proposals were therefore drawn up in Santiago and submitted
to Gaínza to the effect that the country should recognize the
sovereignty of Ferdinand and declare that Chile remained an
integral part of the Spanish domains. Delegates should be sent to
Spain to discuss a basis for composing the present differences, and
in the meantime the existing administration should remain in force.
Such an arrangement was clearly going beyond anything the Viceroy
had authorized, and would amount to giving the Patriots a two years'
truce in which they would have time to recover and reorganize. This
Mackenna, who had been to Santiago to take part in the discussion
with Hillyar, explained in confidence to Bernardo O'Higgins. A few
days later, Captain Hillyar left the capital with an escort of honour
to begin his parleys with the Royalist general.

Gaínza, who had made his headquarters at Talca, was conscious
that his own position had been weakened by the large-scale desertions from his army which had begun to occur once Concepción
and the South had been reoccupied by the Royalists. Many simply
left his camp in the belief that the war was now virtually at an end.

---

[1] For a study of the British Navy's role during this period *see* Donald E. Worcester:
Sea Power and Chilean Independence (University of Florida Press, 1962) and G. S.
Graham and R. A. Humphreys: *The Navy and South America,* 1807–1823 (Navy
Records Society, London, 1962).

There was thus little that Gaínza could do but agree to the opening of negotiations. To bring greater pressure to bear upon him, O'Higgins, who had managed to increase his forces, moved them up to within three leagues of Talca. The first parley between the opposing chiefs took place in a peasant's hut by the shores of the Lircay river. It was an informal affair, with Mackenna and O'Higgins representing the Patriots, Gaínza the Royalists, and Hillyar as the mediator. They dispersed after a friendly exchange of ideas. Two days later, formal negotiations were opened in the presence of the officers' respective legal advisers, whose arguments soon came to dominate the proceedings.

Gaínza showed himself somewhat disposed to accept the proposals put forward by the Chilean leaders, but his *asesor*, the astute Rodríguez Aldea, warned him that the concessions demanded by the other side went far beyond anything which the Viceroy had authorized Hillyar or Gaínza himself to consider. The Patriots, it was true, agreed to recognize the sovereignty of Ferdinand and of the regency acting in his name, and promised to send delegates to the *Cortes*. But they insisted that the present administration should remain in power in Chile, and that the Royalists should evacuate Talca within thirty hours, and the whole province of Concepción within one month. When Gaínza was on the point of consenting, his *asesor* broke off the conference and after a private discussion with his chief, presented a series of amendments which together amounted to the restoration of the old colonial system and the occupation of all the Concepción province until the Viceroy had ratified the pact. At this O'Higgins lost patience and exclaimed: 'This is not dealing openly with us! Then we shall go on with the war!'

Gaínza and his adviser were obliged to withdraw their objections, and the pact was signed at eleven o'clock the same evening. It consisted of sixteen articles including the main demands of the Patriots and a number of secondary clauses regulating such questions as the release of prisoners, the exchange of hostages and guarantees, and a reciprocal amnesty.

The Treaty of Lircay, from which the Patriots stood to gain most, was agreed to by both sides from the most dubious of motives. Each believed and hoped that the other party would honour its undertakings but had little intention of doing so itself. During the negotiations, O'Higgins and Gaínza took a stroll together, wrapped in their great-coats, along the river bank, and O'Higgins was amazed to hear his companion express something like sympathy with the aims which inspired the Patriot cause. In effect, some seven years later, when Gaínza had been appointed Governor-General of Guatemala, he declared himself openly for South American independence. But he was not a strong man, and he felt himself at the mercy of circumstances. Once he had returned to Talca, he yielded to the pressure of his advisers and fellow officers and prepared to repudiate the agreement. He only abandoned his intention of recrossing the Maule and falling back on better positions in Chillán when he realized that he lacked the horses and oxen necessary for the removal of his equipment and saw himself compelled to accept the transport, and thus the control, of the Patriot forces.

The Patriot leaders, for their part, were equally ready to throw over the agreement as soon as it suited them. Even O'Higgins seems to have been prepared to depart from his customary candour in the interests of his sacred cause. It is true that he offered himself as one of the hostages for the guarantee of the treaty—an offer which his own government overruled—and that Rodríguez Aldea assured Gaínza that 'the word of this officer is worth more than any hostage.' Probably he regarded the treaty as tacit breathing space for both sides. He could scarcely have expected that the Viceroy, or the Spanish government, would ever willingly consent to its terms, though he expected Gaínza to honour the undertaking to evacuate Concepción province—or was ready to force him to do so.

In Santiago the news of the truce was received with enthusiasm. Everyone expected a speedy return to the good old days of peace and prosperity. Church bells were set joyfully a-ringing, and a thanksgiving *Te Deum* was celebrated in the Cathedral. Hillyar was given the freedom of the city, whose principal citizens vied with each other for the privilege of entertaining him, and he sailed for England at the end of the month with universal blessings on his head. Only an intractable minority denounced the pact. Brawls between extremists and Royalist sympathizers occurred in the plaza, and discontent spread amongst the army when orders were given to replace the Chilean flag by the old Spanish colours. Some troops publicly trampled those colours under foot, whilst the hussars under Captain Prieto, one of the ablest of the younger officers, tied the cockades to their horses' tails.

In the Royalist camp, the opposition was more serious. Gaínza's orders to prepare the troops for reembarkation caused an angry outcry. Gaínza resolved to play for time in the hope of holding on in Chillán until fresh instructions were received from the Viceroy. He sent a series of prevaricating communications to O'Higgins pleading lack of ships, the bad state of the roads, and a dozen other excuses. O'Higgins grew more and more impatient. The final provocation came when the Royalists sent back his envoys on the grounds that their credentials were not in order. Convinced at last that the enemy had no serious intention of evacuating the province, he urged on his government the immediate resumption of hostilities.

But the Royalists still held one trump card which they now proceeded to play with skill. José Miguel Carrera and his brother Luis, it will be remembered, had fallen into their hands. Lastra and the government rightly feared that their release would inevitably lead to a fresh attempt to usurp power and overthrow the Treaty. This delicate point had come up in the discussions with Gaínza, and both O'Higgins and Mackenna had firmly rejected the insinuation that the Creole trouble-makers should be exempted from the general release. 'These are our own affairs,' Mackenna had announced. 'The release of the Carreras is, in any case, a point of honour for us.' It had finally been agreed that the two brothers should be conveyed to Valparaíso where they would be placed at the disposal of the Patriot government. Thence the dangerous firebrands could be shipped off to Brazil with Captain Hillyar.

Shortly after the signing of the Treaty of Lircay a group of Royalist officers, who had already established friendly relations with their two captives, arranged for them to have an interview with Rodríguez Aldea. The crafty lawyer painted a lurid picture of the malice with which O'Higgins and Mackenna had spoken of them, and of their rivals' plans to have them sent up to Lima where they would be sure to perish in the Viceroy's dungeons. Then, sure that enough fuel had been added to the flames of their already passionate indignation, the officers saw that the prisoners were well provided with money, arms, and horses—even a notorious bandit for a guide—and could make good their escape.

A few days later, two travel-stained figures burst in upon the Patriots' headquarters. O'Higgins embraced them impulsively as old comrades-in-arms, and lodged them in his house. But there could be no denying that their arrival was an embarrassment. The officers around O'Higgins had nothing but black looks and muttered threats for them. Fearing that their appearance in public would sooner or later lead to some untimely incident, O'Higgins felt constrained to ask them not to venture out openly into the street. José Miguel retorted with characteristic arrogance that they were not ashamed to show their faces before anyone, and would know how to look after themselves. Two days later, with a couple of dragoons which O'Higgins had given them as an escort, they rode off towards Santiago. Their stay in Talca had been short, but they had been there long enough to perceive that the truce was unpopular with the army, and had drawn their own conclusions.

Director Lastra was exceedingly angry when he learned that the two brothers were at large and that the Commander-in-Chief had helped them on their journey to Santiago. He sent out patrols to intercept them and wrote a stern reprimand to O'Higgins. 'You must learn in the future to restrain your natural kindliness,' he urged, 'and follow out with punctiliousness the resolutions of the government, which are designed to preserve the glories which you have won.'[1] Of Luis and José Miguel Carrera there was no sign. They had reached the safety of a friendly *hacienda* from where José Miguel soon ventured in disguise to the capital to prepare the coup against the government which he had long been meditating. His brother Luis was caught and placed under arrest, but that made little difference to their plans. On 23 July, Lastra, Mackenna, and the chief supporters of the government were seized by the conspirators. The irrepressible José Miguel Carrera had reassumed power and placed himself once more at the head of a three-man junta.

[1] *Archivo*, Vol. 2, p. 226.

Twelve

The Spanish Reconquest

JOSÉ MIGUEL CARRERA's second dictatorship was characterized by a more violent and vengeful spirit than his first. Poinsett had left Chile, and the Consul's influence was now replaced by that of Doña Javiera Carrera, a woman as intelligent and as restless as her brother, but also more fanatical and vindictive. Realizing that his position was far from secure, Carrera at first feigned a conciliatory attitude. He hoped to play the old game which had served him so well with Rozas, opening negotiations with his antagonists until he had built up enough political and military strength to crush them. But now the task was harder; he had not only to settle accounts with O'Higgins, and the bulk of the Patriot army, but with the Royalists who were daily expecting reinforcements from Peru.

Bernardo O'Higgins, now bitterly conscious of the justice of Lastra's reproaches and his own failure to foresee Carrera's perfidy, summoned a council of war and a *cabildo abierto* in Talca and forthwith resolved to refuse obedience to the new government. But instead of marching on Santiago before the dictator could consolidate his power, he hoped that Carrera would listen to reason and at least agree to some compromise rather than risk precipitating civil war. José Miguel artfully stimulated these expectations by keeping up a flow of seemingly cordial letters. 'My friend,' he wrote,'—whether I can still address you as such I do not know; I have always been a true friend to you, and still am, in spite of our disagreements. Which of us is so mad and so heartless that he would wish to bring ruin upon our native country Chile? I only know that I shall do nothing, as you should do nothing, until we both meet once more to examine our differences.'[1] Under pressure from his officers, and learning that Mackenna had been exiled to the Argentine, O'Higgins' attitude began to harden. Leaving a strong force to contain the enemy on the

[1] *Archivo*, Vol. 2, p. 330.

banks of the Maule, he at last pushed on towards the capital. Carrera sought to detain him by sending fresh envoys, but O'Higgins brushed them aside with a curt reply: 'Let him resign, and the people freely choose their own government.' He had now passed from indecision to impatience, and without waiting for the main body of his forces to come up, O'Higgins led an advance guard of a hundred and fifty men against defensive positions which his rival had established outside Santiago, and which were held with considerable skill by his brother Luis. The clash lasted only an hour, but O'Higgins could not dislodge the enemy, who counter-attacked vigorously. In the skirmish, O'Higgins lost his horse and baggage and only managed with difficulty to extricate his men and rejoin the main army.

The following morning, when the Commander-in-Chief was mustering his troops for a full-scale attack on Santiago, an event occurred which changed the whole face of the campaign. An officer of the Royalist army arrived under a flag of truce bearing an important message. The Viceroy of Peru had repudiated the Treaty of Lircay and had sent a new expedition under Colonel Osorio who was now advancing rapidly from the south and called upon all the Patriot forces to lay down their arms. After delivering this startling news, the officer rode on to repeat his message to Carrera.

Osorio's envoy reached Carrera's headquarters as the brothers were celebrating their 'victory' over O'Higgins. His message was received with more indignation than consternation, its bearer thrown into prison, and preparations were continued to settle accounts with O'Higgins. The news was brought to Mackenna, now on his way to exile, by Luis Carrera. 'Then everything is lost!' exclaimed the Irishman. 'Why should you think we cannot save Chile through our efforts?' retorted Luis, always quick-tempered and boastful. 'Why do you cast doubts on the patriotism of the Chileans?' 'You speak about saving your country, and you begin by filling the prisons with honest men,' Mackenna replied bitterly. 'You talk about preserving unity, but at this very moment you are preparing to attack O'Higgins!'

It was true. On 1 September, Carrera issued a proclamation announcing that the civil war must go on. His furious intolerance of any rival was proving a stronger emotion than his desire to see an independent Chile. O'Higgins, on learning of Osorio's approach, had sent an emissary to Carrera urging that they should compose their differences. He proposed the formation of a provisional govern-

ment under the auspices of the Santiago *cabildo*, which Carrera had
dissolved, and implored Carrera to make the final sacrifice required
by his honour and his country, promising, for his part, to place all
his troops under Carrera's command.[1] Carrera repulsed these overtures with disdain. 'This is really the height of stupidity,' he exclaimed. 'His wits seem to have forsaken him since he became
Commander-in-Chief. To demand that the victorious army, an army
which has just doubled its strength, should agree to its own undoing
is something which only an O'Higgins could expect.' But Bernardo
still believed that compromise was possible. He dropped all his
demands and merely asked that the most unpopular and brutal
member of Carrera's junta, a priest called Uribe, should be replaced.
But even this Carrera haughtily refused to consider. It was clear
that, however desperate might be the plight of both parties in the
face of the common threat, Carrera would never bring himself to
surrender the most trivial of his pretensions. When he at last realized
this, O'Higgins made the decision to sacrifice his principles and pay
the price demanded by his rival for the reestablishment of unity. On
the evening of 3 September, he gathered together a small band of
personal friends and fellow-officers and rode to Carrera's headquarters to place himself unconditionally at the dictator's disposal.
A new manifesto was hurriedly drawn up and issued to the public:
'We have now sealed a pact of eternal reconciliation. The army of
the South is one with the army of the capital!'[2] Together the two
chiefs made the round of the barracks to demonstrate their new-
found unity and raise the morale of the troops, whilst the citizens
of Santiago were exhorted to rally to the colours. Two days later
O'Higgins left the capital to rejoin his troops and take over command of the advance-guard of the united forces.

Satisfied that he had succeeded in imposing his authority on his
rivals, Carrera now set about preparing to meet the Royalist advance.
But his feverish efforts only concealed the basic incompetence of his
leadership. Continuing his tactics of gaining time by trying to delay
the enemy with a stream of conciliatory messages, he could think of
nothing better to do in the capital than to imprison suspected
Royalists and burn an effigy of the Viceroy in the plaza. A bombastic
proclamation somewhat surprisingly branded Osorio and the
invading army as 'traitors to King and Country' and set a price on
their heads. Nothing, however, was done to remedy the deplorable

[1] *Ibid*, p. 339.　　[2] *Ibid*, p. 344–346.

state of the Patriot forces. O'Higgins sent a despatch from the front
complaining that the men were barefoot and in rags, had not touched
a peso of their pay for months, and that 'there was not a serviceable
pot or pan for cooking in the whole army'.[1] Desertions to the
Royalists were frequent, and many of the officers had gone off on
leave and refused to return. O'Higgins' own secretary went over to
Osorio and had the impudence to write a letter urging him to do the
same and promising, as a reward, the post of Governor of Concepción which his father had held before him. Similar inducements
were held out by the astute lawyer Rodríguez Aldea.

Though O'Higgins was staunchly proof against such blandish-
ments, the morale of the Patriot army had never sunk so low. The
last minute reconciliation between the two chiefs had convinced no
one that the breach had really been healed. The two factions still
eyed each other with distrust. Carrera could not believe in the
obvious sincerity of his rival, and noted in his diary that 'his
obstinacy and desire for revenge were equalled only by his ambition.'[2] Distrusting the loyalty of the forces under his command and
in doubt as to the movements of the enemy, Carrera showed himself
incapable of forming any consistent scheme of defence. As Osorio
continued his steady advance, all Concepción province, then Talca,
and a part of Santiago province falling to him without resistance,
Carrera changed his plans no less than five times in a single month.
His combined forces totalled less than four thousand men, half of
whom were raw militiamen who might be expected to flee at the
first shot. Osorio commanded five thousand troops, staffed by
competent officers and including six hundred men of the Talavera
regiment—the first Spanish unit to take part in the fighting—whose
training and morale were greatly superior to those of the Creoles.
Where could he hope to halt and give battle to such an enemy?
Carrera could not make up his mind. He thought of the plain of
Maipo, on the approaches to Santiago, or the pass of Angostura de
Paine, where the *cordillera* and the coastal range drew near to each
other. Then there was the Cachapoal, a shallow river which could
normally be forded but which might possibly be converted into an
effective barrier if the irrigation sluice-gates were opened.

O'Higgins urged Carrera to join him at the front and see for

[1] *Ibid*, p. 373–74.
[2] *Diario militar del general Carrera* in *Collección de Historiadores y de Documentos
relativosa la Independencia de Chile*, Vol. 1 (Santiago, 1900).

himself how the situation was developing. 'You should take up the post befitting the Commander-in-Chief,' he wrote to him, 'and I will be at your side serving as adjutant or in command of some division, small detachment, or simply with gun in hand.'[1] But Carrera, perhaps suspecting that the invitation was a trap, remained with his staff in the rear. As September drew to a close, the Patriot army was loosely grouped behind the line of the Cachapoal. O'Higgins and his first division had taken up positions on the left wing, between one of the fords and the town of Rancagua. The second division, under the command of Juan José Carrera, held the centre of the line but had not advanced near enough to the river to deny the enemy the use of the second ford. A third ford, further down-stream, should also have been guarded by the third division under Colonel Benavente and Luis Carrera, and it was here that during the night of 31 September, Osorio succeeded in throwing over the bulk of his army and then veering right, along the bank of the Cachapoal, towards Rancagua. O'Higgins moved his division forward to meet him, expecting to effect a junction with Juan José's men, and then to join up with the third division. Such indeed had been his instructions. But of Juan José there was no sign, and the enemy were pressing on. Suddenly a courier arrived with a message from Juan José saying that he had taken refuge with his men in Rancagua, and imploring O'Higgins to join him there.

O'Higgins was now faced with a dilemma. Should he disregard this call for help, fall back to join the third division as ordered, and leave the second to certain annihilation at the hands of Osorio's superior forces, or should he join Juan José in what threatened to be the death-trap of Rancagua? His officers urged him to leave the rash grenadier to his fate. Why should he risk his life, and those of the men entrusted to his command, to save a rival from the results of his own folly? 'It is just *because* the Carreras are my greatest enemies,' O'Higgins replied, 'that I cannot abandon them now. Honour is more than life. I could retire now, and the real motive for doing so would be the safety of my brave troops. But that is not how men would interpret it, and the thousand tongues of calumny would soon convince the world that I had betrayed and abandoned a comrade-in-arms because I looked on him as a personal enemy.' He then rode with his men into the town. Juan José met him in the plaza and threw his arms round him, saying; 'Though I am your

[1] *Archivo*, Vol. 2, p. 368.

senior in rank, I place myself under your orders.' 'I accept the command,' O'Higgins replied dryly, and set about the disposition of his troops.

Rancagua, like other Spanish foundations, was built on the usual chess-board pattern of intersecting streets, but it had the peculiarity that the four main streets ran into the plaza, not at the corners of the square, but in the middle of each side, forming the shape of a cross. This offered certain advantages to the defenders, who established their central positions in the plaza. Stout barricades and two guns were placed at the mouth of each of these streets, sharp-shooters took up their position on the roofs, horses, reserves, and ammunition were stationed in the plaza, whilst the tower of the parish church served as an excellent look-out. O'Higgins ordered that the Chilean flag should be hoisted and draped with black as a sign that they would fight to the last man. Although the forces under his command numbered less than half the enemy, they had the advantage of fighting in strong defensive positions where they could be most influenced by the personal example of resolute officers.

The battle opened on 1 October. Osorio's plan was to sweep the defenders out of the square by an impetuous attack launched from the south, with the cavalry waiting to cut down the enemy as they fled northwards to Santiago. The attack was entrusted to the seasoned Talaveras and other picked troops. Only the Royalists' conviction that the Patriots were now so demoralized that they would flee at the first shock could justify the suicidal decision to attempt a frontal attack down streets against cannon and rifle fire at point blank range. They were soon rudely disillusioned. As they advanced towards the plaza, they were mown down in a merciless fire and the street was soon piled with dead and wounded. Assaults down the other three streets were similarly repulsed. The Royalists were forced to withdraw after an hour's fighting more intense than anything hitherto seen in Chile.

Though the Patriots could not know it, Osorio found himself in a serious quandary. He had recently received secret instructions from the Viceroy that a serious situation had arisen in Peru, and that he was therefore to send back the Talaveras and other troops if the war was already over; if it was not, he was to make a truce with the Patriots so as to release the men required. Confident of being able to crush the enemy with one blow, Osorio had decided to postpone obeying these orders. The costly failure of the initial attack now filled him with mortification and he thought of breaking off the action. But his own officers grew indignant at this apparent act of pusillanimity and forced him to resume the fighting. Determined to take no chances this time, Osorio brought up his artillery and ordered the infantry to advance from house to house and along the roofs. The defenders were now exposed to heavier fire but threw back the Royalists at the point of the bayonet. When night fell, both sides snatched what rest they could and set about preparing for the ordeal of the morrow. O'Higgins, sanguine as he was, knew that his force could not hold out for more than one more day. Losses had been heavy, and munitions were running low. The enemy had cut off the water supply, and a well hastily dug in a corner of the plaza had to suffice for the men's needs. A courier managed to slip through the enemy lines with a message for Carrera imploring him to send relief and fresh supplies. By dawn the courier was back with a somewhat enigmatically worded promise of help.

The following morning, the Royalists resumed their house to house advance. There was bitter street fighting, with barricades improvised from the piles of dead. Under the inspiring leadership of O'Higgins and his officers, the Patriots fought with desperate heroism. Just before eleven in the morning, a look-out espied a cloud of dust on the horizon. The exhausted defenders raised a cry of *Viva la Patria* and encouraged each other with the glad news that the Third Division was hastening to their relief. A confused movement in the enemy ranks suggested that Osorio was turning to face the threat in his rear. Then the look-out from the church tower shouted, 'They are retreating—retreating!' 'Who?' cried O'Higgins, anxiously. 'The Third Division,' came the disheartening reply. 'The Third Division are retreating!'

It was only too true. At the very moment when the Royalists had been caught unawares and were thrown into confusion between two fires, the relieving force had broken off the engagement and turned tail. Was it treachery, cowardice, or simply some disastrous blunder? O'Higgins and his beleaguered remnant had no time to speculate on these things, for the enemy, recovered from their sudden fright, were now launching the full fury of their attack against the plaza. With this hope of relief gone, the end could now be only a matter of hours. Osorio's men set light to the houses. There was no water, and the lips of the soldiers were black and the barrels of the cannon so hot that charges exploded on being placed

5

in the muzzle. A spark from a burning roof set off a great explosion in the powder store. The attackers were breaking into the trenches in the plaza itself. At three in the afternoon O'Higgins gave the order for the dragoons and any others able to do so to mount and prepare to fight their way out of the town. Five hundred men made ready. Driving a band of pack- and artillery-mules before them so as to sow confusion, they broke out of the square in a last desperate sortie. O'Higgins' horse was too exhausted to scale the barricades. He dismounted, and an adjutant was struck down at his side. A Royalist soldier rode at him and tried to cut him down, but was himself killed. O'Higgins mounted his assailant's horse and cut his way clear. Juan José, who had played little part in the grim events of the day and had been careful to keep a good horse in reserve, also made good his escape.

Back in the plaza, a scene of merciless carnage was raging. The Royalist soldiery, maddened by the fierce resistance they had encountered, gave no quarter. Prisoners were killed out of hand. The women who had taken refuge in the church were violated and the children massacred. Only with difficulty did Osorio and his officers manage to stay the slaughter and establish order. Flames spread to the house where O'Higgins had improvised his hospital. The wounded who could still move dragged themselves out into the open; the remainder perished in the flames. As he turned to take a last look at the town where he had lost so many of his comrades, O'Higgins saw only a thick column of smoke rising in the stillness of the evening sky.[1]

At eight o'clock in the morning of 3 October, O'Higgins, followed by two hundred exhausted soldiers, entered Santiago and went straight to confer with José Miguel Carrera. It was a brief and stormy encounter. O'Higgins impetuously demanded to know why the Third Division had turned tail in so cowardly and unaccountable a fashion. Carrera retorted that O'Higgins should have seized the opportunity to break out. How, Carrera went on, could he have pressed home the attack with untrained militiamen armed chiefly with lances? Besides, on approaching the town, the noise of battle

[1] O'Higgins has left his own accounts of the battle of Rancagua; a short official report for the information of the Government in Buenos Aires (*Archivo*, Vol. 2, pp. 420–427) and a much later account apparently dictated to his secretary John Thomas during his exile in Peru (*Revista Chilena de Historia y Geografía*, 1914, Vol. 12, pp. 5–59). For a good general account *see* Luis Valencia Avana: *Campaña y batalla de Rancagua* (Santiago, 1964).

at the centre had died down, and they had therefore thought that the defenders had surrendered. There had been other reasons, too, which Carrera did not disclose. He wanted to keep his Third Division intact to serve as the nucleus for a new army which might fight on in Chile's untouched northern province. Whilst O'Higgins was so desperately holding out in Rancagua, Carrera had already begun to send instructions and supplies northwards for this purpose.

Carrera's excuses and counter-charges did not shake O'Higgins' conviction that he had acted with the greatest treachery and cowardice. At Rancagua, someone had thrust an anonymous letter into O'Higgins' hand warning him that there was already a hired assassin in the camp waiting to strike him down in the name of Carrera should he manage to defeat the Royalists. Only with the greatest difficulty could he now restrain his anger and turn the conversation to other matters. What was to be done now? O'Higgins believed that there was nothing for it but to seek safety in the Argentine, where alone it might be possible to reorganize and re-equip the army. He lost no time in sending on his mother and sister to the town of Los Andes, where he promised to join them. Five days later, with a handful of brother officers and a few dragoons, they began the ascent of the Cordillera. Panic had seized Santiago, and hundreds of refugees, many of them not pausing to take provisions or warm clothes, began to stream out towards the mighty mountain chain. Where snow-drifts blocked the track, pack animals and mounted dragoons went ahead to trample down a path. On 12 October they reached the summit of the pass, and spent the night in one of the stone huts which Don Ambrosio had built nearly half a century before. Little could he have imagined that it would some day shelter the woman he had loved, and their son, in this hour of need.

The long descent into the Argentine began, and at length the fugitives received their first message of comfort and encouragement. Juan Mackenna, exiled in Mendoza, had learned of their coming and had sent a peasant to meet them with food and wine, and with a letter informing them that the Governor of the province of Cuyo, Don José San Martín, had accumulated and despatched enough provisions to feed all the Chilean fugitives and the remnants of the Patriot army, to whom he cordially extended the promise of his help and protection. The following day, O'Higgins emerged into the foothills where the two friends met.

Carrera, in the meantime, had evacuated the capital and after destroying its military installations, had set off for the north. Almost the only unit of any real military value remaining under his command was a small detachment of Argentine volunteers. Carrera ordered the officer-in-charge to place sentinels on the road to turn back any fugitives trying to escape across the Andes. The Argentines refused to obey these orders. They saw it was madness to try and carry on the struggle in the north of Chile, and they thought it their duty to bring order out of chaos and do what they could to help the refugees pass the Cordillera in safety. Carrera, furious to see his authority flouted, thought of making a stand round Los Andes, and sent out a rear-guard to delay the advance of the enemy. But after remaining undecided for some time in Los Andes, and seeing no signs of the reinforcements he had expected from Valparaíso and other parts of the country, he suddenly changed his mind and decided that he, too, would cross the Andes into Argentina.

Thirteen

Across the Andes

THE WELCOME OFFERED to the fugitives by the province of Cuyo was a warm one. The province had formed a part of the captaincy-general of Chile until 1778, when it was incorporated in the newly-formed viceroyalty of Buenos Aires. It was still linked to Chile by many ties of kinship, commerce, friendship, and a similarity of social structure and outlook. With its orchards and vineyards, its streams of clear water and the invigorating air from the Cordillera, it was a well-favoured and pleasant place, the more attractive by contrast to the monotony of the pampa and the perils of the Andean passes.

Cuyo had recently received as its Governor a professional soldier, born in the Argentine of Spanish stock: José de San Martín. Amongst the residents of Mendoza with whom the new Governor had already formed friendships was a group of Chilean exiles. In banishing Mackenna, Irisarri, and other personal enemies to Mendoza, Carrera had unwittingly paved the way for his own downfall. The exiles had won the ear of San Martín, who soon came to look at the course of military and political events west of the Andes through their eyes. All that he heard of José Miguel Carrera convinced him of his reckless, ambitious, and unprincipled character, whose overbearing arrogance would make co-operation impossible and could ultimately lead only to the ruin of the Patriot cause. What he heard of Bernardo O'Higgins, on the other hand, predisposed him in his favour. His valour and singleness of purpose, no less than his frankness of character, marked him out as a leader excellently suited to further the grandiose design which had led San Martín to accept the relative obscurity of the governorship of Cuyo: the building up of a well disciplined invasion force which would cross the mountains into Chile, defeat the Royalists, and then strike against the heart of Spanish power in Lima.

133

News of the Rancagua disaster reached Mendoza on 9 October. The city responded nobly to the call for help and lost no time in gathering together provisions and sending a relief column of one thousand pack-mules to meet the fugitives. The Governor himself took the road to Uspallata and hurried some twenty leagues into the Cordillera. Here he encountered streams of fugitives in indescribable misery and confusion, their despair deepened by reports that the Royalists were already on their heels. 'A scene of pitiful disorder, which may well be imagined, met my gaze,' San Martín wrote. 'A mob of scattered soldiery, without leaders or officers and thus unrestrained by any discipline, was struggling for the provisions, cursing and committing all sorts of excesses and almost making them unusable in their fury. Some were crying out aloud against the Carreras, whom they blamed for the loss and destruction of their country. A multitude of old men, women and children weeping with fatigue and exhaustion, fear and dismay. A great number of citizens stoutly maintaining that the Carreras had brought out from Chile more than a million pesos belonging to the State, hidden in the luggage of their numerous adherents, and beseeching me not to permit the theft of funds so essential for the task of reconquering their country.'[1]

Amongst this crowd San Martín encountered O'Higgins, whom he greeted warmly and asked to assert his authority in order to bring some order out of the prevailing confusion. Carrera, whose adherents brought up the rear of the column, sent his brother Juan José to pay his respects to the Governor in the name of 'the government of Chile'. San Martín replied guardedly that he was happy to learn that Don José Miguel and his friends had reached Argentine soil in safety. Shortly afterwards, Carrera called in person, and during an exchange of compliments, expressed pained surprise that San Martín had already treated O'Higgins, his subordinate, as the senior officer. San Martín calmly assured him that his only object had been to put an immediate end to the prevailing confusion amongst the fugitives, and promised that he would do what he could to provide food and supplies for the Chilean army and facilitate its leaders' journey on to Mendoza and Buenos Aires.

But early the next day, San Martín set out for Mendoza leaving orders that O'Higgins was to be regarded as the Chilean Commander-in-Chief, and that the Carreras' luggage was to be searched

[1] Quoted in F. Encina: *Historia General de Chile*, Vol. 7, pp. 113-114.

for the alleged treasure. This was an insult which José Miguel could not forgive. Brushing aside the officer instructed to carry out these orders, he declared that 'he would sooner consign it to the flames than let it be searched.' But the following day, having regained his composure, he sent the baggage to the Mendoza customshouse where the Governor could satisfy himself that it contained nothing belonging to the State. San Martín felt somewhat abashed by this incident (for the funds had been purloined by the Royalists and not by the Carreras) and José Miguel determined to follow up his advantage by sending a stiff note on the following day protesting against the way in which his authority as head of the Chilean state had been disregarded and usurped. San Martín retorted that 'the only authority in a country was that of its own lawful government'.

The battle between the two men was now joined. As the presence of Carrera not only sharpened the rivalry between the two factions in the Chilean army, but also spread dissension amongst the residents of Mendoza, San Martín asked Carrera, in the interests of public order and his own safety, to remove to the neighbouring town of San Luis. José Miguel retorted that 'he would rather be torn in pieces'. For the moment, the balance of military power lay with Carrera, who hoped to use the same tactics against the Governor of Cuyo as he had applied so successfully against the Santiago junta. But he had now a more formidable adversary. Before Carrera could stage his coup, San Martín quietly collected troops and prepared to deal a decisive blow. By mustering the local militia, the adherents of O'Higgins, and the Argentine volunteers in the old Chilean army, San Martín raised a total of one thousand troops with which he surrounded the Carrera faction in their barracks on the morning of 30 October. Faced with a ten minutes' ultimatum, the Carreras were forced to submit. José Miguel, Juan José, their wives, Doña Javiera, and a band of their closest officer friends were then sent under strong escort to San Luis, whilst the rank and file followers were destined for incorporation in the Argentine forces in Buenos Aires. A memorandum enumerating the misdeeds of the Carreras was drawn up, signed by seventy Chilean officers, and entrusted to Mackenna and the able young politician Irisarri who set out to deliver it to the Argentine government in justification of San Martín's drastic action. The rival faction, not to be outdone, sent Colonel Benavente and Luis Carrera to Buenos Aires to put their side of the case.

The struggle was now to win over the Director Supremo of the Argentine. This was Don Gervasio Posadas, an amiable figure-head and uncle to the brilliant but unstable young officer Alvear, who promised to become the rising star of the Argentine revolution, and felt drawn to the Carreras by ties of friendship and similarity of temperament. Posadas received the Carrera emissaries affably but gave only vague promises of satisfying their requests and did nothing to curb the activities of the Governor of Mendoza. Luis, incensed by the detention of his two brothers in San Luis, determined to avenge himself on the chief of the O'Higgins faction in Buenos Aires. He had already attempted to provoke Mackenna to a duel in Talca the previous year, and Juan José had tried as much in Mendoza, but others had intervened to prevent bloodshed. Now he was to have his way. The challenge was given and the duel was fought outside the Argentine capital in the night of 21 November. The Irishman was shot through the neck and his lifeless body deposited outside the gates of the prison.

News of Mackenna's death aroused the keenest indignation. Irisarri tried to procure the arrest of the suspected culprits and an inquest was opened. José Miguel grew alarmed for the safety of his brother and hurried up to Buenos Aires where he had little difficulty in persuading his friend Alvear to induce Posadas to hush up the whole affair. Events now seemed to be moving in favour of the Carreras. Not only had one of the ablest leaders of the opposing band been removed, but they soon had hopes of eliminating San Martín as well. Less than two months after the death of Mackenna, Alvear took over the office of Director Supremo from his uncle. San Martín had been watching which way the wind was blowing and had laid his plans accordingly. Confident of the support which he now commanded in Cuyo, he asked permission to be relieved of his post. Alvear, delighted at the prospect of ridding himself of a possible rival, willingly consented and appointed another governor in his place. But the people of Mendoza refused to accept Alvear's nominee and demanded that San Martín should be reinstated. The new Director, alarmed and still unsure of his position, was forced to acquiesce, and San Martín resumed his office with greatly in-creased prestige. Alvear himself was ousted from power in little more than three months.

The tragic loss of his closest friend and comrade deeply affected O'Higgins. Though neither vindictive nor quarrelsome by nature, he was now implacable in his hatred of the Carreras. The bitter feud amongst the Chilean exiles only rendered San Martín's task of creating a disciplined army more difficult. Most of the exiles had migrated to Buenos Aires, where they hoped to find a modest living in the administration or in commerce. With San Martín's approval, O'Higgins moved there too. His mother and sister insisted on accompanying him, for they feared his impulsive nature might draw on him Mackenna's fate. They had brought their modest savings with them from Chile, and these, eked out with the slender proceeds from sewing, rolling cigarettes, and selling sweetmeats, kept the wolf from the door for the next few months.

Buenos Aires was a lively, bustling, but scarcely an elegant capital city. The churches were large and gloomy, their walls and roofs overgrown with weeds; the treasures of gold and silver which had once adorned their interiors had been sacrificed to the cause of independence and replaced by tinsel ornaments. Samuel Haigh, who arrived there in 1817, found 'there is a wild, unfinished look about it which is anything but pleasing; excepting in a few streets, in the vicinity of the Plaza or Great Square, the houses are low and dirty, and become more so as you approach the environs.'[1] O'Higgins rented a small house near the artillery barracks. It was scarcely big enough for the needs of the three of them but it possessed a flat roof which served as an open-air dormitory for any homeless guests. Others joined the family circle for meals. Amongst those who frequented the modest *tertulia* were old friends from Bernardo's Cadiz days—Juan Pablo Fretes, a revolutionary-minded canon, and his nephew, Juan Florencio Terrada. These men initiated him into the Logia Lautarina, the secret society named after Lautaro, the legendary Araucanian chieftain, and formed with the aim of bringing about the independence of the Spanish American countries. The Lodge had now recovered from Alvear's attempt to use it for his personal ambitions and was once more an instrument devoted to a great cause.

To retain faith, amidst the dreariness of exile, in the triumph of this cause was often far from easy. By 1816, all America, with the sole exception of the viceroyalty of Buenos Aires, had been re-conquered by Spain. In Chile, the mass of the people, still largely royalist in sentiment, and a great part of the aristocracy, accepted the re-establishment of Spanish rule as putting a welcome end to

[1] Samuel Haigh: *Sketches of Buenos Aires, Chile, and Peru* (London, 1829), p. 11.

5*

the exactions and anarchy of Carrera's dictatorship. Since most of the active revolutionaries had fled the country, Osorio, who was by nature conciliatory and magnanimous, was personally in favour of a policy of forget and forgive. But he was under pressure from Abascal on the one hand, and, on the other, from local Royalists bent on settling old scores. Against his better judgment, he was forced to undertake a series of measures which inevitably turned opinion against his régime. Many leading Creoles were exiled to the island of Juan Fernández, and the country groaned under the burden of supporting an army of occupation and the brutalities practised by the rowdies of the Talavera regiment. Men forgot the natural benignity of Osorio in their resentment at the cruel despotism of San Bruno, the notorious Talavera officer.

After an administration lasting less than a year and three months, Osorio quarreled with Abascal and was replaced by Marcó del Pont. The new Governor was incompetent, effeminate, and luxury-loving to a degree which filled the Royalists with embarrassment and exposed the whole apparatus of Spanish rule to public con-tempt. What prompted the Spanish government to appoint such a figure of fun to a post of responsibility it is hard to conjecture. The preamble to the proclamation which he issued on assuming office reads like a Gilbertian burlesque: 'Don Francisco Casimiro Marcó del Pont, Angel, Díaz, and Mendez, Knight of the Order of St James, the Royal Military Order of San Hermenegildo, and the Fleur-de-Lys, Member of the Royal Ronda Equestrian Club, well-deserving of his country to an eminent and heroic degree, Field-Marshal of the Royal Armies, Supreme Governor, Captain-General, President of the Royal Audiencia, General Superintendent Sub-delegate of the Royal Exchequer and of Posts, Mails, and Couriers, and royal Vice-Patron of this Kingdom of Chile . . .' The reality beneath the gilded grandeur of such a functionary was the iron hand of San Bruno and his Talaveras. The régime became more and more unpopular and men began to speak with longing of the return of the Patriots. Rumours of the imminent appearance of a powerful squadron in the Pacific, or of an invasion over the Andes, gained currency and were cunningly stimulated by San Martín. His agents —amongst whom he had skilfully found an outlet for the energies of a number of Carrera's adventurous followers such as the sub-versive genius, Manuel Rodríguez—alarmed the Spaniards by spreading false reports of where and when the invasion was to take place, and by fomenting the emergence of guerrilla bands.

The problem of how and when to return to Chile was the constant preoccupation of the Chilean exiles. The rival factions had each concocted their own plans for which they hoped to enlist Argentine support. That of Carrera, which was presented to the government in Buenos Aires with little delay, was typical of the man. He declared that it would be enough for him to raise a force of five hundred men, with another thousand rifles in reserve, with which he would make for Coquimbo, the key to the untouched northern province, where he was confident that the population would acclaim him with enthusiasm and march on Santiago beneath his command. No attempt was made to work out the plan in detail; everything was left to the inspiration of the moment and the mystic power of the dictator's personality. O'Higgins' plan, on the other hand, was painstaking in the extreme, if almost as impracticable. He worked out an elaborate scheme demanding an army of six thousand men (against the four thousand believed to be in Chile) which should cross the Cordillera at a number of points ranging between Coquimbo, Santiago, and Concepción, whilst a naval expedition was to sail round Cape Horn and land troops on the coast. But there was no explanation as to how this was to be financed, organized, and synchronized, and the project exposed patriot columns to the risk of being destroyed one by one.

Carrera's plan was submitted to San Martín, who not unnaturally dismissed it as chimerical. The Chilean *caudillo*, temporarily abandoning the field to his Argentine rival, decided to try his luck at raising funds and buying ships in the United States, where he counted on Poinsett and others to help him. O'Higgins, too, was tired of the frustrating idleness of life in Buenos Aires and eagerly accepted the invitation offered by San Martín at the end of 1815 to join him in Mendoza. He set off across the pampa with his inseparable companions Doña Isabel and Doña Rosita, and a small escort of cavalry. He bore no resentment that his own plan for the re-invasion of Chile had been but lightly regarded. He was content to play any part assigned to him in the scheme which another had conceived and which was now taking bodily shape in the workshops and drill-grounds of Mendoza.

The transformation which San Martín had wrought in the little Cuyan capital was truly miraculous. An air of martial purposefulness animated the whole city. The local transport industry had been

placed on a war footing and a host of carters and muleteers, with
their immense train of pack-animals, oxen, and waggons, and their
stocks of baggage and saddle equipment, had been mobilized for
the grand design. Every citizen was proud to have a part to play.
The ladies were busy sewing uniforms from cloth woven in specially
constructed mills. The church bells had been melted down to feed
the arsenals where the warlike Franciscan friar Luis Beltrán turned
out his cannon, bayonets, horse-shoes, cartridges, and other warlike
supplies. Even the school-children were drilling enthusiastically in
their playgrounds.

When O'Higgins returned to Mendoza, he found that the
strength of San Martín's army amounted to just over 1,500 troops
of the line, with seventeen cannon. The Cuyo militia totalled over
four thousand, mostly horsemen, but they lacked serious military
training and were fit only for auxiliary duties. The Governor
proposed to increase the strength of his army, but he wished to do so
without denuding the province too seriously of its own man-power.
His skill in financing and equipping his force from the resources of
the province without bleeding it dry was extraordinary. He had so
infected the citizens with his enthusiasm and inspired them with
such a fervent belief in their mission that the levies and taxes were
borne almost cheerfully. One of the Cuyans' greatest sacrifices was
the voluntary surrender, at the Governor's request, of two-thirds of
their negro and mulatto slaves—more than seven hundred in all—
to strengthen the infantry in which the army was most lacking.

San Martín was now also anxious to incorporate as many Chileans
as he could into the army. He had at first preferred to see them
dispersed to Buenos Aires, for fear that they would either cause
trouble in favour of Carrera or else slip furtively back into Chile.
Now that his army was in being, he felt fewer misgivings in in-
corporating the Chilean rank and file in the Argentine units, whilst
forming the officers into cadres to command the new troops he
expected to raise on Chilean soil. O'Higgins was confirmed in his
rank of Brigadier, began to draw regular pay, and was given a small
permanent escort. But for all this, and in spite of the warm personal
friendship which began to develop between the two men, San
Martín was careful to keep him in the background and entrust him
with only minor responsibilities. Too great a consideration shown
him would not only irritate those Chilean officers who still cherished
some sympathy for the Carreras, but would arouse the jealousy of

the Argentine officers, often unduly sensitive in matters of precedence. After all, though no one doubted his personal integrity and
his often heroic valour in the field, could he be said to have the
makings of a true general? O'Higgins was only too conscious of his
shortcomings in this respect, and spent his evenings poring over
manuals of military tactics and strategy.

The task in which he found most satisfaction was that of preparing
the ground for the new camp at Plumerillo whence the Army of the
Andes—such was now its official designation—was to undergo its
final training. Here, one league to the north of Mendoza, trees had
to be felled and store-houses built. O'Higgins threw himself happily
into the work, which recalled to him his labours on his estate at
Las Canteras. The camp was ready by the end of September 1816,
and the troops moved into it to complete the final and most arduous
stage of their training. The disciplined daily routine which followed
was something which the movement for American independence
had not known before. San Martín had made the fortunate discovery
of a man with brilliant aptitudes as an organizer and administrator.
This was José Ignacio Zenteno, a reserved and taciturn Chilean of
abstemious life and unquestioned probity, who had been earning his
living by running a small inn and whose taste for meditation and
ethical speculation had won him the nickname of the Philosopher.
Zenteno, with whom O'Higgins too soon became friendly, served
as San Martín's right-hand man, first as his secretary, and later in
Chile, as O'Higgins' Minister of War.

By the end of 1816, the Army of the Andes had increased its
strength to four thousand men. In training, discipline, morale, and
even in equipment it was superior to any force that had hitherto
been seen in South America. Its composition was preponderantly
Argentine; less than one-tenth were Chilean, and even these fought
under Argentine officers, for O'Higgins and an intrepid young
Captain called Ramón Freire were the only Chileans to hold responsible command. The army was accompanied by a detachment of
miners whose duty it was to repair the track where required for the
passage of the artillery which was transported in special carts and
sledges equipped with anchors to hold them in the steep descents.
More than nine thousand mules were assembled; some to serve as
pack animals, others as mounts for the cavalry, for the horses had
to be kept fresh for use on the other side.

On 18 January, 1817, Colonel Las Heras set off for the Cordillera

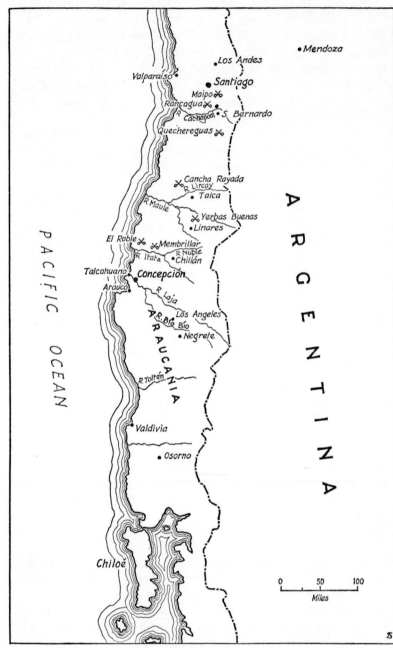

Route of the Army of the Andes

with the first part of the army.[1] His division numbered eight hundred men and he was instructed to make for the Uspallata pass and to join up with the main body of the army at Los Andes. The rest of the army left shortly afterwards, according to a carefully worked out time-table; the 1,350 men of the First Division under Soler, O'Higgins with the 1,000 men of the Second, and San Martín, the Commander-in-Chief, bringing up the rear. The army marched north across a plateau until striking the river Los Patos, whose banks they followed to the summit of the pass 3,500 metres above sea level. On the way, O'Higgins was overtaken by a courier who thrust a letter into his hands. It was from his friend Terrada, now Minister of War for the Argentine, and it informed him that Pueyrredón, the head of the Argentine government, hoped to see him nominated Director Supremo of a liberated Chile. The letter also contained an item of news which indicated that his authority would not pass unchallenged; Carrera had returned from the United States and was believed to be bound for Chile on board an American frigate.

San Martín had chosen the pass of Los Patos as he wished the army to descend as near as possible to the capital and strike the decisive blow before the enemy could rally troops from outlying posts. The summit was reached and passed without a single serious mishap. The victims of frost and mountain sickness were revived by the rough remedies of onions and brandy. Not a single gun was lost. Only the mules and horses suffered heavy toll.

By 2 February O'Higgins could look down into the fertile landscape of his beloved Chile stretching away beneath him in the valley of Putaendo. The first Royalist detachments, caught utterly unawares, were easily routed, and the population came out to welcome the army with gifts of food. O'Higgins distributed stirring proclamations. On 8 February the main army entered San Felipe, and Las Heras Los Andes. San Martín's plan was scrupulously observed. Shortly after, both armies joined forces and encamped in lovely Curimón, south of the Aconcagua river. Here they rested until the artillery train had been brought up.

The total forces at the disposal of Marcó del Pont, the Governor

---

[1] For further particulars of this historic crossing *see* Hans Bertling: *Estudio sobre el paso de la Cordillera por San Martín* (Santiago, 1917), *Documentos Históricos referentes al paso de los Andes* (Concepción, 1908), and Bartolomé Mitre: *Historia de San Martín y de la Emancipación Sudamericana* (Buenos Aires, 1909).

of Chile, numbered little more than four thousand. These were
scattered all over the country, some of them as far south as Concepción, and there were not more than fourteen hundred troops at
the immediate disposal of Maroto, the officer commanding in the
Santiago area. The Royalists had to make a speedy decision as to
where they should try and halt the enemy's advance. There were
two alternatives; the hilly ridge called Chacabuco, linking the
Andes with the coastal range, and Colima, a town lying in the valley
between Chacabuco and Santiago. The latter offered greater space
to manœuvre, and their artillery and reinforcements were already
to hand. But, if the engagement went against them, there would be
no time to reform and the capital would fall.

Chacabuco presented better defensive positions. Two tracks
wound over it towards Santiago; one, to the east, led across the ridge
and down through a defile towards the *hacienda* and village of
Chacabuco. It was the shortest route, but steep and rough. The
second track, more to the west, was gentler and less direct. They
were separated by thickets and precipitous rocks, so that it would be
impossible for any force advancing along one of them to keep contact
with the other. Maroto decided to make his stand at Chacabuco.

San Martín prepared to attack at once. Soler, with the first
division, was ordered to follow the longer track, O'Higgins—his
second division now increased to 1,500 men—the more direct. They
were then to join forces and fall upon the enemy simultaneously,
enveloping the Royalists' centre and left wing, and overwhelming
them by force of numbers. The success of the plan depended on the
Patriots being able to prevent the enemy, once they realized they
were outnumbered, from disengaging and withdrawing to regroup
round Colima, one day's march away, which they could do owing
to their superior mobility.

O'Higgins' ascent of the Chacabuco ridge was accomplished with
difficulty, and the two guns with which his division was equipped
were lost over a precipice. As they at last approached the summit, he
formed his troops into two columns, one under himself and the
other under Colonel Cramer, a veteran of the Napoleonic wars.
Both columns fanned out as they drew near the summit of the ridge
and forced back the enemy defending it. San Martín had now ridden
up to join O'Higgins. He was suffering from one of the bouts of
illness which periodically assailed him, and could only keep his
saddle thanks to a strong dose of opium. O'Higgins asked for

authority to continue pursuing the enemy over the ridge. San Martín consented on condition that he abstained from a general engagement, as Soler's division was still far off.

O'Higgins began his descent in pursuit of the enemy, but the track was so steep and narrow that his men could only go down the gorge in single file. The Patriots believed that the main body of the enemy had taken up positions round the village of Chacabuco. They now saw to their surprise that the enemy had advanced, and that O'Higgins could not move forward without a frontal attack, nor could he retreat without courting disaster. O'Higgins sent back a message to San Martín informing him of the position and of his resolve to press on. He asked for reinforcements and the acceleration of Soler's division. He then advanced to within some three hundred yards of the enemy positions. It was now midday, and the heat reflected from the rocks was intense. O'Higgins regrouped his forces into two infantry columns, with the cavalry in the rear. Both sides opened fire. Though that of the Patriots was effective, the enemy artillery took the heavier toll. There was still no sign of Soler's division or of other reinforcements. The position of O'Higgins' troops grew critical.

Cramer, with his greater military experience, foresaw that the Spaniards would break off the engagement and withdraw to Colima as soon as they perceived the approach of Soler's division. 'General, let us attack with the bayonet!' he urged. O'Higgins, who was slow to apprehend the situation and mindful of San Martín's instructions, hesitated. Cramer renewed his persuasions, and O'Higgins impulsively consented. 'The devil take me if we won't!' he exclaimed and immediately formed his men into two columns of attack, in the Napoleonic style, and led them against the Talaveras on the enemy right wing. The cavalry was ordered to charge against the centre, but they found their way barred by a deep gully which deflected them towards the infantry columns on their left. These, disconcerted by this turn of events, fell back behind a small hill where their officers hurriedly reformed them. The cavalry was then switched against the enemy right wing, whilst the infantry attacked the centre.

Cramer and O'Higgins, each at the head of a column, led their men against the Royalist infantry who had followed up their initial advantage by advancing to new positions. But these they could not hold in the face of O'Higgins' renewed attack. The Royalists began to fall back, whilst the Patriot cavalry, after dispersing some light mounted guerrilla bands, attacked the Talaveras drawn up in square formation and overwhelmed them in spite of determined fire. The Royalist artillery was next overrun. By half past one in the afternoon, the whole line of battle was disrupted and in flight towards Chacabuco. At this moment, Soler's advance troops appeared and began to fall on the enemy left wing. This completed their discomfiture. Within half an hour the battle was over and the Patriot cavalry in full pursuit of the enemy to the gates of Colima.[1]

As O'Higgins was entering Chacabuco, General Soler rode up in great anger and began to reproach him for disobeying the Commander-in-Chief's orders and imperilling the whole army by his rashness. The proud Argentine was furious that he had been robbed of the chance of distinguishing himself in the victory. O'Higgins, mastering his temper with difficulty, replied curtly that this was no time for recriminations, and turned on his heel. When he found San Martín, he asked to be given command of a thousand of Soler's fresh troops with which to cut off the enemy's retreat to Valparaíso, and urged the General to push on at once to Santiago before the Royalists could recover. Had he done so, the whole campaign in Chile might have been ended. But San Martín, ever cautious, was well content with the gains of the day and did not wish to risk his army against any Royalist reserves.

Well might the Commander-in-Chief of the Army of the Andes be satisfied with the results of the victory of Chacabuco. A third of the enemy had been killed or disabled, more than another third taken prisoner, amongst them the notorious San Bruno. At one blow, the Spanish power in Chile had been sent tottering and a great step forward taken towards the final achievement of American independence. When San Martín and O'Higgins entered Santiago at the head of the victorious army, they were acclaimed heroes and liberators by a population frenzied with enthusiasm. San Martín was not habitually given to exaggeration, and it was with pardonable pride that he was able to claim in his official despatch to Buenos Aires: 'In the space of 24 days, we have crossed the highest mountain range in the world, overthrown the tyrants, and given liberty to Chile.'

[1] For full accounts of the battle of Chacabuco see the articles by Francisco Javier Díaz and Alberto Lara in the *Revista Chilena de Historia y Geografía* Nos. 27 and 28, Vols. 23 and 24, 1917.

Fourteen

Director Supremo

ON 15 FEBRUARY, 1817, the chief citizens of Santiago were summoned by proclamation to meet together to elect a new head of state. The choice of the assembly, and of the enthusiastic multitude thronging the plaza outside, was unanimous; it could be none other than the Commander-in-Chief of the victorious Army of the Andes. But San Martín was resolved—and the instructions which he had received from Buenos Aires laid it down—to decline political office and to devote himself instead to the prosecution of the war. His mantle would inevitably fall on O'Higgins. This too had been foreseen and approved. Though he was empowered to make the nomination himself, the Argentine general preferred with characteristic sagacity to leave it to the Chileans to make the choice.

The following day, the assembly received San Martín's courteous refusal and proceeded to acclaim O'Higgins in his place. The crowds took up his name with enthusiasm and brought the news of his nomination to the house of the Conde de la Conquista where he was lodging. The hero of Chacabuco was then escorted back to the assembly with pomp and rejoicing. There he took the oath, swearing 'by the Lord Our God, His four holy gospels, and my word of honour' to be faithful to his high office.

The following days were spent in festivities and carnival. Wherever San Martín, O'Higgins, and their brother officers appeared they were greeted as the saviours of Chile. A princely banquet was offered in their honour by a rich patriot, Don Felipe Santiago del Solar, who roofed over the two courtyards of his house with sails brought up from Valparaíso and improvised candelabras out of clusters of bayonets. Even the turkeys with which the tables were laden carried flags in their gilded beaks, and the guests danced to music provided by the band of the negro volunteers, magnificent

147

in their turbaned uniforms and in the pride of their new-found freedom. A battery of cannon thundered its echo to each toast, and the whole glittering concourse rose to join in singing the national anthem of the Argentine.

But in the very fervour of this rejoicing there lay danger. Patriotism was an intoxicating new sensation, but it could easily be dispersed by the rough winds of adversity or a gust of partisan passion. Now that the Royalist army was in flight and the exiles from the Argentine and Juan Fernández would soon all be home, people assured each other that the war was over and that past tribulations would be forgotten in an era of peace and prosperity. They felt a sense of relief similar to, if more intense than, that occasioned by the coming of the Royalists after Carrera's dictatorship. Few suspected the sacrifices which the new government would soon call on them to make. For San Martín and his comrades, Chacabuco marked less the end of one phase of the struggle than the beginning of another. The task was now to organize a still more ambitious Chilean–Argentine force and to launch it, in a mighty fleet which should first have swept the enemy ships from the sea, against Peru.

How, then, was the integrity of this great design to be assured against the caprice of the majority and the subversion of the Carrera faction? San Martín, following the example of Miranda, sought to find the safeguard in an instrument forged for the very purpose— the Logia Lautarina. We know something of the structure of this secret organization from the copy of its statutes which were found amongst O'Higgins' papers after his death.[1] The avowed object of the Lodge, which had started in the Argentine and established a branch for Chile after Chacabuco, was the independence of America; 'This Society has been established for the purpose of grouping together American gentlemen who, distinguished by the liberality of their ideas and the fervour of their patriotic zeal, shall work together systematically and methodically for the independence and well-being of America, devoting to this most noble end all their strength, their influence, their faculties and talents, loyally sustaining one another, labouring honourably and proceeding with justice under the following conditions...' These conditions included a

[1] See B. Onedo Martínez: *La Logia Lautarina* in the *Revista Chilena de Historia y Geografía*, No. 66, Vol. 62, and Antonio Zúñiga: *La Logia Lautaro y la Independencia de América* (Buenos Aires, 1922).

clause laying down that if one of the Brothers should be elected Head of State, he should reach no decision in matters of grave importance without first consulting the Lodge, and another pledging him to make no senior appointments in the offices of State, judicature, church or army, without the prior approval of the Brothers. For betraying the secrets of the Lodge the penalty prescribed was death.

The Lodge controlled the new Chilean administration as completely as the Party controls the government in a Communist state. Key posts were held everywhere by the Brothers, many of whom were high-ranking officers like Las Heras and Quintana. In the first popular enthusiasm for the liberators from beyond the Andes, this was accepted without demur, but as time went on, these sentiments gave way to resentment and finally to a pronounced anti-Argentine reaction. The gratitude of a nation dissolved under the thousand irritations provoked by the tactlessness and arrogance of many Argentine officers. This in time added greatly to the difficulties of O'Higgins' administration and contributed to the loss of its popularity.

But so long as the mood of elation over the victory of Chacabuco lasted, popular resentment was directed only against the oppressors of yesterday. The ludicrous Marcó had been captured and escorted, with ironic courtesy, to the Argentine. He was regarded as no more than the grotesque figure-head of Spanish power, and popular anger turned against his caucus of advisers, two of the most notorious of whom were publicly executed. Other reprisals were less drastic. A Commission was set up to investigate the conduct of alleged Royalists, and those who could not clear themselves were excluded from public office, whilst the property of those who had fled the country was confiscated. A few, such as the intriguing lawyer Rodríguez Aldea, who had once been at Gaínza's elbow, succeeded in ingratiating themselves with the new Director.

But if O'Higgins was not the man to harbour old grudges, he could show himself inflexible to the point of harshness with those whom he considered to be still a menace to the cause. He was particularly dissatisfied with the part which the Church had played, and still showed signs of wishing to play, in the struggle. A number of clergy, it is true, had sided with the Patriots, sometimes fervently. Others, such as the Franciscans of Chillán, had opposed them with equal fanaticism. The hierarchy of the Church, headed by Bishop

Rodríguez Zorrilla of Santiago, had thrown its influence on the side of the King. The people of Chile were still, for the most part, piously attached to their priests and the traditional observances of the faith. Prudence counselled that the new government should do its utmost to conciliate the Church and avoid anything likely to offend the religious sentiments of the people. But O'Higgins and San Martín regarded the Bishop as too dangerous an enemy to be allowed to remain in the country, and he was immediately exiled to Mendoza. His successor, with the approval of O'Higgins, began to introduce a whole series of reforms designed to curb the more superstitious and bigoted practices of the Church. To the common people, who reverenced their bishop and delighted in processions and the cult of images which the new Director frowned upon, O'Higgins and his friends began to appear as godless men.[1]

In his zeal to break with the colonial heritage of Spain, O'Higgins went even further. His irregular birth, with which his enemies never ceased to taunt him, his education, and his own unassuming tastes, had never predisposed him in favour of the aristocracy. His unsuccessful attempts to secure a certificate of legitimacy and the right to his father's titles had only sharpened the edge of his antagonism. More prudent advisers, such as Zenteno, who shared his egalitarian views but thought it unwise to offend a powerful section of the landed gentry, counselled moderation. But O'Higgins was adamant. 'Aristocracy is naturally abhorrent to me,' he wrote, 'and adored equality is my idol.'[2] On 22 March, he issued a decree ordering the removal of all armorial bearings from the doors of private houses. Five months later, all titles held by 'so-called Counts, Marquises, nobles or knights of this or that order' were declared to be abolished. Public services were in future to be re-rewarded by a Legion of Merit more in keeping with the spirit of the times.

But the cause of independence was not to be won by controversial reforms. The enemy, though shattered, was still not crushed. The handful who had escaped the disaster of Chacabuco were now already regrouping in the South, where an able Royalist officer,

[1] For a discussion of O'Higgins' own religious convictions see D. Barros Arana and C. Errázuriz: *Una Controversia sobre la religiosidad de O'Higgins* in the *Boletín de la Academia de Historia*, No. 23, 1942, and J. Eyzaguirre: *La Actitud Religiosa de don Bernardo O'Higgins* in *Historia* (Catholic University of Chile) 1961, pp. 7–46.

[2] *Archivo*, Vol. i, p. 208

Ordóñez, had rallied them in the port of Talcahuano. A small Patriot force under Las Heras proved powerless to dislodge him, and Ordóñez continued to raise fresh troops and restore morale in expectation of reinforcements from Peru. Why, we may wonder, had not the Patriots followed up their initial advantage and pressed home the pursuit of the enemy before they could recover? O'Higgins' natural pugnacity was more suited to this task than to the more subtle labours of legislation. The explanation is perhaps to be found in the complex character of San Martín, and in the influence which the Commander-in-Chief of the Army of the Andes exercised over O'Higgins and the other members of the Lodge. The genius of the general lay in his capacity for prudent and detailed planning, the mustering, step by step, of the resources he calculated to be necessary for the fulfilment of his strategic purposes. So careful was he to avoid taking any step which might imperil his designs, that he let unexpected opportunities slip and declined the most legitimate risks, even where the prizes were greatest. Though hardy and abstemious by nature, he was also prone to attacks of physical and nervous prostration—acute rheumatic pains, sudden vomitings, and severe haemorrhages—which more than once made the doctors despair of his life. Now, after the mighty achievement of raising an army, bringing it safely across the Andes, and leading it to victory at Chacabuco, when his prestige and popularity were at their height, a mood of utter exhaustion and depression settled upon him. On 26 February, he wrote to the government at Buenos Aires asking as his only reward for the successful campaign the permission to retire and spend the few remaining days of his life in peace. A fortnight later, he set out in person for Buenos Aires, leaving the Lodge to take whatever major decisions it thought fit for the further prosecution of the war.

The military situation was now clearly deteriorating to the dis-advantage of the Patriots. Ordóñez had mustered more than a thousand troops of the line in Talcahuano. He had sealed an alliance with the Araucanians who furnished him with food and supplies, and reinforcements were expected to arrive at any moment from Peru. It was imperative for the Patriots to dislodge him before this occurred. Las Heras sent messages urging that more troops should be sent south without delay. The Lodge realized that the situation had become critical and decided that O'Higgins should delegate his political power to Colonel Quintana, one of the Brothers, and himself take the field at once with all the forces he could raise.

In the middle of April O'Higgins left Santiago and began the long march south to join Las Heras. His progress was slow, as the country through which he passed had to be cleared of bandits and the local administration strengthened. Much of the province, even when pacified, remained Royalist at heart. Chillán, proud of its resistance in the great siege, was still secretly loyal to the King. Even the city of Concepción, where O'Higgins made his headquarters for the offensive against Talcahuano, received the Patriots coldly. As he moved south, despatches reached him from Las Heras urging him to quicken his pace. Finally, an exhausted courier thrust a message into his hands informing him that Ordóñez had attempted a sally in force against Las Heras, but had been repulsed, with the loss of three guns and much war material. Las Heras implored him to hurry on to complete the rout before the enemy could fall back on Talcahuano. But O'Higgins' advance-guard rode up to join Las Heras' troops just as the Royalists had regained the safety of their defences.

O'Higgins' satisfaction over this set-back to the Royalists was soon outweighed by his anxiety on discovering the extraordinary strength of their position at Talcahuano and the wretched condition of the Patriot army. The port lay on a promontory, defended by a deep moat spanned by a drawbridge and protected by thirty well-placed guns. The hills which rose behind contained other formidable defences. After a careful reconnaissance, O'Higgins resolved to attempt an amphibious operation. Whilst his troops delivered a frontal assault, other detachments, manning eight launches which he proposed to bring up overland from the nearest river, would try to gain possession of the ships moored in Talcahuano harbour. But the rainy season was at its height, the roads were little better than swamps, and the launches which the patriots dragged along on rollers were soon bogged down and had to be abandoned. The frontal attack was initiated by a heavy cannonade which lasted all through the night. The Patriots had managed to reconquer the area to the south of the besieged town, thus cutting it off from its Araucanian allies, and O'Higgins hoped that the despondency caused by this loss, combined with the effect of the cannonade, would lead the Royalists to capitulate. But Ordóñez was a resolute officer, and his positions were strong. When dawn came, the

Royalists seemed as full of fight, and their positions as impregnable, as ever. O'Higgins reluctantly decided that there was nothing for it but to break off the close siege and withdraw to winter quarters in Concepción.

The war now degenerated into an affair of guerrilla bands, with the Royalists and their Araucanian allies growing ever bolder in their sallies. O'Higgins tried in vain to suppress them with the sternest measures, and no quarter was given to captured guerrillas. A final assault was even attempted on the Royalist stronghold and the command entrusted to Brayer, a Frenchman who had risen from the ranks to become a general in Napoleon's army. But this met with no more success than O'Higgins' earlier attack.

The tedious months dragged by, without any hope of the campaign being brought to a conclusion. 'We are almost swimming in water,' O'Higgins wrote irritably to a friend. 'We are cut off on all sides. The smallest streams have swollen into impassable rivers. It has been raining without stopping the last twenty days.'[1]

Would this war of attrition, with its train of economic exhaustion and ferocious internecine strife, never be brought to an end? O'Higgins' thoughts turned increasingly to the hope that Spain might be induced to desist from attempting to reimpose her authority through the mediation of a friendly foreign power. On 20 November he took up his pen to address an appeal to the Prince Regent of Great Britain, 'a prince who has the honour of presiding over the most free and the most powerful people of the globe'. The injustice with which Spain persisted in treating her subjects in America, he declared, 'has animated the Americans with such a spirit of liberty as causes them to look with indifference on the destruction of their homes and the annihilation of their fortunes... Should Chile be indebted to Your Royal Highness's influence for the recovery of her rights, and should the ships of Englishmen freely resort to our ports, so as that under the safeguards of a liberal Constitution we could offer the gold yielded by the mountains of this country in exchange for the products of Your Royal Highness's industrious subjects, then I flatter myself,' he concluded, 'would such channels be opened as would repair partially the losses of Europe, useful knowledge would be disseminated in these beautiful regions and the people of Chile would, in the political and commercial treaties, consent to such advantageous conditions as

[1] *Ibid*, Vol. 8, p. 17.

gratitude would owe to those who had mediated the Independence of America.'[1]

The half-ruined and hostile city of Concepción, where this appeal for British mediation and promise of attractive commercial prospects was penned, offered little consolation to the Patriot forces quartered there. O'Higgins had left his mother and sister in Santiago, and in his loneliness and frustration began to seek solace in the company of Doña Rosario Puga y Vidaurre, the daughter of one of his brother officers.[2] She was a flighty red-haired young woman of twenty-one who had left her husband to lead the life of a courtesan. People knew her by the nick-name of *punta de diamante* — 'diamond-sharp'. Bernardo, inexperienced in the wiles of such women, fell rapidly under her spell. Was he, in this untimely liaison, unconsciously emulating his father's adventure with Doña Isabel— the adventure to which he owed the chance of his own birth?

Disturbing reports began to reach Concepción from Santiago. The Carrera faction, encouraged by the return of José Miguel from the United States to Montevideo, was once more active. Manuel Rodríguez, whose restless conspiratorial spirit San Martín had turned to good account by sending him to organize subversive activity in Chile before the coming of the Army of the Andes, was at large, and everything suggested that his agitation was now directed against O'Higgins' administration. San Martín was back again in Chile, but still refused to play any direct part in its political life. The rule of Colonel Quintana, whom the Lodge had selected as O'Higgins' deputy, was growing more and more unpopular. Though loyally accepting the decisions of the Lodge, O'Higgins was filled with misgivings. 'The country resents the fact that it is not being governed by a Chilean,' he wrote to San Martín.[3]

Most serious of all was the news, which the Patriots had long expected, that a new Royalist expedition was on its way from Peru. Abascal had been succeeded as Viceroy by Pezuela, who decided to entrust the command of the expedition to Osorio. A supreme effort was to be made to reoccupy Chile at all costs and repair the consequences of Chacabuco. An army of over three thousand troops,

[1] This letter was enclosed with a formal note from San Martín to Castlereagh dated January, 1818. C. K. Webster: *Britain and the Independence of Latin America*, 1812–30, (London, 1938) Vol. 1, p. 554.

[2] Her full name was María del Rosario Melchora Puga y Vidaurre. *See* M. Balbontín and Opazo Maturana: *Cinco Mujeres en la Vida de O'Higgins* (Santiago, 1964).

[3] Quoted by Eyzaguirre, *op. cit.*, p. 192.

some of them veterans from Spain, and the remainder Peruvians, was raised and shipped off to join Ordóñez in Talcahuano. Their plan was to engage and destroy O'Higgins' force in the south, then to re-embark and land south of Valparaíso, so that they could march at once on the capital.

The Chilean Patriots had their spies in Lima, even in the Viceroy's own secretariat, thanks to whom they were kept accurately informed as to the strength and objective of the new expedition. The report that it had sailed was received with confidence, even with satisfaction, by San Martín who believed that his forces were strong enough to dispose of it effectively. He could now count on a total of some 9,000 troops in Chile. Confidence in his own leadership was unshaken, and his own health and spirits had begun to improve miraculously in response to the new challenge. 'As soon as I learned of the coming of the *matuchos*,' he wrote to O'Higgins, 'all my pains and aches left me. That is a good omen.'[1]

To forestall the danger that Osorio might land higher up on the coast and cut off O'Higgins' army from that of San Martín, it was decided that the army of the south should break off the siege of Talcahuano and retire northwards with all possible speed. It was to be a withdrawal not only of the army, but of the entire civilian population, with all its livestock and supplies, so that nothing but a desert should be left to the advancing enemy. O'Higgins issued a proclamation calling upon the people to make this supreme sacrifice for their country. Then, with the exception of the convinced Royalists who preferred to take to the woods and hide until Osorio's men arrived, the great exodus began. The army set out on its long march, accompanied by a multitude of fifty thousand civilians with their flocks and belongings. O'Higgins was the last to leave Concepción. Doña Rosario accompanied him.

O'Higgins' thoughts inevitably went back to the retreats of former campaigns, but this time he was resolved that there should be no truce, no compromise with the enemy. Too much blood had now been shed in the cause of emancipation for there to be any half-measures. The time was ripe, now that this new emergency was upon them, to affirm openly and unequivocally, the aims for which they were fighting. For some time past, his friends in Santiago had been working out the text for a formal Declaration of Independence. When his troops entered Talca at the beginning of February,

[1] Quoted by Encina, *op. cit.*, Vol. 7, p. 460.

O'Higgins affixed his signature to the document which affirmed
Chile to be 'a free, independent, and Sovereign State, separated for
ever from the Crown of Spain, with full powers to adopt that form
of government which most closely conforms to its interest.'[1]

Whilst O'Higgins was approaching from the south, San Martín
decided to move his army of 4,400 men to positions four leagues
south of Valparaíso. From there he could repulse any landing
directed against the capital, or else switch to the line of the Maule,
or other good defensive positions, to join forces with O'Higgins if
Osorio decided to advance overland. In the meantime, he continued
to intensify the training of his troops and build up their numbers.

Osorio's advance towards Santiago was slow. He had been
delayed more than a month in Concepción through the difficulties
of collecting sufficient horses and other means of transport as a
result of the patriots' scorched earth policy. When at last he had
managed to find some, chiefly through the help of the Araucanians,
he pushed on slowly, and without encountering opposition, to the
banks of the Maule. Here he wished to pause and take up strong
defensive positions. But his more impetuous officers showed
obvious signs of intending to depose him for alleged pusillanimity
unless he continued his advance. San Martín, now satisfied that no
coastal landing would be attempted, marched to join O'Higgins.
Their forces together numbered 6,600, all apparently in good heart
and good fighting trim.

When his advance-guard made contact with the Patriot army,
Osorio realized that his misgivings had been justified and he began
to fall back on the Maule. Both armies now moved south, parallel,
with about two leagues between them. The Royalists, seeing that
they would be prevented from reaching the river, made for Talca
instead. San Martín tried to check this by ordering a cavalry charge
against their rear-guard. The Royalists met it with resolute infantry
fire and counter-charged. The Patriot cavalry, though some three
times as numerous, was somewhat surprisingly put to flight. This
was in part due to the nature of the ground, seared with gullies,
which gave the place its name of Cancha Rayada.

San Martín was anxious to bring the Royalists to battle before
they entrenched themselves in Talca that night. O'Higgins too was
itching to attack, and was authorized to bring his artillery to play
on them and engage them with light forces until more infantry

[1] The Declaration is actually dated Concepción, 1 January, 1818.

could be brought up for a general assault. But the enemy turned to face this new menace with spirit, and San Martín, conscious of the exhaustion of his troops and the fading daylight, ordered O'Higgins to break off the engagement. The decisive battle would be fought on the following day—or so at least he thought.

The Royalists were now conscious of the danger of their position. The cautious Osorio had been overruled, their advance had been too rash, and they now found themselves up against a united and superior Patriot Army. They lacked the means of resisting a serious siege in Talca, yet they would be cut to pieces if they continued their withdrawal to the Maule. They saw their only hope of escape in launching an immediate frontal attack whilst the Patriots were least expecting them. The plan was to thrust forward in three infantry columns, totalling two thousand men, whilst a force of five hundred cavalry was held in readiness to pursue the fugitives. Ordóñez, more experienced in this sort of fighting than Osorio, took over command of the operation.

San Martín's spies had reported that something was afoot in the Royalist camp, and he decided to deploy some of his troops to the flank so as to envelop the enemy if they attacked. But the operation was not completed in time. The division commanded by O'Higgins was caught on the move, the Royalists bore right through it, scattering the artillery and cavalry in confusion, towards a small hill where San Martín had pitched his headquarters, together with the military hospital, the stores, and some reserves. The peninsular troops, with their greater experience of night fighting, showed themselves more than a match for the Patriots, though Ordóñez' second column, veering slightly to the east to make contact with the enemy, struck troops of their own first column and engaged them in a hot fire before the mistake was realized. Despite this set-back, the advantage which the Royalists had secured over the panic-stricken Patriots was almost complete. Only O'Higgins managed to rally a battalion of fusiliers and hold his ground until a ball shattered his right arm. Weakened by loss of blood and suffering intense pain, he was helped back to join San Martín who was hastily issuing orders for a general retreat.

The pursuit of the Patriots continued to the banks of the Lircay river, where Ordóñez stopped to reorganize. His losses had been some fourteen officers and three hundred soldiers, with another seven hundred scattered. The Patriot losses had been slightly less, but their discomfiture and the destruction of their equipment were far more serious. Most of their artillery and munitions had disappeared in the night. On the banks of the Lircay alone the Royalists captured more than 800 pack-mules.

The disaster suffered by the Patriot forces, when there had been every reason to anticipate a decisive victory, was as unaccountable as it was sudden. The dismay and discouragement to which it gave rise were correspondingly great. Even senior officers, who should have endeavoured to restore confidence, were amongst the first to regard it as irreparable and to think only of saving their own skins. Brayer, veteran of a dozen Napoleonic campaigns, had already been stripped of his command by San Martín, and did not stop in his flight until he had crossed the Argentine frontier. Monteagudo, whom San Martín had made his *auditor de guerra*, followed suit, spreading defeatism in his wake. O'Higgins, whose wound made progress slow and painful, came up with San Martín on the banks of the Lircay, and the two friends pushed on together all through the night. Early the next morning, at the village of Quecheraguas, they received the first reassuring news; the first division, under the command of Las Heras, had escaped intact. Together with other scattered units, it would join up with them that evening. O'Higgins, obstinate and pugnacious in defeat, as ever, was all for digging in at Quechereguas and awaiting the enemy attack. But San Martín realized that fresh troops must be brought up, munitions accumulated, and morale re-established, before another clash could be risked.

The same afternoon, O'Higgins received the first proper attention to his arm. His surgeon was an English volunteer, James Paroissien, who told him he would not lose it. Twenty hours' hard riding had left O'Higgins weak and feverish. Paroissien tried to console him by remarking that, in the last resort, the army could always retire as before across the Andes. 'No, not that,' replied O'Higgins vehemently. 'One taste of exile is enough. As long as I remain alive and have a single Chilean to follow me, I shall go on fighting against the enemy in Chile.'[1]

By nine o'clock that evening, O'Higgins and San Martín had reached the town of San Fernando. Together with Las Heras' division and the other units they had rallied, their forces numbered

---

[1] Barros Arana: *Historia General de Chile* (Santiago, 1884–1902), Vol. XI, pp. 388 389*n*.

some four thousand. Discipline and morale were steadily re-established. When, two days later, the Commander-in-Chief visited Las Heras' camps where the men were assembled to hear Easter mass, he was greeted with tumultuous applause.

But in the capital panic reigned. News of the disaster of Cancha Rayada had been brought by an officer who breathlessly described how the entire Patriot army had been hopelessly routed. Soon fugitives began to pour in and each added his contribution to the store of rumours; San Martín and O'Higgins had been taken prisoner, they had escaped by sea from Valparaíso, they were dead, in flight over the Andes. An 'eye-witness' recounted how he had seen the Commander-in-Chief shoot himself.

Whilst the plaza filled with agitated crowds demanding news, those who had property to lose or considered themselves specially compromised began feverishly to pack their things and make off towards the mountains. The streets were crowded with baggage-mules and carriages, and with groups of dishevelled and tear-stained women crying for news of their menfolk in the army. Only Royalist sympathizers smilingly assured each other that better days would soon be here. Cries of *Viva el rey* were again heard in the streets.

The government did what it could to curb the panic. A despatch from San Martín was at last received, read aloud in the main square, and handed around to convince the people that it was genuine. The general declared that the reverse had not affected Las Heras' division, and that the whole army was reforming and was confident of victory. Patriot hopes began to revive, but the panic had given just the opportunity which the Carrerist faction, led by the turbu-lent Manuel Rodríguez, had been hoping for. He persuaded the populace that the government was luke-warm in its measures to meet the crisis, and got himself appointed, first, adjutant to Luis de la Cruz, who had succeeded Quintana as acting Director, then co-Director himself. Opening wide the arsenals to the riff-raff of the city, he announced the formation of a new emergency detachment which he christened the Death's-head Hussars. But in the great battle which was about to decide the fate of Chile, the vaunted Hussars fired not a single shot, for their real aim was to husband their strength to overthrow the government of O'Higgins and restore the Carreras to power. By emptying the arsenals, they prevented the militia from arming and hastening to reinforce San Martín's army. Zañartu, a shrewd supporter of O'Higgins, sensing the danger

of a political coup whilst the whole fortune of the war hung in the
balance, sent an urgent message to the Director Supremo to hurry
back to the capital.

At noon on 24 March, O'Higgins, pale from exhaustion and the
pain of his wound, appeared before the *cabildo* and the chief citizens
to signify the formal resumption of his functions as Director
Supremo. The Carrerists had hinted darkly at deposing him by
force, but his mere presence was enough to dominate the assembly
and rekindle confidence in his leadership. His stocky figure and
bandaged arm seemed the very symbol of the country's will to
defend its independence. O'Higgins described in quiet and earnest
tones how the army had suffered a reverse at Cancha Rayada but
how it had rallied and was now preparing for a second and decisive
battle. 'All this I have seen myself,' he concluded, 'and I am firmly
convinced that we shall be victorious in this second battle if each
of you does your utmost to help. I am not asking for money. I shall
ask nothing until our conduct in the battle which will be fought to
decide the fate of ourselves and our children first shows you that
we have done our duty. I only ask you to be whole-heartedly with
us.'

When he had finished addressing the assembly, O'Higgins set
about recalling the arms that Manuel Rodríguez had so imprudently
distributed amongst the populace and hastened the arrival of a
fresh consignment from Mendoza. Two thousand regular troops
were summoned from Valparaíso and other centres, and the militia
called out for auxiliary duties. On the evening of 25 March, San
Martín, accompanied by his adjutant O'Brien and a small cavalry
detachment, entered the capital. He held a brief conference with
O'Higgins and then took up his quarters in the Bishop's Palace. On
the way, he addressed the crowds who thronged around him,
assuring them that he now commanded an army of more than
four thousand disciplined men, and that the reinforcements they
were expecting would ensure victory. Two days later, he left for
the front at the head of two thousand troops collected by O'Higgins,
whilst the Director stayed on still frantically assembling stores,
arms, and supplies of every description. To guard against any
attempt by the enemy to evade the Patriot army and occupy
Santiago, trenches were hastily dug and rough fortifications thrown
up at the approaches to the city. A report was received that the
enemy were advancing along the Valparaíso road and O'Higgins

was urged to seek safety in San Martín's camp. 'No—I'll stay here,' he replied quietly. 'If the enemy attack, I shall die at my post.' The same resolute spirit now inspired the whole army. Their deficiencies in arms and equipment had been made good, and so confident were they in ultimate victory that San Martín could permit himself to jest with his friend. 'It's all very well for you if we're beaten,' he remarked to O'Higgins with mock seriousness. 'You'll be pardoned as the son of a Viceroy. But for fellows like me there'll be no mercy.'

The battle of Maipo[1] was fought on 5 April. 'Not a cloud obscured the bright and everlasting blue of the sky,' wrote the English merchant Samuel Haigh, who happened to be in Santiago at the time.[2] 'Birds were singing, and the fragrance of the orange blossoms shed a delightful perfume in the breeze; there was that balmy softness in the air so peculiar to the clime; the church bells were ringing for mass, and religious feeling crept over the senses...it seemed like sacrilege that such a holy quiet should be disturbed by the loud din of battle.'

Osorio's opening move was to try to cut the road to Santiago and isolate the Patriot army from its base. San Martín countered by a rapid advance in close columns. The Royalists then paused and took up positions on a ridge by the farm and village of El Espejo. At about eleven o'clock a fierce cannonade announced the start of the battle. The advantage at first seemed to lie with the Royalists. But when, at midday, O'Higgins rode out of Santiago at the head of a thousand mounted militiamen, he saw with relief that the enemy were being driven back behind El Espejo. Spurring his horse on to where the Chilean flag marked San Martín's headquarters, he threw his arms round the General and gasped out his gratitude for the victory. Both then rode forward towards El Espejo where fierce resistance was being offered by the enemy, quarter being neither given nor expected until the officers managed to stop the carnage and receive the surrender of the enemy.

Losses on both sides had been severe. Of the 4,500 enemy troops with which Osorio had begun operations, no less than one third had been killed and nearly 2,300 made prisoner. The Patriots lost

[1] It is also known as the Battle of Maipú. *See* Elías Lizana: *Cómo debe denominarse la Batalla—Maipú o Maipo?* in *Revista Chilena de Historia y Geografía*, Vol. 10, No. 14 1914). For a detailed study of the battle, *see* Luis Merino: *La Batalla de Maipú* (Santiago, 1909).

[2] Haigh, *op. cit.*, p. 219.

eight hundred killed and a thousand wounded. Haigh, who had hastened out of Santiago to view the scene, adds a gruesome foot-note: 'Although scarcely two hours had elapsed since the action, the *huasos* of the country (who had all the time been hovering about on horseback, just beyond the range of shot) were engaged in stripping the bodies of the dying and dead; indeed, many of the latter were already naked, and the natives were riding off with their spoils.'[1]

The victory was complete, though it had been purchased at a high price. The last of the Royalist expeditions from Peru had been routed, the defeat of Cancha Rayada avenged, and the work of Chacabuco completed.

[1] *Ibid*, pp. 233–234.

Fifteen

The Fall of the Carreras

THE TRAIN OF fateful events which had been set in motion when the Army of the Andes began its historic march had been watched with mounting incredulity, envy and resentment by the four exiled Carreras. To José Miguel, Juan José, Luis, and Doña Javiera it was unthinkable that there could be any emancipation of Chile in which they were not assigned the leading roles. Liberation at the hands of others seemed a vile usurpation of their natural rights and a betrayal of the national interests. If they loved their country, it was because Chile enjoyed the distinction of having given them birth, and was destined to be the scene of their greatest triumphs. The unconditional loyalty of the people of Chile to their persons they took for granted, without feeling any obligation to earn it by disinterested statesmanship or real military ability. They were firmly convinced that José Miguel had but to show himself again in Chile for the entire nation to acclaim him and turn its back on Osorio, San Martín, O'Higgins, or whoever else might have dared to usurp his natural primacy.

But to return to Chile, José Miguel realized (for he was shrewd enough when not blinded by passion) that he would need the help of a friendly government. So long as his rival San Martín had the ear of the Director Supremo of the Argentine, Carrera thought he would best find this help in the United States. There he counted on Poinsett and other friends to assist him to raise volunteers, purchase ships, and enlist the sympathy of the authorities. Poinsett had always believed that Carrera was the best man to guide Chile's destinies, and to guide them not only to national independence but in a direction most likely to serve the interests of the United States. O'Higgins, on the other hand, seemed to him less desirable as a head of state in view of his British sympathies, although his Republican convictions and malleable character might be turned to good account by skilful advisers. 'O'Higgins,' he once wrote to a friend, 'is not an Englishman in his politics, and is easily led and most firmly attached to republican principles, more so than our friend Carrera. The latter possesses more intellect and more vigour of character and is the only man I know there capable of carrying the revolution to a successful termination, but his Republicanism was due to my ascendant over him and I found on that subject that he was difficult to govern. O'Higgins is a well-disposed man, and a skilful agent can render him subservient to all his views; he must be managed and dealt gently with in these discussions.'[1] But the United States government, though eager to reap whatever economic advantages might result from the emancipation of the Spanish colonies, was anxious to preserve strict neutrality in the struggle. Carrera found, to his chagrin, that his admirers were neither so numerous nor so influential as he had supposed, and not all his persuasive talk and charm of manner could win the advantages he hoped for. Only after great effort and ruinous expense did he manage to return to Buenos Aires with the corvette *Clifton*, of 400 tons, a couple of dozen volunteers, and the promise of other ships and arms to follow.[2]

Two weeks later the news of Chacabuco reached Buenos Aires, to the jubilation of the populace and the ill-disguised irritation of the ex-dictator. He still cherished a mad-cap scheme for sailing into the Pacific and landing somewhere on the coast of Chile. Pueyrredón and the Argentine government, realizing that his appearance in Chile would only lead to another attempt to seize power and plunge the Patriot cause in renewed anarchy, did everything possible to detain him with long drawn-out negotiations. Carrera boasted that a powerful squadron of American ships would soon arrive bearing arms and ammunition, but as the days passed without any sign of the vaunted armada, he changed his tune and offered to sell the *Clifton*, and another small vessel which was all he had received from the United States. Pueyrredón, impressed with this apparently generous and patriotic gesture, wrote to San

[1] Letter of 31 October, 1817: *Hispanic American Historical Review*, Vol. 43, 1963, p. 407.
[2] The assistance furnished to the cause of Chilean independence in general by well-wishers from the United States was however by no means negligible. *See* W. H. Neumann: *U.S. aid to the Chilean Wars of Independence, Hispanic American Historical Review*, Vol. 27, 1947, pp. 204–19, and E. Pereira Salas: *La actuación de los oficiales norteamericanos en nuestras costas* (Santiago, 1936).

Martín recommending that the Chilean government should pay the Carrera brothers a pension in recognition of their past services. Could the proud, imperious José Miguel really have suffered a change of heart? The ex-dictator even wrote to the abhorred O'Higgins no less than three letters full of conciliatory phrases expressing his wish to hurry to Chile to play his part in the final campaign against Spain.

O'Higgins, who had so long and so candidly taken the promises of the *caudillo* at their face value, was now irreconcilable. The return of the Carreras, he was convinced, would spell the ruin of the patriot cause. 'The crafty ambition of the Carreras,' he hastened to warn Pueyrredón, 'has managed to win some favour with the government of the United Provinces, who have been taken in by the cunning and double-dealing of men who ought to be branded as outlaws for bringing ruin and tyranny upon Chile and then delivering her to the brutal fury of the Spaniards. They are detested by the population of this country who would be quick to lament their own fate and the conduct of this government if they suspected it of showing any disposition to favour the Carreras...The honour of Chile demands that they should be called to account rather than loaded with favours of which they are unworthy.'[1] But despite these harsh words, O'Higgins agreed that a modest pension might be paid out to them provided they kept away from Chile.

José Miguel's brief reconciliation with Pueyrredón had however already come to an end. A third ship, the *Savage*, joined Carrera in the second half of March, and its master, anxious to get the best price for the vessel and its cargo, thought he would find the highest bidder in Chile. He therefore decided to sail on into the Pacific and tried to persuade the captain of the *Clifton* to do the same. One of the ship's officers reported what was afoot to the Argentine government, and added that José Miguel was behind the plot, and was scheming to land in Chile and attempt a coup against O'Higgins. Pueyrredón was incensed. He ordered the arrest of the brothers and proposed to ship the whole family off to the United States. But José Miguel, exercising his inimitable powers of fascination, succeeded—as he had done more than once before—in winning over the officers who were sent to guard him, and fled to Montevideo.

Doña Javiera was now the heart and soul of the Carrerist faction

[1] Encina, *op. cit.*, Vol. 7, p. 439.

in the Argentine. Her house opposite the church of Santo Domingo in Buenos Aires became the centre for mysterious comings and goings. Jewels were sold and couriers despatched to her brother in Montevideo and to fellow-plotters in Chile. A desperate plan began to take shape. Juan José and Luís were to return secretly to Chile, secure the persons of San Martín and O'Higgins, and force them to resign. If the first surprise failed, guerrilla war would be fomented throughout the country. As soon as the government had been seized, the Army of the Andes would be sent back to the Argentine, and a new army of 10,000 Chileans raised in its stead to undertake the conquest of Peru. The head of state and Commander-in-Chief, it went without saying, would be José Miguel. The latter, however, was kept in ignorance of the plot until it was far advanced, and his first reaction on learning of it was one of horror. It was not that he had any aversion to the use of violence; on the contrary, it was the weapon he personally preferred to handle. But he was too well aware of the incompetence of the plotters to have much hope of its success. 'This will be the ruin of my brothers,' he wrote in alarm, and with prophetic insight, to his sister. 'They are not cut out for such things. They have neither the prudence, nor the resources for it, and the time is not ripe.' But though his reason warned him against it, the challenge to rash adventure was more than he could resist.

The plot was discovered simultaneously in Chile and the Argentine. Both Luis and Juan José, who were making their way separately and in disguise towards the Chilean frontier, were apprehended and imprisoned in Mendoza. The news only served to confirm O'Higgins' forebodings. 'Nothing which you tell me about the Carreras surprises me in the least,' he wrote to San Martín. 'They have always been the same, and only death will change them. So long as they are alive, the country will be torn with incessant convulsions...If fortune has favoured us now with revealing their dark designs and disposing their capture, it may not be so propitious next time. A swift and exemplary punishment is the only cure for this grave evil. Let the three iniquitous Carreras disappear from our midst. Let them be brought to judgment and die, for this they deserve more than the greatest enemies of America. Let their followers be expelled to countries which are less worthy than ours to be free.'[1]

O'Higgins' outburst of anger soon gave way to calmer reflections.

[1] *Archivo*, Vol. 8, p. 40.

When William Worthington,[1] who had succeeded Poinsett as the United States' Consul, called on him to intercede for the prisoners, the Director Supremo courteously replied that he would like to exercise clemency but that, since the case was *sub judice*, it would be improper for him to intervene at the moment. 'The Carreras may be patriots,' he added shrewdly, 'but it is common knowledge that they look on Chile as their personal property and would rather see it ruined than saved by anybody but themselves.' Now that the conspiracy had been nipped in the bud, O'Higgins felt that the wisest course would be to hush up the whole affair as far as possible. A commission headed by Zenteno was set up and secretly charged with this very purpose. The fellow-conspirators apprehended in Chile were treated with the greatest leniency, and the incorrigible Manuel Rodríguez was not only released but actually entrusted with a responsible office. To make martyrs of their opponents would only fan the fires of civil strife and hamper the prosecution of the war. Besides, in Chile (in contrast to other parts of South America) violent punishments for purely political crimes were almost unknown; the only precedents had been set by José Miguel himself when he ordered the executions of Royalist sympathizers in Concepción. So long as Luis and Juan José could be kept under lock and key in Mendoza, and then shipped off, together with their brother if possible, to some distant country where they could no longer stir up trouble, all would be well. San Martín wrote repeatedly to the Governor of Mendoza urging him to exercise the utmost vigilance. He also asked that the prisoners should be well treated.

In Buenos Aires, Doña Javiera and José Miguel moved heaven and earth to persuade the Argentine government to release their brothers, or at least to order their removal to some other spot whence their escape might be contrived. But the very arrogance of their demands exasperated the authorities and the months dragged fruitlessly by. At length, yielding to the secret counsels of Javiera and their brother, the two prisoners decided to attempt an escape by subverting the guard. Luis, more daring than his elder brother, even plotted to shoot the Governor and replace him by an officer who would countenance the formation of a new expedition to Chile to overthrow the hated rivals. Juan José, who had grown sick of the hazards and hardships of exile, showed little enthusiasm for his brother's plot. 'Only let them send me back to my country as free

[1] See E. Pereira Salas: *La Misión Worthington en Chile*, 1818–19 (Santiago, 1936).

as when I left it,' he wrote in a moving letter to his wife. 'Only let me stay quietly on my estates and they can be sure that they will not so much as know I'm still alive. If I break my word, I myself will propose the penalty; they can shoot me.'

Luis' daring plot came within an ace of success. The citizens of Mendoza, whom the Carreras had treated arrogantly as a race of carters and muleteers, were deeply alarmed. They feared that the trouble-makers would sooner or later succeed in escaping and would then avenge themselves on their enemies. Alarm deepened to panic when the news of the disaster of Cancha Rayada reached the town, and the first fugitives began to arrive, as in the days after the battle of Rancagua. Rumour had it that the triumphant Spanish army was at their heels and would soon pour over the frontier. Luzuriaga, the Governor, felt the situation slipping beyond his frightened grasp. It was at this point that a sinister and forceful character came upon the scene and resolved to put a drastic end to the problem.

The new-comer was Bernardo Monteagudo, San Martín's *auditor de guerra*, who had taken such precipitate flight after the field of Cancha Rayada. This Argentine-born mulatto, who combined in his person the destructive instincts of the terrorist with utter ruthlessness in the pursuit of power and the indulgence of his own passions, was the evil genius of the Revolution. A trail of crime and assassination marked his passage through each country— Argentine, Chile, and Peru—in which he sought his fortune, until the storm of hatred aroused by his misdeeds culminated in the dagger-thrust which ended his sinister career. This man had no personal animosity against the Carreras. He had indeed at one time been friendly with José Miguel. But he saw in the momentary helplessness of the two brothers an opportunity of satisfying his own sadistic lusts and at the same time currying favour, as he thought, with San Martín and O'Higgins. He therefore bent all his energies to securing their speedy execution.

Prompted by the subtle persuasions of Monteagudo and their own increasing panic, the *cabildo* of Mendoza declared that the public safety demanded the immediate execution of Juan José and Luis Carrera. The hesitations of the Governor were overcome by the threat that inactivity would brand him as 'an accomplice in the subversion of two states.' The prisoners were informed of their fate and received the sentence with incredulity, horror, and rage.

Luis was the first to calm himself and accept his destiny with an almost mystic resignation. After confessing himself, he embraced his brother who ceased his torrent of mingled supplications, threats, and insults, and became calm too. Then they both went out to face the firing squad. Barely four hours later, a courier arrived with news of the victory of Maipo and instructions from San Martín to suspend proceedings against the Carrera brothers until further notice.

In Santiago, events had moved to the pattern of an ironic fate. Taking advantage of the mood of jubilation and relief following the battle of Maipo, the wife of Juan José approached first San Martín and then O'Higgins with a petition for the immediate pardon and release of the brothers. Mastering his old resentment, O'Higgins consented. Although his wound kept him confined to bed, he wrote off at once to Luzuriaga asking that the prisoners should be set at liberty. Four days later—on 14 April—he received the Governor's despatch informing him that they had been shot.[1]

The news of the Mendoza executions aroused passionate indignation in Santiago. In spite of the antagonism which the personal rule of José Miguel had excited amongst the aristocracy, his family was amongst the most influential in the country and the killing of the two brothers was regarded as an insidious blow against the leading social caste. The magnanimity of O'Higgins in apparently consenting to their release was now interpreted as the most cynical hypocrisy, for few doubted that the execution had been carried out on the secret orders of the Director Supremo and General San Martín. It was a reminder of the dictatorial powers wielded by the head of state when there was a growing desire throughout the land for a return to more constitutional ways. Others saw in the executions the sinister hand of the Lodge.

Popular unrest, fanned by the Carrerist faction, came to a head when an excited mob penetrated into the courtyard of the Director's palace. O'Higgins' adjutants confronted it boldly and put the ringleaders under arrest. O'Higgins himself got out of bed and struggled into his uniform. Then he summoned the dissident spokesmen and accused them angrily of stirring up sedition and anarchy, whilst the whole country needed to make its supreme effort against Peru. How could a wrangling junta or congress command the authority

---

[1] For a full account of the activities of the exiled Carrera brothers and their ultimate fate, see B. Vicuña Mackenna: *El Ostracismo de los Carreras* (Santiago, 1938).

necessary to organize the great expedition and complete the work
of emancipation? He told them he had no wish to retain power—
the burden of high office was already becoming an intolerable
strain—but until the common task was completed, he must remain.
Then, with a vague promise that he would consider introducing
some provisional constitutional machinery whilst the emergency
lasted, he dismissed them.

Now that José Miguel was in exile and his brothers dead, the
chief trouble-maker was Manuel Rodríguez. As a young man fresh
from the university, Rodríguez had thrown himself with ardour
into the revolutionary cause and had served as secretary to the junta
of which both Carrera and O'Higgins had been members. Sharing
the turbulence, the irresponsibility, and the conspiratorial genius
of José Miguel, he had none of the latter's arrogance and imperious
pride. In spite of his continuous provocations, he had still retained
the friendship both of O'Higgins and San Martín. The latter had
known how to turn his skill as an an agitator to account, but after
Chacabuco, Rodríguez had tried to set himself up as an independent
caudillo in the San Fernando region and had had to be subdued by
force. O'Higgins warned him that unless he mended his unruly
ways he would one day fall foul of the government and end his
life in front of a firing squad. 'You have really seen to the bottom
of my character,' Rodríguez admitted with disarming candour. 'I
am one of those who believe that a republican government ought
to be changed once every six months, or at the most every year,
and to bring this about, we would do everything in our power. So
deep-rooted in me is this conviction, that if I were Head of State
and could find no one to lead a revolt against me, I would lead one
myself. Don't you know that I even tried to lead a revolt against my
friends the Carreras?'

'Yes, I know, and that's why I want you to leave the country,'
O'Higgins replied, and offered to send him to Europe or North
America with a generous allowance to enable him to complete his
studies. Manuel Rodríguez, after some demur, appeared to accept,
but a few days later he eluded his guards and went into hiding.
There he remained until he managed to make his peace once more
with O'Higgins and San Martín, who even made him for a time his
auditor de guerra after the defection of Monteagudo. But to refrain
from sedition was beyond the powers of Rodríguez. He threw
himself into the abortive Carrera plot of 1817, tried to overthrow

the government with the help of his Death's-head Hussars in the critical days after Cancha Rayada, and finally headed the malcontents when the news of the execution of Juan José and Luis reached Chile.

If San Martín and O'Higgins had been inclined to show too much indulgence towards the incorrigible conspirator, the other members of the Lodge shared no such sentiments. Without the knowledge of the Director Supremo and the Commander-in-Chief, they resolved that the time had come to quench the fire-brand for ever. Monteagudo, fresh from his bloody work at Mendoza, and a certain Colonel Alvarado assumed the responsibility for his elimination. Rodríguez was again under arrest, after his latest attempt against the government. Alvarado gave orders that he should be sent to Quillota, half-way between Valparaíso and the capital, and gave secret instructions to the officer escorting him that he was to be shot on the pretext that he had attempted to escape. This officer was a certain Lieutenant Navarro, a Spaniard who had thrown in his lot with the Patriots. Knowing that he had no family or powerful friends to protect him and that his origins might be held against him, Navarro was frightened into obeying the orders imparted to him personally by Monteagudo and his colonel. The deed was done outside the village of Tiltil, a fictitious report of the attempted 'escape' was sent to the Director, and Navarro was smuggled out of the country.

News of the murder of Manuel Rodríguez—for no one believed the official version of the affair—affected O'Higgins almost as deeply as the common people, for whom the young guerrilla was an almost legendary hero. O'Higgins was as innocent of his murder as he was of the executions at Mendoza. Yet what could he do? His tongue, no less than his hands, was tied by the terrible loyalty he had sworn to the Lodge. Its statutes plighted the Brothers 'to aid and protect each other in all conflicts which may arise in civil life and support each other's opinions; should this run counter to public opinion, they must at least keep silence'. So the Director Supremo kept silence, and folk took this as evidence of his complicity in the crime.

The assassination of Manuel Rodríguez left only José Miguel Carrera to carry on the implacable feud against O'Higgins. The execution of his two brothers had moved him to the very core of his being. Henceforth, his life was dominated by the craving for revenge. Everything else—the cause of American emancipation, even the recovery of high office for himself—was subordinate to this overmastering passion. At first, from his enforced exile in Montevideo, he could only give vent to his fury by penning envenomed tirades inciting the people of Chile to rise against his rivals. 'Chile has now no other enemies than these vile oppressors,' he thundered. 'The blood of the Carreras cries for vengeance. Vengeance, fellow countrymen! Hatred eternal for the despots of South America!' Broadsheets were smuggled across the Andes with the purpose of exacerbating local dislike of the Argentines: 'Chile is to be a mere colony of Buenos Aires, as she once was a colony of Spain...From the Argentine they send governors for your provinces, magistrates for your towns, generals and armies for your frontiers.'

For several months this verbal bombardment continued unabated, but José Miguel knew that words alone could not overthrow his enemies and he waited impatiently for the opportunity to play a more active role. 'I am going to strike,' he wrote to his sister Javiera in July, 1818. 'I am going to avenge myself and avenge you.' But how and where could he strike? The easiest target now seemed to be Pueyrredón's government, which had backed and befriended San Martín, and was now sinking into impotence as the country fell beneath the sway of warring factions and increasing anarchy. But even Pueyrredón's approaching fall could not satisfy him. He needed to settle accounts with his enemies with a more sudden, dramatic blow. At last, chance seemed to bring an instrument to hand. Doña Javiera's house was still the rendezvous for desperate adventurers of every sort, and a small band of these were finally persuaded to make their way into Chile and strike down the chief figures in the government. But Pueyrredón still had the strength and the vigilance to foil the plot. The conspirators were seized as they were setting out across the pampa. One was killed on the spot, and two others were tried and executed. Doña Javiera, and a number of other accomplices, were thrown into prison.

After this fresh failure, José Miguel found an outlet for his energies in the troubled waters of Argentine politics. Any rebellious *caudillo* or provincial chief eager to defy the authority of Buenos Aires could count on his help. By the beginning of 1820, events seemed to be sweeping him once more to the fore. Pueyrredón and his group had disappeared beneath the waves of anarchy and

Carrera's old friend Alvear was recalled from exile to take military command. The country was to be reorganized as a loose confederation, local *caudillos* being left to rule their respective provinces as they wished, without interference from the capital. Despite the violent protests of Zañartu, Santiago's representative in Buenos Aires, José Miguel was allowed to organize a force of six hundred men, mainly Chileans, called the Legión Chilena, with which he proposed to return to his native country and overthrow its government. But the scene became more and more confused. Revolts and counter-revolts shook all parts of the Argentine. Opinion in the capital turned against Alvear, who was again thrown out, and against the menace of the Legión Chilena and its arrogant leader. Carrera decided to take the pampa as his future theatre of operations.

Across the grassy wastes of the great Argentine plain surged Carrera's motley host, now seizing and plundering a settlement, now repulsed by the more strongly defended forts. Soon only a handful of his vaunted Legión remained, but his ranks were swollen with a great concourse of Indian braves attracted by the prospect of booty. All strategic objectives had now been frankly abandoned, for the Indians refused to pass the Cordillera, and Carrera found himself the chieftain of a vast marauding band, powerless or unwilling to control its destructive fury. His hordes fell upon the fortified town of Salto, massacred the men and raped the women, not sparing even those who had sought refuge in the church, and carried off the surviving children and women into captivity. Horror, fear, and indignation spread through the whole Argentine.

The brunt of these depredations was borne by the province of Cuyo. O'Higgins made desperate efforts to raise arms and munitions and send them over the mountains to Mendoza. Finally, after bitter fighting, the Governor of Mendoza managed to rout Carrera's horde, and the *caudillo* himself was seized and handed over by his own unruly officers. José Miguel was brought into Mendoza amidst the imprecations of the populace. The court martial set up to try him did its work quickly. Spurning the consolations of the priests and the exultations of the hostile crowd, he entered the courtyard where his brothers had met their death, exactly ten years since José Miguel had begun his public career by launching his first coup against the moderate junta in Santiago. The memory of that brief and troubled spell of greatness—a greatness of which he was still proudly conscious even in death—led him to exclaim as he faced the firing squad: 'I die for the liberty of America!'[1] After the execution, the corpse was quartered and the limbs publicly displayed as a warning to other malefactors.

The news of José Miguel's end filled O'Higgins with grim satisfaction. 'For you has been destined the glory of exterminating the band of anarchists and its terrible ringleader, which has laid waste these provinces and regions and impeded the liberty and independence of America,' he wrote to the Governor of Mendoza.[2] 'These men dared to rend their country limb from limb, and in just retribution fell victim to their own fierce and wanton audacity. Such monsters must be crushed beneath the full weight of rightful authority, justice and the execration of the whole world.'

But had the victory been so complete? Was José Miguel Carrera to be wholly denied his vengeance? He had left two fatal legacies which, though O'Higgins could not foresee it, were to bring his rival's most cherished design to the verge of destruction and cause his ultimate downfall. The first was the legacy of the Argentine anarchy and exhaustion, which Carrera had done so much to foment, and which was to prevent that country from making its due contribution to the expedition against Peru. The second was the legacy of resentment aroused in the Chilean aristocracy by O'Higgins' suspected complicity in Carrera's death. In his lifetime, many had feared and hated him; now that he could no longer harm them, there was a revulsion of feeling in his favour. The pillars of the house of state still stood, seemingly as firm as ever. But if the dying Samson had not pulled them down with him, he had shaken their foundations. Another shock might bring the whole edifice crashing about the head of his victorious rival.

---

[1] José Benito Lamas: *Ultimos momentos del general J. M. Carrera* in the *Revista Chilean de Historia y Geografía*, (No. 44, Vol. 40, 1921).

[2] *Encina, op. cit.*, Vol. 8, p. 474.

Sixteen

The Birth of a Navy

THE INVASION OF Peru demanded one essential and formidable pre-requisite—the formation of a strong navy. This O'Higgins, who had once thought of a naval career for himself and had personal experience of the helplessness of an inadequately defended convoy in the face of well-armed war-ships, had long realized. 'This victory,' he wrote after Chacabuco, 'and a hundred others, will be of no account unless we gain command of the sea.' Indifferent strategist as he was, O'Higgins showed in this an appreciation of a truth which Spain had long ignored at her peril. It is strange that a race which had performed such prodigies of discovery and exploration and had won a far-flung empire whose stability largely depended on her ocean highways should have failed to grasp the real nature and importance of sea-power. Perhaps the Spaniard had always been at heart a soldier rather than a sailor; the disaster of the Invincible Armada demonstrated the superiority of a navy over the greatest sea-army, but Spain still refused to learn the lesson. In her American dominions, she never built up a squadron capable of dealing with the corsairs. She formed no effective cadres of naval personnel, never looked at her problems with the eyes of a naval strategist. Yet it was clear that other powers might use their naval superiority to seize a foothold in her territories. Ambrosio O'Higgins had been obsessed with this danger. Writing to the Secretary of the Navy in November, 1797, he complained of the 'pair of miserable ships' which constituted all the Spanish navy in his viceroyalty, and warned the Minister that neither they nor any of the merchant vessels he had been arming would have a chance against even a couple of enemy frigates.

If the Spaniards' navy was traditionally weak, the Patriots' was as yet non-existent. They had no warships, no money with which to purchase them, no naval tradition, no trained officers, no crews except for a few sailors from fishing and coastal vessels. The only way to acquire ships was either to capture them from the enemy, or to buy from neutrals through a combination of government promissory notes, loans from foreign merchants anxious to share in the prize money, and whatever ready cash could be raised by the ransoms of Spanish traders, and through the sale of confiscated cargoes and captured prizes. A start had been made by the capture of the *Aguila*, a Spanish brig which put into Valparaíso in February, 1817, and the commissioning of the *Rambler* of Providence as a privateer. O'Higgins set himself to the formidable task of building up the navy with admirable tenacity and resourcefulness.[1] An important purchase was made whilst Osorio's army was still advancing on the capital. An East Indiaman of 800 tons and thirty-four guns called the *Windham* was bought in Valparaíso, rechristened the *Lautaro*, manned by a mixed crew of English, North Americans and Chileans, and placed under the command of Lieutenant William O'Brien, late of the Royal Navy.

The first naval action to be fought under the Chilean flag was truly heroic. Valparaíso was being blockaded by the royalist frigate *Esmeralda* and the brigantine *Pezuela*. The *Lautaro* attacked and boarded the *Esmeralda* with great gallantry and then turned to pursue the other ship. In the meantime, the crew of the *Esmeralda*, which greatly outnumbered the Chilean boarding-party, recovered from their surprise and managed to regain control. O'Brien fell, mortally wounded, but encouraging his men with shouts of 'Don't leave her, lads; the frigate is ours!' Both the Spanish ships managed to break off the engagement and put into Talcahuano. But the Patriots did not lose their labours, as they captured a Spanish brig on the voyage back. The sale of the prize and her cargo, together with the ransom of the Spanish merchants on board, paid off most of the purchase price of the *Lautaro* and that of another small vessel to which the name of *Pueyrredón* was given.

With this initial encouragement, other ships were gradually purchased; the *Chacabuco* (ex-*Coquimbo*) and *Araucano* (ex-*Columbus*); the *San Martín* (ex-*Cumberland*), a large vessel of 1,350 tons and forty-four guns; the *Intrépido*, of eighteen guns, sent by Pueyrredón. O'Higgins, ably seconded by Zenteno, his Minister of War, accomplished miracles of organization and supply, assembling equipment, armament, and provisions in the midst of a bankrupt country and in

[1] Luis Uribe Orrego: *Los Orígenes de nuestra marina nacional* (Santiago, 1892).

the teeth of a thousand difficulties. The officers recruited for the new navy were mainly English volunteers, the ratings Chilean, English, American, and other nationalities. The command was given to a twenty-eight year old Chilean, Manuel Blanco Encalada, whose dash and enthusiasm were supported by an experience only of land operations.

In the autumn of 1817, King Ferdinand VII resolved to send an army of over 12,000 men under General O'Donnell to attempt the reconquest of the River Plate, and an expeditionary force of 2,000 to reinforce the Royalists in Chile. The project was unpopular from the start and grossly mismanaged. It was not until the following May that the *Reina María Isabel*, ten guns, sailed with a convoy of eleven transports and over 2,000 men for Talcahuano. The morale of the expedition was poor. On one transport the men mutinied, killed their officers, and handed over the ship to the Patriots in Buenos Aires. The ship's papers and operational plans were delivered with all speed to O'Higgins, whilst the remaining transports, suffering from scurvy and indiscipline, struggled on round Cape Horn and entered the Pacific in a lamentable condition.

The port of Talcahuano had, in the meantime, been abandoned by Osorio, in accordance with the Viceroy's instructions. The handful of soldiers which he had left there were ordered to fall back into Araucanian territory if attacked. This was a fateful decision, as it meant the definite abandonment of Chile to the Patriots. Had the Royalists held on, their presence in the South would have tied down San Martín's troops and perhaps have prevented the expeditionary force from sailing against Peru. It would also have continued to offer a base for reinforcements from Spain or Lima. But now the Patriots were able to trap the Spanish ships as they sailed into port, believing it still to be loyal to the Crown. A battle squadron consisting of the *San Martín*, the *Lautaro*, the *Chacabuco*, and the *Araucano*, flying the Spanish flag to deceive the enemy, captured the *Reina María Isabel* and five transports undamaged, the remainder having sailed on direct to Callao.

News of this success was greeted with tremendous enthusiasm throughout Chile, greatly increasing the waning prestige of the Director Supremo and reconciling the public to the sacrifices demanded of them for the creation of the Navy. But was the stroke no more than beginner's luck? Could the dominion of the Pacific be so easily wrested from the hands of the enemy? O'Higgins was aware

that fortune was fickle and that what the fleet needed above all was
the presence of an experienced professional commander. This he had
indeed foreseen and hoped shortly to arrange. At the beginning of
the year, his envoy in England had written to him that he had
succeeded in securing for Chile the services of Lord Cochrane—'a
man whose reputation alone will be the terror of Spain and a pillar
of American liberty'. O'Higgins had been in two minds as to whether
to endorse the contract or not. Cochrane was reputed to be undoubtedly one of the most brilliant officers of the day. But he had
also fallen foul of the British government whose goodwill Chile
needed for the negotiating of a million-pound loan. It looked as if a
choice might have to be made between the admiral and the loan, and
it was even considered whether the famous sailor should be presented
with the Chilean island of Juan Fernández in compensation for a
broken contract. O'Higgins finally decided to risk it. Cochrane was
already on the way; if fortune favoured, Chile would get her admiral
and the million pounds as well.

Parallel with the formation of the navy went the building up of the
expeditionary force. Here, too, the first problem was to find the
money. Ten days after the victory of Maipo, San Martín, accompanied by his adjutant O'Brien, set out for Buenos Aires. On the
way, he paused to make a small bonfire of the correspondence captured from Osorio. This comprised letters sent to the Royalist chief
by sympathisers in Santiago anxious to come to terms with the
presumed victor in the coming battle. In our age of card-indexes and
security dossiers, such magnanimity seems strange indeed.

After a month's discussions with Pueyrredón and other Argentine
leaders, San Martín started back for Chile. Of the million pesos
which the expedition to Peru would probably cost, it was agreed that
each country should contribute half. On reaching Mendoza, where
he learned that heavy falls of snow blocked the passes into
Chile, San Martín received unwelcome news. Pueyrredón wrote
to say that the growing anarchy into which the Argentine was
sinking made it quite impossible to raise the sum of 500,000 pesos
'though I should fill the prisons with Capitalists.' The General was
seized with indignation and despondency. He replied that, in the
changed circumstances and the precarious state of his health, he
could no longer remain in command of the Army of the Andes.
The news that San Martín had presented his resignation was received with consternation both in Buenos Aires and Santiago, where

it seemed that his withdrawal would precipitate the dispersal of the Argentine units and probably lead to the abandonment of the whole enterprise. The impression on O'Higgins was particularly profound. He wrote that the news had 'pierced him like an arrow', and urged his friend to reconsider his decision. He declared that San Martín had been chosen by Providence to accomplish the emancipation of Spanish America and must not deny the call. 'Yes, my dear friend,' he concluded, 'whatever may have been the reason for your offering to resign and lies within the power of your comrade in this country to put right, I pledge myself to do. I will see that your health improves, for this benign climate will set it to rights and cure all sorts of ailments. I implore you, in the name of our friendship and of our fatherland, to come as soon as you can and bring relief to the anguish which I now suffer—the only possible relief of consenting to do what I implore of you.'[1]

In Buenos Aires, the real reason behind San Martín's threatened resignation was realized only too well, and superhuman efforts were promised to raise funds. But at the same time a development occurred which comforted Pueyrredón and the Lodge with the possibility that the Expedition might not be essential after all. The alarming spread of anarchy and economic exhaustion raised the question of how the country was to be organized once complete independence was assured. Would not a Republic be powerless to restore and maintain order? Fantastic schemes were canvassed. Should it not be possible to revive the old Inca Empire, thereby ensuring the loyalty of the Indians? Or would some form of monarchy be preferable? Pueyrredón and most of the Argentine leaders favoured the latter solution and even sent their emissary to Europe to sound the great powers on the subject. Another envoy confided the proposal to San Martín and pressed him to win over O'Higgins to the idea.

San Martín was personally by no means opposed in principle to the establishment of monarchies in South America, but he took the realistic view that it would be useless to expect any solution without first entirely crushing the power of Spain. He therefore resolved to press on with his preparations for the Expedition, and in October, 1818 he was back again in Santiago after an absence of six months. To broach the idea of a monarchy to O'Higgins was a delicate matter, in spite of the deference with which the Director Supremo always accepted his friend's suggestions. O'Higgins was known to

[1] *Archivo*, Vol. 8, pp. 80–81.

be a convinced republican, and any suggestion of introducing a monarchy in Chile would be coldly received. San Martín began by trying to talk O'Higgins round privately. Much as he disapproved of the proposal, O'Higgins did not wish to give a frank refusal and risk provoking another offer of resignation (a form of pressure which San Martín readily employed to further his plans). He reluctantly agreed to instruct Irisarri, the Chilean envoy in Europe, to make discreet enquiries as to a suitable prince. But when these instructions had been drawn up, O'Higgins could not bring himself to sign them, and Irisarri, judging them to be invalid without the Director's signature, sent them back to Santiago. By then, O'Higgins had hardened against the project and withdrew his instructions.

So the tempting prospect of compromise was abandoned and warlike preparations were resumed. By the time San Martín had returned to Santiago, O'Higgins had not only formed the nucleus of the fleet, but had increased the strength of the army to nearly 7,500 men. If San Martín was secretly pleased with this progress, he had subtle reasons of his own for not showing it. A new body—the Senate—had been called into being with the dual purpose of assisting the Director Supremo and curbing his despotic tendencies. After protesting that it would bring the country to the verge of ruin, the Senate agreed to San Martín's request for half a million pesos. But when he urged that this contribution should be increased to make good the Argentine's incapacity to pay, he met with a firm refusal. San Martín now saw all his plans jeopardized through lack of funds. The most tortuous of stratagems occurred to him for extracting the money from Buenos Aires; he would frighten his government by painting a grotesque picture of Chilean incompetence and the necessity, if funds were not forthcoming, of recalling all Argentine units. It was a dangerous game to play, and we can only suppose that it was the nervous and physical exhaustion which increasingly succeeded his periods of creative exertion that blinded the general to his folly. In the middle of December he reported to Pueyrredón that lack of resources was bringing the army to the verge of disruption. 'If this help is not forthcoming,' he concluded, 'let us at least save the army.' The following month, when Pueyrredón had been succeeded by Rondeau, he complained (quite unjustly) that O'Higgins had not strengthened the army by a single soldier during the last six months, nor supplied a peso towards its expenses. 'The government shows a total bankruptcy in its conduct of public affairs,' he asserted. 'Its administration is loathed and hated by the entire population.' He repeated his suggestion that the Argentine element in the army should be withdrawn, on the pretext, if necessary, that a new Spanish expedition was on its way to Buenos Aires.

Could the General have realized what an irreparable disaster would follow if the Argentine government, instead of forwarding funds, took him at his word and recalled their troops? There are other passages from his correspondence at this time which show that he knew, in his moments of lucidity, that the results could only be wholesale desertions and a disastrous collapse of morale. The inevitable at last occurred. The Argentine government, accustomed as it was to put implicit trust in the General's suggestions, issued the order for the Army of the Andes to return. They were convinced by San Martín's despatches that it would never be in a fit state to wage a successful campaign in Peru, and they invoked the pretext he had suggested of an imaginary Spanish expedition.

The news fell amongst O'Higgins and the Brothers of the Lodge with the force of a thunderbolt. Little suspecting the tortuous motives which had prompted San Martín to put forward the fatal suggestion himself, he implored his friend to use all his influence to reverse the decision. 'I am at my wits' end over the return of the Army across the Andes,' he wrote to him. 'I fully realize the needs of Buenos Aires and the risks which threaten her; but this State too remains in imminent peril. I know that Buenos Aires is merely asking for what is her own, and gratitude compels us not only to take this step to help her, but also to put all our resources at her disposal, even if it means the ruin of Chile.'[1]

San Martín's eyes were at last opened. He realized—but too late—the dangers into which his too subtle intrigues had led him. Had O'Higgins been less candid a friend, less inspired with heartfelt gratitude and loyalty to his Argentine comrades, the Chilean might have demurred and tried to keep the troops in his own country. But the order to withdraw was given and obeyed. When at last San Martín intervened with Buenos Aires and requested at least a partial cancellation of the order, over 1,200 Argentine troops had already retired to Mendoza, and many had deserted en route. The discipline and fighting spirit of those which remained in Chile suffered a disastrous decline.

[1] *Ibid*, p. 92.

The progress of the navy was more encouraging. At the end of November, 1818, Lord Cochrane arrived in Valparaíso, and O'Higgins hurried down to that port to invest him with the rank of Vice-Admiral and Commander-in-Chief of the Fleet. Blanco Encalada remained as his second-in-command. After a round of lavish entertainment in Valparaíso, Cochrane and his officers were invited up to Santiago to taste the hospitality of the capital. O'Higgins gave a banquet for them in the Governor's palace, as his father had entertained Vancouver and his party twenty-three years before. A round of picnics was organized and a special performance of Othello staged in an improvised theatre to demonstrate the Chileans' appreciation of English culture.

But beneath the genial welcome there was opposition to the new admiral. The Brothers of the Lodge were not convinced that the English lord was wholeheartedly loyal to the cause, and one of their number, an Argentine called Alvarez Jonte, was appointed his secretary, with secret instructions to keep a strict eye on him. With O'Higgins' laborious but pedantic Minister of War, Zenteno, the impulsive Cochrane soon quarrelled. Even amongst the officers of his own fleet there was a hostile faction, led by Captain Guise who had coveted the command for himself. Only with O'Higgins, who was ready to overlook the asperities of his character in admiration of Cochrane's undoubted genius, did his relations remain consistently friendly.

The Admiral soon left the capital in order to devote himself to the task of getting the fleet ready to put to sea. From Valparaíso he bombarded the Minister of War with a series of complaints, proposals and demands. The lucky improvisations of the squadron's first sally had to give way to planning, organization, discipline, and the costly and varied equipment of a fleet in fighting trim. It was not until the beginning of 1820 that instructions were issued that the fleet should sail. Cochrane's last act was to write to the Director Supremo begging him to take Lady Cochrane and his son under his protection should he be killed in action. O'Higgins gave his solemn assurance and anxiously awaited the admiral's despatches.

The outset of the voyage was not auspicious. A mutiny broke out on board the *Lautaro*, the crew of which refused to sail, and there was trouble on the *Chacabuco*, where the men had a mind to turn pirate. The unrest was dominated with some difficulty, and the expedition continued on its way to Callao. There Cochrane found the Spanish ships sheltering under the powerful guns of the fort. He reported to O'Higgins that he had engaged them in a gunfire duel, and that although no material advantage had been gained, the morale of officers and men, and their conduct in the action, had surpassed his expectations. This, at least, was encouraging. But there was soon bad news to come.

At the end of May, Blanco Encalada suddenly reappeared off Valparaíso. The Admiral had left him to continue the blockade of Callao, whilst he sailed on to carry out operations further up the coast of Peru. Blanco Encalada excused his disobedience on the plea that he found himself short of supplies, since the ship's provisions had been adulterated by profiteers, and he was therefore obliged to break off the blockade and return to Chile.

O'Higgins was furious. He brushed aside Blanco Encalada's excuses and ordered his arrest and court martial. Then he hurried down to Valparaíso and threw himself into the task of re-victualling and re-equipping the ships.

Three weeks later, Cochrane himself was back in Valparaíso and there were fresh troubles. The feud with Captain Guise was increasing in bitterness, and the Admiral had caught Alvarez Jonte, the Lodge's watch-dog, prying into his personal papers and had thrown him under arrest. Cochrane demanded an increase in salary and the full value, instead of a part-share with the State, of any prizes captured at sea. The men would turn corsair, he explained, unless they could be sure of a more generous slice of the booty.

But a new issue had arisen to dwarf these petty bickerings. In his ill-advised and tortuous attempts to extort funds from his government by threatening the withdrawal of the Army of the Andes, San Martín had suggested that the pretext of a new Spanish invasion should be invented. It now seemed that an ironic fate was taking its revenge by turning fiction into fact. Reports reached America that Spain was mustering a powerful army of twenty thousand men or more to be launched first against the River Plate provinces, then against Chile, and if necesary, against Peru. If these reports, which were confused and contradictory, proved correct, as San Martín feared they might, he was convinced that no force which the Patriots could put into the field would have the slightest chance of success. At the end of July, 1819, he wrote to O'Higgins urging him to send the Chilean fleet round Cape Horn to try and intercept the Spanish armada in the Atlantic. This Cochrane stoutly refused to consider, and O'Higgins, now for the first time opposing the suggestions of his friend and mentor, wholeheartedly agreed with the Admiral. In the first place, the motley crowd of adventurers who had enlisted for the chance of prize money would never consent to face the greater hardships and uncertainties of such a voyage. And if the fleet were to sail, Chile would be left at the mercy of the Viceroy's squadron.

Fortunately, the difficulty was resolved when fresh reports revealed that plague and revolt had disrupted the Spanish fleet and prevented it from sailing. Cochrane's ships would remain then in the Pacific, but how best could they be used? Here opinion was divided. O'Higgins advocated a frontal attack against the Spanish squadron in an attempt to destroy it outright. Zenteno approved the plan, but imposed a condition which would render it unfeasible; the ships were not to venture within range of the shore batteries of Callao, under which the enemy were sheltering. Cochrane himself favoured a plan combining prudence and audacity. Part of the fleet was to continue the blockade of Callao, whilst daring raids should be made at other points on the coast to disrupt the enemy and incite the population. The latter would in all probability have proved the most effective plan, but Cochrane was obliged to accept the proposals of O'Higgins and his Minister.

By the beginning of September, the six ships of the fleet were again ready for action. Their re-equipment had only been achieved by dint of superhuman efforts, but O'Higgins was well pleased with the results and confident that they would soon bring success. 'Cochrane assures me that on the twenty-fourth of this month, shortly after eight in the evening, the shipping in Callao will all be ablaze, and that by the 15th October I shall have received his despatch,' he wrote to San Martín. 'I am sure that Cochrane will be as good as his word.'[1] But the exertions of the preceding weeks had taken toll of the Director's health, and at the end of September O'Higgins fell seriously ill with an attack of apoplexy and a return of his old rheumatic complaints. Only thanks to the devoted care of his mother and sister was he slowly nursed back to health.

Cochrane had pinned his hopes of destroying the Spanish fleet to the new invention of rockets which he had used with success against the French in Europe. A number of these weapons were constructed under his instructions in Valparaíso, but an attempt to employ them against the enemy squadron in Callao ended in failure. A second

[1] *Ibid*, p. 116.

attempt met with no better result. The admiral found himself sadly frustrated. His instructions categorically forbade him to venture his ships within reach of the shore batteries. How then could he come to grips with the enemy? He tried to provoke the Viceroy by a high-sounding challenge to send his ships out to sea, to avoid a holocaust of the civilian population. The Viceroy not unnaturally refused, and added an insulting post-script to his message, as an editor might admonish an irresponsible letter-writer: 'This correspondence is now closed.'

Cochrane's next move was to write to the Director Supremo offering his resignation unless greater freedom of action could be granted him. San Martín, who had begun to take a dislike to the English admiral and his overbearing ways, advised O'Higgins to accept the resignation and entrust the blockade of Callao, which he thought should be sufficient to compel the Spaniards to surrender, to Blanco Encalada. But O'Higgins, now increasingly aware that his friend's judgment was not infallible, declined the advice. His confidence in Cochrane was soon to be brilliantly justified. The Admiral, refusing to continue his humiliating inactivity in front of the Callao fortress, decided on a characteristically audacious and unexpected feat. Many hundreds of miles to the south, the fortress of Valdivia was still holding out for the Royalists. The chain of forts, with their numerous cannon and strong garrison, were generally assumed to be impregnable. Leaving part of his squadron to continue the blockade, Cochrane slipped off to make a preliminary reconnaissance and to communicate his plans to O'Higgins and to Freire, the officer commanding the Patriot forces in the south of Chile. O'Higgins gave his enthusiastic aproval, and Freire lent two hundred and fifty men to co-operate with Cochrane's assault party. Soon after, the Director Supremo received a message that the hazardous undertaking had been crowned with overwhelming success, and that the bastion of Royalist power was in the hands of the Patriots.

The capture of Valdivia—the triumph of audacity, so different in essence from San Martín's triumphs of prudent foresight—won for Cochrane an immense and instant popularity. His daring appealed to the ardent temperament of the Chileans, and the masses believed that if he were entrusted with the supreme command of the Peruvian expedition, he would infallibly repeat the same successes on a still grander scale. The Admiral had secured the most coveted possession of a war leader—the unquestioning conviction of the masses that he

could lead them only to victory. Even the Senate and the Chilean
aristocracy were carried away by the popular enthusiasm, and San
Martín himself, after two years of delay and uncertainty, at last
decided that he would wait no longer and that the invasion of Peru
should be attempted with Chilean resources alone.

The Argentine government was now not only a broken reed as far
as the Expedition was concerned, but an active threat to its realization. East of the Andes, hopeless anarchy prevailed and there was
constant agitation that what remained of the Army of the Andes
should be recalled to fight under the banner of one or other of the
warring factions. At the beginning of 1820, San Martín left the
Argentine, giving as his reason the need to restore his health by
taking the Chilean waters. His own position had become somewhat
anomalous. He was still the Commander-in-Chief, but the government under whom he was to act had now ceased to be an effective
force. He summoned his officers together and explained that, in such
circumstances, he could no longer continue to serve as their chief and
they should therefore elect one of their number as General. The
precarious state of his health, he added, precluded him from standing
for election. But in spite of this perhaps not very sincere refusal, he
was unanimously acclaimed and pressed to continue in office. The
old Army of the Andes was then fused with the more recent units
raised by O'Higgins, Argentine officers were assured of equivalent
rank under the Chilean flag, and the whole force received the
designation of the Army for the Liberation of Peru.

The equipment of the new Army had been facilitated by the end
of the hostilities between England and the American colonies, since
arms-merchants were now eager to find a new market for their wares
in South America. As no financial help was clearly to be expected
from the Argentine, and Chilean resources were being eaten up by
the expense of supporting the growing army, the Senate at last
decided, thanks to the unremitting persuasions of O'Higgins, to
pledge the nations' credit to the hilt and make the supreme effort of
financing the whole cost of the Expedition. In May, the army began
to muster at Quillota, in preparation for embarking. Though
weakened by some last minute desertions, it numbered just over
four thousand men and nearly three hundred officers, with thirty-
five guns, fifteen thousand rifles for Peruvian recruits, funds sufficient to pay the army for four months, and ample supplies of food
and fodder. In equipment and weapons it was superior to the old

Army of the Andes or any other army hitherto put into the field against the Spaniards.

Only in morale and the quality of its leadership did the Expeditionary Force belie something of its outward splendour. The Commander-in-Chief was no longer the man of outstanding intellect and will who had created his army and led it to victory over one of the greatest mountain ranges in the world. He was falling more and more under the influence of the sinister Monteagudo who was now one of the most powerful figures in his entourage. O'Higgins, loyal as ever in his admiration and affection, was bound to realize that there was something amiss. 'General San Martín is making a very slow recovery,' he wrote to Zañartu in February, 1820.[1] But he trusted that, under the spur of danger and opportunity, the old vigour and sagacity would assert themselves over the deadly lassitude of opium. In this confidence O'Higgins brushed aside the suggestion that he himself should sail with the expedition as its Commander-in-Chief, taking San Martín as his chief-of-staff. Instead, he invested him with the supreme Chilean rank—that of Captain-General—and with full powers over both naval and military forces. Secret instructions empowered him to remove even Cochrane in the event of the latter's insubordination. The Senate had drawn up detailed directives for the Commander-in-Chief, but O'Higgins declined to pass them on and contented himself with reaffirming that 'the only and exclusive purpose of this glorious enterprise is to liberate Peru from the shameful servitude to the Spanish sceptre,' and that the army must therefore regard itself as liberators and behave accordingly, concentrating on the total destruction of the Spanish forces as opportunity should permit.

On 10 August the great embarkation began. The Bay of Valparaíso was filled with an unprecedented and ordered activity. Ten days later, San Martín paid a visit of ceremony to each ship, the Chilean flag was hoisted, and at two o'clock in the afternoon, the admiral's flag-ship, the *O'Higgins*, set sail with a favourable breeze. The Commander-in-Chief closed the rear in the *San Martín*. O'Higgins, his mother and sister by his side, watched the departure of the armada with deep emotion. Tradition attributes to him the following farewell:[2] 'Four small ships once gave Spain the dominion of America; these will wrest it from her.'

---

[1] *Ibid*, Vol. 6, p. 307.
[2] Another source gives a slightly different version of the saying on the departure of Blanco Enclada's first squadron.

Seventeen

The War in Peru

PERU WAS STIRRED by the same revolutionary currents that had swept over the other Spanish colonies, but her inhabitants had not been carried away by the popular enthusiasm for national independence. How indeed could there be a sense of nationhood in a country made up of so many differing regions, castes, races, and sectional interests? The bleak plateau of Upper Peru, and the scorched, coastal regions of Lower Peru were two different worlds: even the south and the north of Lower Peru were divided by far-reaching differences. The total population of the country (including Charcas, detached from the La Plata vice-royalty after the revolution) numbered some 2,800,000. Of these roughly half were pure-blooded natives, for whom a change of white masters could mean but little. There were also about 800,000 mestizos of ambivalent loyalties, some tens of thousands of negroes (slaves or freed men), and about 350,000 pure or almost pure whites. The latter comprised Creoles and Spaniards, separated by deep animosity. Even the Spaniards were divided amongst themselves, for some were conservatives and absolutists, others liberals and advocates of Spain's new constitutional liberties.

Lima still regarded itself as superior to any other city of the New World. It was proud of being the court of the Viceregal world (Peru boasted no less than eighty-two titles of Castilian nobility) and mindful of the profitable economic privileges it had enjoyed. Five years before, the iron hand of Abascal had seemingly suppressed the revolution throughout almost the whole of South America. But the price of victory had been economic and military exhaustion. The best Peruvian troops had been sacrificed on the fields of Chacabuco and Maipo. Trade was ruined by the blockade, corsairs preyed on shipping and commerce, and most of the rich merchants had already smuggled their capital out of the country. The exchequer was all but bankrupt. The *Esmeralda* and other fine ships of the Spanish navy were immobilized beneath the guns of the Callao fortress not through cowardice but because there was simply not enough money to make them seaworthy.

The number of troops at the disposal of the Viceroy reached the apparently formidable total of 17,000, of which 7,000 were concentrated in Lima. But the configuration of the country, with its stretches of desert and vast mountain ranges, made it impossible to regroup and rally these scattered units. Moreover, their discipline and morale were lamentable. Nevertheless, San Martín did not dare to risk his four thousand well trained troops in a decisive engagement against an enemy so numerically superior. He believed that time was on his side and that he had only to use the weapons of bluff and intrigue for the Viceroy's army to melt away and allow him to enter Lima without bloodshed. This, he was convinced, would be the end of the war. These tactics might have stood a better chance of success had the Commander-in-Chief been in possession of his original astuteness and organizing powers, and had the army been able to count on the united resources of Chile and the Argentine for the prosecution of a prolonged campaign.

O'Higgins shared much the same illusion. He was persuaded that the Expedition had only to show itself off the coast of Peru for the population to rise and force the Viceroy to capitulate, or at least to sue for a truce. The proclamation which he had prepared for distribution in Peru informed the inhabitants somewhat grandiloquently that 'Liberty, the daughter of heaven, is about to descend upon your lands', and exhorted them to give the goddess a rousing welcome. 'I am certain that our army will not have to fire a single shot,' he wrote off to his Minister of War. 'Everything indicates that the liberty of America will be won without further bloodshed.' Always prone to attribute to others the desire to shake free of the Spanish yoke which was the guiding passion of his own life, he failed to understand that a city which owed its splendour and prosperity to the favour of the Crown would look with mixed feelings on the crusade for national independence. Only Cochrane was shrewd enough to realize that a series of resolute hammer blows would be needed to bring about the collapse of the enemy. He asked in vain for the command of a couple of thousand men with which to strike at different points on the coast in rapid succession.

Pezuela, the Viceroy, had considerable strategic insight. He was one of the few Spanish generals to realize that the campaign would be decided by sea-power, and he feared for the defeat of the vice-royalty as soon as Chile started to create a fleet. These views he urged on the Spanish government with great force, arguing that 'without the control of the sea, the salvation of these lands is impossible.' He therefore determined to hold on to Lima and Callao as long as possible, whilst La Serna, Canterac, and other Royalist leaders favoured a withdrawal to Upper Peru, where they hoped to continue the struggle, although the lack of any sea base would mean that reinforcements would never reach them from Spain.

The campaign opened according to San Martín's plan.[1] The Expeditionary Force reached the Bay of Paracas, south of Lima, in good order and began to disembark. But, except for the slaves, the population showed no particular enthusiasm to enlist in the ranks of their liberators. Negotiations were tentatively started with the Viceroy, whilst San Martín's spies brought him reports of the position in the capital. There all seemed to favour the Patriot cause; the Royalists were in great consternation, and the citizens eagerly expectant. But still San Martín hesitated, hoping to achieve the bloodless victory in which he believed. His changing moods of elation and discouragement are mirrored in his despatches to O'Higgins.

Three events then occurred to strengthen his hand. First, the port of Guayaquil, with its garrison of 1,500 men, declared itself for the Patriots; secondly, Cochrane, by a stroke of incredible daring, succeeded in capturing the *Esmeralda* under the very noses of the defenders of Callao; and thirdly, the Numancia Battalion of the Viceroy's army, comprising 650 Colombians and Venezuelans, went over to him *en bloc*. San Martín decided to re-embark his troops and land again at Ancón, north of Lima, making a threatening demonstration in front of Callao on the way. The garrison of Trujillo, following the example of Guayaquil, declared itself for the Patriot cause under the command of the Marqués de Torre Tagle, a vacillating nobleman and former school-mate of O'Higgins whom the latter had been secretly urging to take this course for some time. Finally, Pezuela himself was deposed by a group of Spanish officers who accused the Viceroy of being luke-warm and incompetent.

But these successes were purchased at a high price. The site of San Martín's camp at Ancón was an unhealthy one, and his ranks were dangerously thinned by fever. 'Our army has been reduced by

---

[1] For a detailed study of the campaign *see* Gonzalo Bulnes: *Historia de la Expedición Libertadora del Perú,* 1817–22 (Santiago, 1887).

1,500 sick and the same number of convalescents,' he informed O'Higgins. 'My own health is very poor, and I have every reason to believe that if things go on in this way I shall soon be finished.' His only consolation was that the plight of the Lima garrison was still more grave. Shortage of food and the spread of epidemics had completed the exasperation of the civil population and the demoralization of the Royalist army. Negotiations continued with the new Viceroy, La Serna, to whom San Martín proposed the complete independence of Peru beneath a prince of the Spanish royal house. Such a proposal La Serna could not accept without reference to Spain, and since the position in Lima was rapidly becoming untenable, he decided to evacuate the capital and continue resistance in the interior. On 2 July, with no pitched battle fought but the war still unterminated, San Martín entered the City of the Kings. The independence of Peru was proclaimed, and the Commander-in-Chief of the expeditionary army assumed the military and civil leadership of the new state, under the title of Protector.

But the rule of the Protector was jeopardized from the outset by two blunders, one military, the other political. The military blunder was to permit La Serna's uniformed skeletons, who could have been easily destroyed even by San Martín's weakened forces, to withdraw to the sierra, where they could regain their strength and raise fresh recruits. Though the Royalists no longer had much hope of ultimate victory, they could still drag out the war in long, bitter, and exhausting campaigns. San Martín's political blunder, the outcome of an intellect and will increasingly undermined by the use of opium, was to give a free hand to Monteagudo and his camarilla. The sinister mulatto had already incurred the loathing of Chileans and Argentines by his crimes, and was soon to bring like odium on the administration of the Protector. To San Martín he showed the most servile adulation but in his heart of hearts he despised and hated him. When not blinded by passion, his mind was clear and vigorous. But the corrupt, pleasure-loving society of the capital offered too many temptations to his vain and sensuous nature, and he lorded it with unbridled insolence until an assassin cut short his scandalous career.

The nefarious influence of Monteagudo was apparent even to the distant and not very perceptive O'Higgins. 'And now, my friend,' he wrote to San Martín in words which recall the warnings he had once himself received against the perfidy of Carrera, 'I must counsel you to moderate your natural kindness towards such men as

Monteagudo, which induces you to protect individuals who keep faith with no one and only involve us in constant embarrassments.'[1] But the Protector paid little heed, and O'Higgins soon forgot his forebodings in his enthusiasm at the news of the fall of Lima. Rejoicing was intensified by the sight of the four Chilean flags captured by the Spaniards at Rancagua and discovered in a Lima church by San Martín who had sent back the trophies to Santiago. 'If this were the last day of my life,' O'Higgins announced with heartfelt sincerity at the official banquet held to celebrate the event, 'I could die more proudly than in the ranks of Mars.' He felt San Martín's triumph as his own—for did not the capture of Lima set the seal on the freedom of South America?—and vowed again his eternal gratitude and friendship. As for San Martín's decision to assume the office of Protector of Peru, O'Higgins wrote that 'the greatest benefit you can confer on these countries is to assume the burden of ruling them.'

But there were many others in Chile who saw things in a very different light. They were uneasy over the dominant influence wielded by Monteagudo, whilst there was not a single Chilean of note amongst San Martín's advisers. The Commander-in-Chief had promised that the Expeditionary Force would live off the land once it had reached Peru, but he was now bombarding the exhausted country with demands for further supplies and reinforcements. Most disturbing of all, the head of an army preponderantly Chilean, and an officer holding the highest Chilean military rank, had suddenly made himself the head of another state without so much as consulting the government for which he was supposed to be acting. This was surely a most extraordinary state of affairs, and one which gave grounds for anxiety as to the fate of the Expeditionary Force. The latter was now without proper leadership and in danger of succumbing to the enemy who were busy reorganizing in the interior.

The effect of the Peruvian campaign was aggravating the already desperate condition of Chile and threatening the personal position of the Director Supremo. The sustained effort of forming a navy and sending the Expeditionary Force had utterly exhausted the country. Instead of being allowed time to recover, it was now harassed with fresh demands from Peru, with calls for help against the marauding hordes of Carrera in Cuyo province, and, above all, with the war still raging in the south of Chile, where Royalists, Araucanians, and bandits were making common cause under a bloodthirsty ruffian

[1] *Archivo*, Vol. 8, p. 83.

called Benavides. Freire, the local commander of the Patriot forces, was a gallant officer, but bereft of strategic or political sense and quite incapable of pacifying the country. The once fertile province of Concepción was no more than a waste, ranged by bands of marauders and groups of famished women, children, and old men, an open wound, through which the little blood still remaining in the body of the state oozed painfully away.

The economic and financial prostration of the country was complete. What money there was had passed into the hands of foreign merchants and a few war profiteers. Fields were left untilled through shortage of labour, and O'Higgins had commissioned his envoys in Europe to send Irish, Swiss, or any other settlers out to Chile with all possible speed. The income from customs was pledged for years to come to pay off the state's debts. O'Higgins was not exaggerating when he wrote to San Martín in May, 1821: 'There is no one here who has money to lend, even at 40% interest. There is no money to pay our army in the south; since the expedition left, public servants, including myself, have had no salary paid to them. Things have got to such a pitch that I even have the humiliation of having to find someone to lend me 500 pesos every month for my own needs.'[1]

In the midst of this universal distress, O'Higgins had striven to carry out a number of drastic reforms. Some proved of lasting benefit. Setting batches of prisoners to work in the capital, he continued the work of improvement begun by his father, and the fine main boulevard traversing the city bears his name to this day. The building of the Maipo canal, which converted a vast stretch of waste at the approaches to Santiago into fertile agricultural land, was another favourite scheme. But many of his measures, such as his encouragement of elementary education, achieved only a partial and temporary success owing to the disturbed conditions of the country, or aroused the opposition of the more conservative sections of the population. This was particularly true of the attempts which the Director made to reduce the prevailing religious bigotry, which he sternly disapproved of both on its own account, and as a legacy from the centuries of Spanish colonialism.

Pueyrredón had once given him the sound advice never to tamper with the established religion. If he was at heart too sincerely devout a man ever to think of attacking the foundations, he was unwise

[1] *Ibid*, p. 129.

7

enough to consider reforming what he considered the inessentials or
excesses of religion. To see the pomp of their processions and the
licence of their carnivals curtailed, and their dead buried in new-
fangled cemeteries instead of beneath the church floor angered the
populace and led to the legend of the government's impiety.
O'Higgins toyed with such projects as abolishing all auricular con-
fession and the celibacy of the clergy, and was only restrained from
airing them in public by his childhood friend, Casimiro Albano, now
himself a dignitary of the church. Other reforms which he openly
advocated, such as the State's official guarantee of freedom of wor-
ship, so as to attract Anglo-Saxon immigrants, were over-ruled by
the Senate. Even his patronage of the worthy James Thomson, who
founded a number of schools on the Lancasterian principle but also
worked for the Bible Society, was frowned upon in pious circles.[1]
But O'Higgins had set himself strict limits to the reforms which he
would like to see introduced. When an American merchant, Jeremiah
Robinson, suggested to him that he might find a way out of Chile's
economic plight by secularizing church property, he was offended at
the impropriety of the proposal.[2] He showed himself anxious, too,
for a reconciliation with the exiled Bishop of Santiago, Rodríguez
Zorrilla, and called him back from Mendoza.

Widespread economic misery, the drain of the war in the south,
the unpopularity of many of the Director's attempted reforms,
suspicions of San Martín's intentions in Peru—all these made for
the growing unpopularity of the O'Higgins' administration. The
landed aristocracy, who had surrendered all participation in the
government in their relief and enthusiasm after Chacabuco, soon
regretted it and began to press for a share of power. The
threat from Osorio's second invasion had momentarily reconciled
them to the Director's autocratic rule, but after Maipo, the
old agitation was renewed. O'Higgins responded by agreeing
first to the appointment of Ministers to relieve him of respon-
sibilty for the detailed transactions of departmental business; then,
in October, 1818, to a provisional constitution providing for the
establishment of a five-man Senate with advisory and some super-
visory powers. The old colonial administrative machine was to be

[1] See W. E. Browning: *Joseph Lancaster, James Thomson, the Lancasterian system...
with reference to Hispanic America* in *Hispanic American Historical Review*, IV (1921)
pp. 49–98.

[2] E. Pereira Salas: *Jeremias Robinson, agente norteamericano en Chile*, 1818–23
(Santiago, 1939).

retained for the time being with only the minimum of essential changes, the former Spanish laws were regarded as still in force, except in so far as they visibly conflicted with the spirit of the Revolution, whilst the old *audiencia* was replaced by new tribunals. The provisional constitution guaranteed the rights of the individual by a sort of *habeas corpus*, private property was protected, and freedom of the press proclaimed.

Though O'Higgins had returned from Europe with democratic and republican sympathies and had once fought hard for the establishment of a congress, experience had convinced him that radical innovations only led to anarchy and dangerously weakened the national war effort. 'In times of revolution,' he remarked to an American who urged him to introduce the republican form of government and full congressional procedure, 'it is dangerous to carry through fundamental changes suddenly, however reasonable and desirable they may be in themselves. This is to risk losing everything.' He strove, rather, to combine zeal for reform with an innate respect for order. But where his father had so admirably succeeded in preserving just this delicate balance, Bernardo, less adroit and confronted with more difficult circumstances, sometimes found himself driven into the most questionable compromises. Yielding to the clamour of more radical reformists, he finally issued a proclamation announcing elections to a constituent assembly, but secret instructions to the provincial governors clearly indicated the names of the candidates he wished to see elected. When, therefore, the assembly was solemnly convened in June, 1822, the Director could safely resign his powers to it, confident that he would be unanimously confirmed in his almost absolute exercise of them.

But while the Director thus evaded the delegation of his real authority to any congress he lacked that delight in power for its own sake which would have given the necessary coherence and drive to his government. San Martín, who knew his friend through and through, once remarked of him that 'there was more wax than steel in his heart.' True, he could show admirable constancy where the dominating passion of his life—the independence of South America —was concerned, but in the tactical details of attaining the goal he instinctively turned for guidance to some stronger or more experienced mind. In England, the mentor had been Miranda; in Chile, Mackenna, then San Martín, and the brothers of the Lodge. But now San Martín was committed to another destiny, his powers

were failing, and the Brothers had mostly followed him to Peru. If
O'Higgins now found himself free of the tutelage of the Lodge,
whose decisions had often involved unhappy consequences for
Chile, that was all to the good. But to whom should he now turn for
the support and guidance that his nature craved?

The answer was as unexpected as it was regrettable; to Gaínza's
former *asesor* and ex-member of Osorio's loyal *audiencia*, the
master of chicanery and intrigue, Rodríguez Aldea.[1] Born in Chillán,
the birthplace of O'Higgins (a link which he was not slow to exploit
in worming his way into the Director's good graces), the lawyer had
been educated in Lima and entered the fray as a convinced Royalist.
He had used his influence first to prevent Gaínza from signing the
Pact of Lircay, and then, when back in Lima, to have his chief condemned for having done so. But his own conduct had not escaped
censure, and though Osorio had appointed him a member of the
audiencia, he again fell under suspicion – this time, on the charge of
having accepted bribes from implicated Patriots. The victory of
Chacabuco convinced him that the Royalist cause was lost, and he
quickly became a fervent convert to the other side. The Director was
not the man to harbour grudges and granted his request to be
allowed to return to Chile. By ingratiating himself first with Doña
Isabel and Doña Rosita, the intriguing lawyer soon won the Director's confidence and finished, thanks to his subtle intelligence,
capacity for hard work, and a genuine admiration for his chief, by
exerting an extraordinary ascendency over him.

It is difficult to imagine two characters more dissimilar than the
two natives of Chillán. Rodríguez Aldea was quick-witted, specious,
and possessed of an intuitive grasp of other men's character, particularly of their weaknesses, which he was an adept at exploiting.
His conception of solving a problem was to play off one person, or
one group, against another. He was confident that he could talk his
way out of any difficulty. He had an innate love of intrigue and
chicanery which led him to prefer the tortuous for its own sake. He
was versatile but meretricious; a jack-of-all-trades who might have
been useful as the assistant to a strong man but was disastrous as the
master of a weak one. He was hard-working, flexible, and able to
learn by experience; capable of occasionally introducing a beneficial
measure – such as declaring Valparaíso to be a free port – but lacking

[1] *See* Francisco de P. Rodríguez Velasco: *Biografía del doctor don José Antonio
Rodríguez Aldea* (Santiago, 1862).

real administrative ability or statesmanship, ignorant of social and economic affairs, and totally devoid of principles. He was shamelessly corrupt himself, and even implicated Doña Rosita, less prudent and scrupulous than her brother, in his shady deals, though she managed to draw back before her fingers were too badly burnt. Rodríguez Aldea, in short, was one of the long line of intriguing opportunists who cause honest folk in South America to wash their hands of politics as a 'dirty business'.

How could a man of good sense and personal integrity fall beneath the spell of the Chillán lawyer? Cochrane, who had an eagle eye for the weaknesses of his friends no less than those of his enemies, suggests a likely explanation: 'Being himself above meanness, he was led to rely on the honesty of others from the uprightness of his own motives. Though in every way disposed to believe, with Burke, that "what is morally wrong can never be politically right," he was led to believe that a crooked policy was a necessary evil of government; and as such a policy was adverse to his own nature, he was the more easily induced to surrender the administration to others who were free from his conscientious principles.'[1]

What was certain was that the ascendency of the Minister, who passed from the department of Finance to that of War, (relegating Zenteno to the Governorship of Valparaíso) to the accompaniment of increasing scandals, was arousing a national resentment which threatened to engulf the Director Supremo himself. At the end of November, 1822, Cochrane wrote to warn him of the approaching storm. 'I wish to give Your Excellency one more proof of my attachment by imploring you to open your eyes to the general discontent prevailing amongst all classes regarding both the declared and the secret measures of Minister Rodríguez, who has fallen in the public esteem, though he does not realize it, lower than Monteagudo himself, when the populace demanded his resignation and then his punishment. Should Your Excellency then attempt to continue your protection of him, you will yourself be involved in the most serious harm, possibly leading to the destruction of your work and of your personal endeavours for the welfare of the state.'[2]

O'Higgins, who had been quick to see the danger to San Martín through the latter's tolerance of the notorious Monteagudo, remained curiously blind to the parallel perils of his own position.

[1] *Narrative of Service in Chile, Peru and Brasil* (London, 1849) p. 71.
[2] Correspondence with Lord Cochrane, *Archivo Vicuña Mackenna*, Vols. 85–88.

Cochrane sent him a second letter of warning, curter in tone than the first, and then washed his hands of the imminent disaster by presenting his own resignation. At the beginning of the new year, popular clamour forced the hated Minister to resign. But it was too late; the irreparable harm had already been done.

Eighteen

Troubles at Home

THE BURDEN OF OFFICE, which the Director Supremo shared with his unpopular Minister, was growing daily more intolerable. 'I am kept busy with papers and business the whole day long,' he wrote to Irisarri, his London envoy, in March, 1822, 'from six in the morning to eleven at night, with only a break for lunch and a rest. It has been such a strain that I feel I cannot keep it up much longer... My own salary is more than a year in arrears, and I have the mortification of having to borrow from my friends for my daily necessities, a thing which has never happened to me before in private life.'[1]

The old palace of the Governors of Chile, which had once been his father's residence, now housed the Director, his mother and sister, and their household. It boasted more European comforts and refinements than in the days when Vancouver had complained of its inches-thick dust. When that observant traveller Maria Graham[2] called on the Director's family, she found that 'the rooms are handsomely but plainly furnished; English cast-iron grates; Scotch carpets; some French china and time-pieces, little or nothing that looked Spanish, still less Chileno.' The house also contained a few incongruously extravagant objects, such as an elaborate bed with silk hangings, which had been purchased from a French cabinet-maker, probably on the initiative of the more extravagant Doña Rosita, for 6,000 francs. But the Director's personal tastes were simple. He had always been a great lover of music, and even in his campaigns had found solace in the accordion which he carried with him. The musical *tertulias* which Doña Rosita was fond of arranging now offered him his rare moments of relaxation.

[1] *Archivo*, Vol. 4, pp. 520–22.
[2] Maria Graham, the author of *Little Arthur's History of England*, has left an interesting account of her experiences in Chile and her impressions of the leading personages of the day in her *Journal of a residence in Chile during the year 1822* (London, 1824). *See* p. 206.

Doña Rosita supervised the management of her brother's house with bustling efficiency. She was short and rather stockily built, like Bernardo, and her brusque ways had won her the nickname of 'the general in petticoats'. She was somewhat plain-featured, and had inherited nothing of the delicate grace of her perennially youthful mother. Doña Isabel cared little for politics but passionately for her son, and she was ready to share uncomplainingly in any sacrifice which he saw fit to make for the cause to which he had vowed his life. Her mission was to lavish on him the care and affection which no other woman could give. Bernardo's ill-starred affair with Doña Rosario Puga had soon come to an end, and the light-of-love had taken a new lover from the ranks of the Carrera faction. The fruit of her brief liaison with Bernardo was an infant, Pedro Demetrio, born a few months after the victory of Maipo. The care of this child had been entrusted to a priest, Father Domingo Jara. But though Bernardo seemed strangely indifferent to the existence of his natural son, Doña Isabel kept an affectionate eye on his upbringing, and later took him to join the O'Higgins household. The latter already included two little Araucanian girls, orphaned in the savage fighting of the South, whom Bernardo had adopted and treated as his own daughters.

'In private intercourse he was affable, unassuming and cautious,' wrote his friend José María de la Cruz, who knew O'Higgins well at this time of his life.[1] 'He liked better to listen than to speak, and he had a peculiar talent for summing up in a few words the ideas or points under discussion; and another peculiarity, that is to say, his ability to present to the world a countenance reflecting nothing of the amusement or gaiety customary among intimates, which resulted in his being classed as reserved...In his home life he was invariably the same. I never knew him to speak sharply to his servants, and some of them he treated as if they had been relatives of the family. He idolized his mother, treating her with a consideration and respect such as I have never known in anyone of his age. When he used to come from the office he would walk up and down in the inner court-yard, where he would find his mother's parrot and parrakeet and, taking one in his hand and the other on his shoulder, he would begin

---

[1] See Miguel Luis Amunátegui Reyes: *Don Bernardo O'Higgins juzgado por algunos de sus contemporáneos* (Santiago, 1917), also published in the *Revista Chilena de Historia y Geografía*, Vol. 24, No. 28, 1917, containing a long letter from de la Cruz giving interesting biographical details about O'Higgins.

to talk to them, the conversation usually consisting of chidings on account of the disputes in which they had been involved. The two pets were his table companions practically every day; he would place one on either side of him and feed them himself.'

Maria Graham, who visited the Director at the small country estate which he had acquired just outside Santiago, noted that he generally preferred to dress in his general's uniform and that he was 'short and fat, yet very active; his blue eyes, light hair, and ruddy and rather coarse complexion do not belie his Irish extraction; whilst his small and short hands and feet belong to his Araucanian pedigree.' He was happy when he could leave his work in the capital and indulge his taste for improving the land and farm buildings of his estate. He liked to think that these country labours encouraged the public to feel confidence in the stability of his administration and its concern for the agricultural development which should be the basis of its prosperity. From his garden he could see the plain of Maipo, bringing memories of the great battle, and what was of more immediate interest now—the improvements resulting from the new irrigation works. The farm-house was clean, plain, but comfortable. 'The Director, when here, sleeps on a little portable camp-bed,' noted Maria Graham, 'and to judge by his room, is not very studious of personal accommodation.'[1]

O'Higgins' modest country house was soon to shelter an illustrious guest—no less a personage than General San Martín, who had returned from Peru, disillusioned and broken in health, at the end of October, 1822, and had then fallen dangerously ill with typhoid. The course of events which led to his withdrawal from public life we must now pause to relate. The Spanish officers who had retreated to the interior of Peru reorganized their forces with such success that they had managed to relieve the beleagured garrison at Callao and make off with a great quantity of indispensable war material. Though the garrison capitulated to the Patriots soon afterwards—an event which Monteagudo grandiloquently announced as signifying the end of the war—Admiral Cochrane had taken a more gloomily realistic view. 'The war is not over in Peru,' he wrote to O'Higgins, 'on the contrary, if the new government persists in following the path it has chosen, my opinion is that the war has scarcely begun...If this

[1] Maria Graham, *op. cit.*, pp. 206–208.

7*

country is lost, it will be due to the measures taken by the Protector.'[1]

The tension between the Protector and the Admiral rose to a climax, deliberately fanned by the iniquitous Monteagudo. The latter, who bore a grudge against Chile for the contempt and hatred in which he was held there, schemed to have the Admiral removed, the fleet dissolved and made over to Peru. To this end, he encouraged Guise and the other anti-Cochrane officers in the navy and prevailed on San Martín to foment the general discontent by withholding funds for the payment of officers and personnel. Cochrane, who now held the lowest opinion of the Protector's abilities and moral character, demanded satisfaction in a series of sharp notes and a final stormy interview in which he championed the claims of Chile against the pretensions of one who was now head of another State. When his demands for the payment of the fleet were again refused, Cochrane determined to take the law into his own hands. The Royalists' relief of Callao had filled the Patriots with alarm, and the public funds, and much private wealth, had been hastily sent aboard the fleet for safe-keeping. This money, including 60,000 pesos of Monteagudo's ill-gotten fortune, the admiral now impounded and with it proceeded to pay the fleet. With the capitulation of the Callao garrison, the necessity of continuing the blockade ceased. At the beginning of October, Cochrane dispersed the fleet, sending two ships back at once to Chile, another to Guayaquil, to be careened, and set off in chase of some enemy vessels with the remainder.

These acts of defiance had moved the Protector to impotent fury. He wrote off to O'Higgins demanding that Cochrane should be stripped of his rank and proclaimed a pirate. But the facts of the case had become widely known in Chile and deepened the indignation against San Martín and his Minister. O'Higgins bent his efforts to saving what he could of the fleet, and sent off supplies and fresh officers to replace the followers of Guise who had now ostentatiously left their ships to put themselves at the disposal of San Martín. To Cochrane he sent a friendly letter: 'I would have done the same, had I been in your place, so I repeat that everything has my approbation, and I give you and the worthy officers under your orders my warmest thanks for your loyalty and heroism in the cause of Chile...' O'Higgins finished by promising them all rewards of land and money on their return. 'You have no reason to receive orders from Lima, either direct or indirect,' he concluded, 'since from the moment of

[1] Encuna, *op. cit.*, Vol. 8, p. 253.

the declaration of the independence of that country under the protectorship of San Martín, the provisional power entrusted to him over the fleet ceased.'[1] Then, wishing to reconcile his own, and the public's, approval of Cochrane's actions with his old loyalty towards San Martín, he wrote the latter a letter counselling restraint and patience. 'We must by no means declare him a pirate,' he urged, 'as he might then turn the blockade against us or make common cause with some other country.' When at length the Admiral returned to Valparaíso, where he was accorded a great popular ovation, O'Higgins hurried down to the port to do him honour. A loan was raised from amongst the local merchant community so that the crews could be paid off. The ships were dismantled, and the Admiral's resignation finally accepted. The fleet which had cost the country so many sacrifices and had born the expeditionary force to Peru with such high hopes, ceased to exist.

In the political firmament too, the Protector's star was waning, dimmed by the brilliance of Simón Bolívar. What passed between the two men at their historic meeting at Guayaquil has never been reliably disclosed, but it is clear that the encounter convinced San Martín, as he admitted to his friend Guido before leaving Peru, that 'there is not room enough in Peru both for Bolívar and myself.' Their personalities and policies were too irreconcilably different. If both strove for the same prize—the independence of America from Spanish rule—the one had moved towards it with the prudent deliberation of the chess-player, the other with the inspired audacity of a great gambler. But now the hand of the master was faltering; he fumbled his pieces and the combination he had planned for the final victory looked like turning into stale-mate or worse. Bolívar, in the plenitude of his genius, was confident that he had but to venture one more bid and the game would be his. In resolving to abandon the field to his rival, the final sacrifice which the common cause demanded of him, the Protector did so with a heavy heart and not without some misgivings. 'Write to our friend O'Higgins as soon as you can,' he told Cruz on returning from Guayaquil, 'and tell him that the Liberator is not the man we thought him to be.' Then, having laid down all his military and civil powers with the resolve to retire for ever into private life, he took up his pen to justify his actions. 'You will reproach me,' he wrote to O'Higgins, 'for not having completed the work begun. You are right enough, but I am

[1] *Ibid*, pp. 271–272.

still more in the right. Believe me, my friend, I am tired of being
called a tyrant, a would-be king, emperor, and the devil knows what.
Besides, my health has gone to pieces, and the atmosphere of this
country has brought me to the edge of the grave. After all,' he concluded, adapting the familiar adage of Pliny, 'I gave my youth to
Spain, and my manhood to my country, so I think I have earned the
right to spend my old age as I please.'[1]

More than two years had passed since the General had set sail
from Valparaíso at the head of the expeditionary army—two years of
mingled triumph, failure and uncertainty which had done much to
alter the esteem in which he had been held by the Chileans. The
army was still far from home and final victory was not yet in sight.
Lord Cochrane wrote to the Director urging that the ex-Protector
should be indicted for misconduct. The Carrera faction increased
the clamour against their old enemy, and it was widely expected that
some sensational incident would occur between the admiral and the
general. But Cochrane withdrew to the estate which had been given
him at Quinteros Bay, and O'Higgins sent his own carriage and an
escort of honour to bring San Martín to the capital. Then, whilst a
virulent attack of typhoid laid the general at death's door, public
opinion against him gradually subsided, and in after years, San
Martín was able to write to Zenteno: 'I shall never forget the kind
sympathy shown me by the inhabitants of Santiago during my grave
illness when I returned from Peru.' In the second half of January he
was sufficiently recovered to leave for Mendoza with the intention of
settling quietly on a small estate in the Andean foothills. But the
disturbed state of the country and the malice of his enemies caused
him soon to leave for Europe, where he lived in modest retirement
until his death nearly twenty years later.

The Director Supremo now felt the loneliness and insecurity of
his position more keenly than ever. San Martín and Cochrane had
gone, the brothers of the Lodge had been dispersed, Rodríguez
Aldea had been driven from office by the popular clamour; even his
old enemies the Carreras, with whom his fate had been so closely
linked in the early days of the revolution, were no more. Old friends,
such as Freire, the commander of the Chilean army in the south,
could now be counted among his enemies. The politicians around
him, if still respectful, were almost all united in opposition to his
rule and impatiently awaiting its end. The superstitious and fickle

[1] *Archivo*, Vol. 8, p. 208.

populace was persuaded that his government had aroused the wrath of heaven and threatened to bring the divine vengeance upon the whole country because of its sins. This was dramatically demonstrated in the middle of November by an event which nearly cost the Director his life and dealt a final blow at the prosperity of the country and the prestige of O'Higgins' administration.

The population of Valparaíso had grown astonishingly during the past dozen years from five and a half thousand to three times that size. This was due in large measure to the wealth and enterprise of the foreign merchant communities which gave to the place something of a European appearance. 'English tailors, shoe-makers, and inn-keepers hang out their sign in every street,' observed Maria Graham, 'and the preponderance of the English language over every other spoken in the chief streets would make one fancy Valparaíso a coast town in Britain.' Even in the house of the Governor were to be found 'an English carpet, an English grate, even English coals'.[1] But the lower classes, still attached to their old ways and superstitions, looked with suspicion on the intrusion of these foreigners and heretics.

The 19 November had been an exceptionally still and sultry day, and the inhabitants of Valparaíso had noticed that the tide had been abnormally high. At half past ten at night, an ominous rumbling followed by a slight tremor brought everyone hurrying out into the streets. A moment later, a violent shock sent all the churches and most of the private houses in the city crashing to the ground, to the sinister accompaniment of a sort of subterranean thunder-clap, the din of falling masonry, and the panic-stricken shrieks of the people. Fires broke out and flames soon illuminated the scene of destruction, whilst the panic was increased by the sight of a great meteor crossing the heavens. For three long minutes the earth rocked to and fro, and the sea withdrew to come hurtling against the coast in three towering waves. No less than thirty-six lesser shocks followed during the rest of that terrible night.

O'Higgins, who had come down to Valparaíso shortly before, escaped from the governor's palace at the first shock, but stumbled on the threshold and was pulled clear by his adjutant only a moment before the building collapsed behind him. He was joined soon afterwards by Cochrane who came ashore to put his services at the disposal of the Director, and had a tent pitched for him on the hillside. Dawn found the whole population huddled round their priests on the slopes

[1] Maria Graham, *op. cit.*, p. 165.

above the ruined town, confessing their sins aloud or passively telling their rosary. Some were scourging themselves in penance; others still frantically clasped the crucifix or image they had seized before rushing from their homes.

In the devastated town itself, bands of marauders were sacking the houses and calling out for the blood of the impious *gringos* and heretics who had brought this visitation on their city. The riot looked so dangerous that the Director issued an immediate proclamation declaring that anyone caught threatening the life or property of a foreigner would be shot on the spot. Gradually, by dint of severity and hurriedly improvised relief measures, order and confidence were restored. The city slowly began to rise again from its ruins. Though some seven hundred houses had been wholly destroyed, the total number of casualties did not exceed one hundred. The Director strove to counteract the bigotry and superstition of the people by having articles inserted in the press explaining the natural causes of the catastrophe. He put an end to the processions of penitents and flagellants, whose violent cries and dishevelled appearance added to the terror of the population. But although the official gazette declared in an excess of fulsome loyalty, that 'the misfortunes which have occurred are insignificant compared with the escape of the person of the Director, who was in imminent danger of being crushed by a falling wall', the mass of the people saw in the disaster the hand of God. A group of monks drew up a petition for the expulsion of all English and Americans. Other malcontents reminded each other how the Director had ordered the execution of the three assassins of an unfortunate English merchant in the capital, and hinted that the tyrant, himself the bastard son of a *gringo*, was secretly planning to hand over the whole of Chile to his 'fellow-countrymen', the English. The triumphs, the heroism, the honesty and unremitting labours of the man were forgotten; he and all his works were pronounced to be of the devil and meet to be swept away if their country and their souls were to be saved.

Nineteen

The Fall of the Director

THE DECISIVE BLOW was struck, as had happened so often in the past, from the South. Traditional jealousy of the capital was now sharpened by the desperate misery of famine and lawlessness. Freire was powerless to pacify the region, and indeed himself became infected with its discontent. He bitterly taxed the government with failing to send him funds and reinforcements and complained that O'Higgins' all-powerful Minister treated his urgent requests with insolent indifference. A visit to Santiago only made matters worse. He even exchanged harsh words with O'Higgins, and the latter's many enemies were not slow to play on Freire's sense of grievance and injured pride. It seems probable too that he now harboured a bitter personal grudge against his former friend. The younger man had become enamoured of an heiress in the capital, the old Conde de la Conquista's granddaughter, who had lost her father on the field of Maipo and thus became a ward of the Director. Whether Freire, who was a reserved man, had confided his hopes to O'Higgins we do not know, but the girl's hand was bestowed on another officer. Freire returned to Concepción apparently reconciled with the Director. 'I respect and love you as father of the Republic and my own benefactor,' he wrote to him shortly afterwards. O'Higgins felt no reason to doubt his words, for Freire had always been his favourite and protégé, one of the loyalest as well as the most gallant of his officers, from the earliest days of the war and during the difficult years of their Argentine exile.

Shortly after returning to Concepción, Freire sent a letter to Cochrane, with whom he had co-operated in the capture of Valdivia, voicing his complaints against the Director Supremo and appealing for the Admiral's support in overthrowing the régime. Cochrane's reply was to warn O'Higgins. But his warning—even if the Director was prepared to heed it—came too late. News reached the capital that Concepción was in a state of open rebellion. But even then O'Higgins could not bring himself to believe that his old comrade-in-arms was implicated in it, and he wrote urging him to take stern measures against the malcontents. Freire now showed his hand by issuing a proclamation expressing solidarity with the Concepción *cabildo* and condemning O'Higgins for 'the usurpation of power which you exercise against the wishes of the people.' The proclamation ended with a fulsome denial that Freire had any aspirations to take over supreme political power himself. Freire also wrote off to San Martín asking him to intervene in the dispute. The general replied that his ill health and his decision to withdraw from politics prevented him from playing any part in Chilean affairs, but he counselled Freire to exercise moderation and compromise, adding that his long acquaintance with O'Higgins' character had shown him that the Director could be stubborn and violent when forcibly opposed, but was always tractable enough if rightly approached.

When O'Higgins at last realized the true nature and gravity of the revolt, he began mustering the military forces at his disposal. Messages were sent to summon the garrisons of Valdivia and Valparaíso, and the Governor of Mendoza also offered to send help. But these preparations to suppress the sedition were half-hearted affairs, for the Director was all but resolved to resign his office. The resignation of San Martín had pointed the way which he himself secretly aspired to follow. Six years of ceaseless exertions, which had won no other reward than the ingratitude and final hostility of the people, made him long to rid himself of his heavy responsibilities. He had never wished for power for its own sake, but only in order to achieve his country's emancipation from Spain. This great cause had still to receive its crown, and O'Higgins' only fear was that his going would plunge Chile into anarchy and misery. If he could but find some safeguard against this peril, then he would gladly go. This he had already confided to San Martín.

In the meantime, Coquimbo and other parts of the country had already followed the lead of Concepción. The faithful Zenteno wrote to him at the beginning of January from Valparaíso: 'To speak with the frankness of a true friend, this city is just as much for the revolution as is Concepción.' The attitude of the aristocracy of Santiago was less clear. They were equally eager to overthrow the Director Supremo, but less certain as to whom they wanted in his place. Certainly not the dictatorship of Freire, the Concepción politicians, and the army of the South. So they entered into negotiations with the insurgents, whilst secretly planning the reversion of power to themselves.

The concessions which O'Higgins made to allay the storm were too late and too inadequate. On 7 January Rodríguez Aldea resigned; ten days later, a series of unpopular economic measures was repealed. But the revolutionaries of Concepción, learning of their support in other parts of the country, only hardened in their attitude. Freire addressed a new letter to the Director couched in the most violent language. O'Higgins replied with dignity and restraint, recalling their old friendship and gently upbraiding him. 'Could you really imagine that threats, and the steps you have already taken, could intimidate me?' he asked him. 'You and everyone know whether I can look death in the face. But an act of ingratitude has more power to move me than a gun levelled at my breast. Now I have drained the cup of bitterness to its dregs.' The letter ended with an appeal to Freire to send his delegates to discuss how their differences could be composed and harmony re-established. At the same time, he nominated delegates of his own with full powers including the right to discuss the Director's resignation.

Even with these drastic concessions, agreement was not easily reached. If the Director Supremo was to go, who should succeed him? O'Higgins himself was still convinced that critical times demanded that power should be in the hands of one man, and he would have preferred to resign in favour of Freire or another suitable successor. The Concepción delegates demanded that power should be vested in the junta which they represented. Whilst discussions on this point were in progress, the capital decided to settle matters for itself. The movement was headed by Guzmán, the *intendente* of Santiago, and a *cabildo abierto* was summoned for 28 January. A number of military leaders had already given the malcontents assurances that their troops would remain scrupulously neutral in the event of an open clash with the Director.

Between ten and eleven in the morning of 28 January the chief citizens of Santiago began to assemble in the rooms of the *cabildo* and of the *intendencia* which, after the damage caused by the recent earthquake, were temporarily housed in the Bishop's Palace. Proceedings opened in an atmosphere of timidity until confidence was inspired by the arrival of Colonel Pereira, the commander of the Director's Guard of Honour, who publicly repeated his promise that his troops would not open fire against the assembly or attempt to dissolve it by force. The Carrerist faction was already murmuring that the crimes of Mendoza must be avenged, and that the Director should pay for them with his life. But Pereira sternly added that his troops would only remain neutral if the person of O'Higgins was respected.

The assembly had now grown to number about two hundred persons and decided to transfer its session to the larger hall of the Consulado, where the recent Constituent Assembly and the old Congress of 1810 had met. A commission of twelve members, headed by Guzmán, went to the Director's palace and requested O'Higgins to attend. Between one and two o'clock the commission returned, somewhat crestfallen, to report that it had been roughly treated by O'Higgins who had declared that he refused to recognize 'a handful of demagogues and café-waiters' as a representative body. The assembly now began to lose confidence, and feared that the Director would try to regain control of the troops and dissolve the meeting by force. One young officer, seeing that some of the faint-hearts were already trying to slink away, drew his sword and barred the door. Anxious crowds gathered outside. It was only with difficulty that the more robust spirits persuaded the assembly to keep their resolve and send another appeal to the Director.

O'Higgins was in no mood to listen to requests or petitions. He had just received a report (later found to be unfounded) that a Carrerist officer had raised a troop of horse and was marching on the city. This increased his anger, and he violently denounced the assembly as illegal. He then ordered his guard to resist with arms any movement of the populace against the palace and set about restoring his authority over the other troops. Finding that Merlo, the commander of his escort, had been in touch with the dissidents, he tore off his badges of rank and degraded him in front of the troops, appointing a reliable officer in his place. This drastic action made a vivid impression on the soldiers who recognized in the Director the hero of Rancagua, Chacabuco, and a score of other battles, and broke out into spontaneous cheers.

O'Higgins hurried to his room and changed into his full-dress uniform of Captain-General of Chile, with the insignia as head of state. He then mounted and rode off with his adjutants to the barracks housing the dragoons and the Guard of Honour, where Pereira had connived at the attitude of a group of dissident officers and placed others known to be loyal to the Director under arrest. Pushing aside a sentry who tried to bar his way, O'Higgins forced his way into the barracks, and confronted some hundred mutinous officers and men in the courtyard. He upbraided them harshly and put the officers under arrest. He then strode on into the barracks, to the acclaim of the troops inside, released the loyal officers, and exchanged a few curt words with Pereira. Then, confining the rest of the troops to barracks, and taking only two companies with him, he rode off, with Pereira at his side, towards the Consulado.

It was now three in the afternoon. With the Escort and the Guard of Honour unconditionally under the Director's authority the assembly felt its courage ebbing. O'Higgins took his stand in the plaza, at the head of his soldiers, and refused to parley with the malcontents. Two more delegations were sent out to him but met with no more success than the earlier ones. The assembly then tried to approach O'Higgins through his mother, but Doña Isabel replied that her son was old and sensible enough to make up his own mind, and that she would rather see him dead than dishonoured. Rodríguez Aldea was next persuaded to write a note to him, pointing out that resistance could only prolong his rule for a few days more, and that it was wiser to accede to the popular clamour at once. A messenger was also sent to fetch Luis de la Cruz, a close friend of O'Higgins, who was on his way to Valparaíso. Cruz hurried back and was just in time to intercept an order which O'Higgins had sent to the assembly warning it to disperse immediately or it would be forced to do so. Cruz stopped the messenger and went to talk to O'Higgins in the square. After some minutes' earnest conversation, it seemed that the Director had changed his mind and was now willing to hear what the assembly had to say. Although still angry at the form in which the opposition to his rule had taken, he at least had the satisfaction of knowing that his troops remained loyal. He still hoped that the representatives he had sent to negotiate with the Concepción delegates would reach agreement. The prospect of handing over his powers to a man like Freire, in spite of the perfidy of the latter's conduct towards his old chief, still seemed to him a lesser evil than rule by popular assembly.

Leaving the troops stationed in the square, O'Higgins entered the Consulado building with Cruz and Pereira at his side. He walked quietly through the crowd, some of whom made no attempt to disguise their hostility, and took his place beneath the canopy which marked the seat of the former President of the Congress. He then courteously saluted the gathering, telling them that he had been misinformed as to the respectable persons who constituted it, and asked in a firm voice: 'What is the purpose of this assembly?' At first there was silence, then a citizen called Mariano Egaña replied: 'The people, Sir, fully esteem your important services and look on Your Excellency as the father of the country. But mindful of the difficult situation through which it is passing, and the civil war and destructive anarchy which threaten it, they respectfully request you to put an end to these ills by resigning the high office which you hold.'

O'Higgins answered that although the assembly was composed of distinguished citizens of Santiago, he could not regard it as having any right to represent the country as a whole. He was answered that the whole country, both the northern and the southern provinces, insisted on a change of government and the summoning of a congress. The Director, knowing that his delegates were at that moment negotiating with the representatives of the South, would not yield. 'What right have your spokesmen to claim to represent the entire nation, which has given them no such mandate?' he asked. 'Since I exercise the supreme authority of the Republic, I can only surrender it into the hands of representatives which it has appointed. What is done here the nation may repudiate tomorrow.'

A score of voices were raised that Concepción and other parts of the country demanded the Director's resignation. In the tumult, Dr Vera, who had once been a friend of O'Higgins, but now harboured an old grudge against him, began to whisper ominously in the ear of his comrades, 'the Ides of March! The Ides of March!' O'Higgins, seeing the hostile mood of the assembly, cried above the uproar: 'I am not intimidated by seditious cries and threats. I despise death today as I have despised it on the field of battle. But I refuse to take part in public arguments like this. If you seriously wish to discuss the situation of the country and find a remedy for its ills, elect some responsible spokesman who can discuss serious matters seriously.'

A dozen men were then selected by the assembly and a long discussion began. O'Higgins kept repeating that he had no wish to remain in office but that he could only hand over power to a properly representative body. His opponents brushed aside this argument and kept insisting that he should resign. When things seemed to have

reached a dead-lock, a letter was brought to him. O'Higgins retired
to a side room to read it. In all probability it was the note written by
Rodríguez Aldea, or perhaps a message to say that his delegates had
failed to reach agreement with the South. When O'Higgins re-entered
the hall, his attitude had visibly changed. He announced that he now
agreed to hand over his authority to a body representing the people
of Santiago, providing it proved capable of keeping order. The news
was passed to the waiting crowds outside who received it with
clamorous enthusiasm, and chorused their consent to the formation
of a junta to represent the capital.

Three members of the assembly were next chosen to form this
temporary junta with the task of summoning a national congress at
the earliest possible moment. A statement confirming the Director's
resignation was drawn up and signed by O'Higgins and Egaña. It
was then read aloud, the hall now being full to overflowing.
O'Higgins took the junta's oath of office, and divested himself of his
insignia. He then addressed the assembly in a few simple words. 'If
it has not been granted me to consolidate the new institutions of the
Republic,' he said, 'I have at least the satisfaction of leaving it free
and independent, respected abroad, and covered with the glory won
by its victorious arms. I thank heaven for the favours it has granted
my government and I pray that it may protect those who are to
follow me.'

O'Higgins took off his sash of office and, placing it on the table in
front of him, continued: 'Now I am a private citizen. During the
time of my government I have wielded almost absolute powers. I ask
you to believe me that whatever wrongs I may have done have been
the result of the difficult conditions in which it was my lot to govern,
and not the fruit of evil passions. I am ready to answer for any
accusations you wish to make against me. And if the wrongs I have
done can be purged by my blood then take of me the vengeance you
will. Here is my breast!'

With a violent and dramatic gesture, O'Higgins wrenched open
his tunic and confronted the assembly.

'We hold nothing against you—nothing!' shouted the crowd, and
the old cries of *Viva O'Higgins!* which had resounded after the
triumphs of war were heard again. By the time the tumult had died
down, O'Higgins had regained his calm. Remarking quietly that
there was no further need for him to remain, he walked out of the
hall.

Never had the Director Supremo appeared greater than in this hour of his fall. As in the bloodstained square of Rancagua, his stature seemed only to attain its full height in the bitterness of defeat. If the exercise of his high office had inevitably raised up many enemies, his manner of relinquishing it created an unexpected reaction in his favour, even momentarily subduing the rancour of his bitterest foes. He was accompanied back to the palace by almost the entire assembly, to rousing shouts of *viva*. An atmosphere of indescribable relief and optimism spread through the city. The threat of civil war had been averted, the people had triumphed, and a glorious victory won without one drop of bloodshed! To the cheering crowds, it seemed that only an era of peace, prosperity, and freedom could lie ahead.

But to the fallen Director, the succeeding days brought nothing but fresh anxieties and humiliations. He had moved out of the palace and was lodging privately with a wealthy kinsman of his old friend Martínez de Rozas, but even so it seemed to him that his continued presence in the capital could only fan the flames of political discord. O'Higgins decided that it would be wiser to move to Valparaíso, though this meant leaving his mother and Rosita behind, since the latter had fallen gravely ill. The new junta still treated him with respect and courtesy, and placed an escort of honour at his disposal. All that was now left to him seemed to be an honourable retirement. His first thought had been to ask for the command of a new contingent of troops which was to be sent to Peru. This would have restored him to active service in the field and given him fresh opportunity to show his fervour for the cause of American emancipation which he was just as willing to fight for in the Argentine pampa or the mountains of Peru as in his native Chile. But the command was not given him. The junta, whose position was far from secure, was reluctant to entrust troops to the ex-Director.

In Valparaíso O'Higgins was given a cordial welcome by his old friend Zenteno, but only a few hours after his arrival, a squadron of ships was seen to enter the bay and it was learned that Freire had arrived in person with the army of the South. The Governor and an adjutant of O'Higgins went on board to pay their respects to the *caudillo* but were coldy received. Freire refused to recognize the authority of the junta to whom O'Higgins had transferred his powers.

The following day, an officer and a detachment of troops were sent ashore to place the ex-Director under arrest.

Events had now taken a singularly ironic turn. O'Higgins had wished to choose Freire as his successor, but had been forced to cede to the junta: Freire was now clearly prepared to vent his spleen not only on the junta but on his fallen protector as well. Had O'Higgins been less of an *anima candida* he would have understood that what the proud soldier refused to accept as a favour he would strive to secure by force. When the officer charged with his arrest arrived, O'Higgins was sitting quietly at lunch and he asked to be conducted to Freire himself. The interview between the former friends was brief and formal and confined to the exchange of a few civilities. He was then escorted back to his lodgings and placed under house arrest. It was only after the intervention of mutual friends that Freire consented to restore to him some measure of freedom. In the meantime, the Carrera faction was agitating to have the ex-Director subjected to the old Spanish practice of the *juicio de residencia*, in which he would have to justify the conduct of his high office. Though his conscience was clear, O'Higgins bitterly resented the ingratitude and vindictiveness of fellow-citizens for whose liberties he had fought so hard. 'The humiliations and loss of liberty which I have suffered since giving up office,' he wrote to San Martín, in reply to his friend's letter congratulating him on his resignation, 'have shown me what I may expect in future from my country, though I would not exchange these last thirteen years of sacrifice and unheard-of effort for anything in the world.'[1]

His sense of isolation was intensified by a physical collapse. Acute headaches and temporary loss of sight kept him confined to a darkened room. But gradually his natural resilience gained the upper hand. News from Santiago was more encouraging; Rosita had made a good recovery and would soon be able to travel. Both she and Doña Isabel wrote to assure him that they would never forsake him and were ready to accompany him again into exile in case of need. If his compatriots had turned from him, there were others who still remained loyal in their friendship. Venancio, an Indian chief who had accompanied O'Higgins on so many of his campaigns, wrote in his quaint Spanish, extolling the memory of Bernardo's father and exhorting him 'not for anything in the world to lose heart, and when you

[1] *Archivo*, Vol. 8, p. 156.

have no other refuge left, you can still count on your Araucanians.[1] There were others too, amongst the new-comers to Chile, eager to offer their friendship to the fallen Director; Thomas Sutcliffe, a volunteer whom O'Higgins generously helped with letters of intro- duction and with the gift of his own sword, pistols, and other accoutrements; an eccentric and gifted Irishman calling himself John Thomas, who had once known and admired Don Ambrosio O'Higgins and now took such a liking to his son that he there and then decided to accompany him into exile.

For exile it was clearly to be. For the moment, until the vexatious question of whether he was to be subjected or not to the indignity of *residencia* was settled, O'Higgins could not leave the country. But his thoughts turned to Europe, where he might still be useful to the cause of emancipation by winning influential friends and recruiting settlers. Personal resentment could never for long cloud the bright- ness of his wider vision. Even the petty-minded and ambitious Freire he was prepared to forgive if only his rule could guarantee Chile order and prosperity. 'Yes, my friend,' he wrote to him at the begin- ning of April, when he learnt that the Santiago junta had agreed to hand over power to the *caudillo* without bloodshed, 'only you can restore it to its former glory...'[2]

With surer intuition, O'Higgins looked to Bolívar to complete the final conquest of Peru which San Martín had failed to achieve. From Valparaíso he wrote to the Liberator to wish him well in the great enterprise and to explain the reasons which had led to his own resignation. He had no regrets over relinquishing office, O'Higgins explained; it was only the way in which it was forced upon him that caused him some bitterness. 'I have felt more at home on the field of battle,' he went on to confess. 'I know nothing of these tortuous arts by which a man may aspire to govern a state torn by envy, parties, and factions. This evil is almost always unavoidable in newly-fledged governments, which must look to themselves for sustenance and growth; men are always reluctant to recognize one of themselves as a superior, even when they have elected him themselves. It is useless to grant institutions and guarantees, for these they despise and con- demn. My experience and what scant understanding of politics I

---

[1] For the role of the Araucanians during the war of independence *see* Tomás Guevara: *Los Araucanos en la revolución de la independencia* (Anales de la Universidad de Chile, 1910).
[2] Quoted by Eyzaguirre, *op. cit.*, p. 381.

possess have convinced me that our peoples will only find well-being under compulsion; but my repugnance for compulsion is so great that I am loth to employ it even to achieve their well-being.'[1] By the middle of July—nearly six months after his dramatic renunciation of office—O'Higgins was free to leave Chile. The clamour for the ex-Director's *residencia* had been finally stilled, and a passport, couched in honourable terms and authorizing him to leave the country, granted by the now triumphant Freire. Doña Isabel and Rosita, fully restored to health, had rejoined him in Valparaíso. On 17 July, O'Higgins embarked with his family, including the two adopted Araucanian girls and the four-year old Pedro Demetrio, on the British frigate *Fly* bound for Peru. Zenteno and a small band of friends gathered to give the exiles an affectionate send-off. The captain of the *Fly* wished to accord the ex-Director the honours of a full naval salute, but O'Higgins courteously declined. As the frigate weighed anchor and drew out of the bay from which he had watched the departure of the great expedition not three years before, O'Higgins could barely control his emotion. 'To whatever shores I may be carried,' he declared in a short farewell message, 'I shall always be with you and my beloved country; I shall ever remain its subject, and your fellow-citizen.'[2]

[1] De la Cruz: *Epistolario de Bernardo O'Higgins*, Vol. 2, pp. 214–218.
[2] *Proclama de Despedida.* See José Zamudio: *Fuentes bibliográficas para el estudio de la vida y de la época de Bernardo O'Higgins, Boletín de la Academia Chilena de la Historia*, No. 25, 1943, p. 58.

Twenty

In Exile

SINCE THE DEPARTURE of San Martín from Peru, the military and political situation in that country had lamentably declined. The Protector had resigned his powers to a Constituent Assembly which in turn had elected a *junta de gobierno*, but the latter's authority had been undermined by internal faction and by the reverses inflicted on the Patriot armies at Torata and Moquegua. An ambitous opportunist, José de la Riva Agüero, had then seized power and was bent on smashing the influence of Congress, which, in its extremity, turned to Bolívar.

The Royalists were not slow to take advantage of these dissensions. General Canterac mounted a counter-attack from the interior, marched on Lima, and forced Riva Agüero and Congress to take refuge behind the ramparts of Callao. But danger intensified rather than diminished the quarrels of the Peruvians. Declaring that Riva Agüero was deprived of his mandate, the members of Congress sailed for Trujillo with the intention of reforming their government. Riva Agüero followed hard on their heels, proclaimed the dissolution of Congress, and arrested as many delegates as he could lay hands on. Canterac, meanwhile, had decided to withdraw once more to the sierra, since his forces were not strong enough to capture Callao and he was unable to hold out indefinitely in Lima. The populace of Lima, prompted by those members of Congress who had escaped falling into the hands of Riva Agüero, proclaimed the latter to have been succeeded as head of the government by the Marqués de Torre Tagle. The Peruvian forces in the Lima area thus came under the command of Torre Tagle, whilst Riva Agüero held power in the north, and a third force, composed of Colombians and Chileans under Bolívar's brilliant lieutenant, Sucre, marched on Arequipa in the south, with the object of joining forces with another rising *caudillo*, Santa Cruz, and bringing the Royalists to battle. But Santa

Cruz failed to effect a junction with Sucre's army and suffered an ignominious defeat. Such was the anarchic state of Peru when Bolívar, amidst the delirious enthusiasm of the populace, arrived in Callao. Torre Tagle hastened to declare himself under the orders of the Liberator, whilst a provincial revolt amongst his own entourage removed the troublesome Riva Agüero from the scene.

O'Higgins arrived at Callao on 24 July, 1823, and before disembarking sent a formal note to the Chilean representative informing him of his coming and requesting permission to break his journey for a short time in Peru. The wording of the note, in which O'Higgins declared himself to be 'desirous of proceeding to Ireland to reside there for some time in the bosom of my family', throws a curious light on the confused state of his mind and the vagueness of his plans at this time. Bernardo O'Higgins, we know, had never set foot in Ireland, and had none but distant relatives there whom he had never seen and who were in all probability quite unaware of his existence. What then had suddenly inspired him with this sudden nostalgia for a fictitious fatherland? Most probably it was the feeling of being rejected by his Chilean countrymen. Even at the moment of his greatest popularity, and despite the sacrifices he had made for the freedom of Chile, O'Higgins had always remained in a sense something of a foreigner, as San Martín had remained a foreigner, and was felt to be such by those around him. He was separated from them by the blood which flowed in his veins, by his English education, and even by the quality of his patriotism which had as its aim the liberation of all America, and not of Chile only, from Spanish rule. It was the realization, soon after his arrival in Peru, that this aim was still far from being fulfilled that made him quickly revise his vague plans of sailing on to Europe.

After disembarking at Callao, O'Higgins drove along the fine new carriage road which his father had had built between the port and the capital. He took a keen pride in this, as in all the other achievements of Don Ambrosio, and had ordered the Chilean Expeditionary Army to commemorate it by erecting a suitably inscribed plaque. In Lima he was warmly received by the Marqués de Torre Tagle whom O'Higgins could now look upon not only as an old school-mate but as a kinsman, as he had married the widow of Bernardo's cousin, Demetrio O'Higgins. Bernardo was seldom a penetrating judge of character, and these ties may have blinded him to the grave unreliability of the Marqués as a leader of the Patriot movement. Torre

Tagle's loyalty to the cause was never more than skin deep, and events were soon to put his weakness and opportunism to a severe test.

As a token of their gratitude to the chief creator of the Chilean Expeditionary Army, the Peruvians had voted O'Higgins the estates of Montalván and Cuiba, in the fertile valley of Cañete, to the south of Lima. But these now lay ravaged and ruined, and the enemy was again actually in possession of their territory. O'Higgins therefore decided to stay for the time being in Lima, where he anxiously watched the course of events. He lodged in the house which San Martín had formerly occupied, and though that too had suffered from enemy depredations, he installed himself there with his household. In the chief reception room a portrait of the Protector stood as constant reminder of what another fickle populace had lost, and was paying for in faction and military disaster, by the departure of his friend.

But Lima was now pinning its hopes on one who seemed greater even than San Martín. Bolívar had been invited to take over supreme power as the one man capable of saving the country from its deepening chaos. The Liberator now stood at the height of his prestige, eager to face the greatest challenge and opportunity of his career. To the acclamations of the people and the offers of the Peruvian leaders he responded with studied modesty, declining the proffered honours and emoluments, but accepting supreme office. In the banquet given in his honour, Bolívar was careful to give a toast to his departed rival the Protector, and spoke warmly of O'Higgins whose labours had made the Chilean Expedition possible. His real feelings seem, at this time, to have been less cordial. From what he had heard of the ex-Director—and his sources were mainly the violently prejudiced followers of Carrera—he judged him to be little more than a puppet moved by San Martín. But, though he refrained from making too great a show of friendship with the Chilean exile for fear of antagonising the jealous Freire, Bolívar wished to preserve good relations with him, as he needed his support for various of his projects. First, there was the need of more Chilean troops. Bolívar asked O'Higgins, who willingly agreed, to write to Freire requesting reinforcements. These, to the number of 2,500 men, were eventually sent, but the reverses suffered in the south of Peru and the danger that they would be used by one side or another in a civil war led to their speedy recall.

O'Higgins was soon to give the Liberator other proofs of his admiration and disinterested desire to be of service. That Bolívar and San Martín had been personal rivals for power and incompatible in temperament was no matter. They were the twin master-builders of American independence. If fate had cast his lot with the one who had now withdrawn from the scene, O'Higgins was still prepared to offer his wholehearted support to the other. When Bolívar left Lima for Trujillo to prepare the campaign which later culminated in the decisive victory of Ayacucho, O'Higgins made up his mind to follow him. How could he remain idle if there was still fighting to be done? Moreover the situation in the capital was sufficiently disturbing to make him wish to remove his family to greater safety. Alarming reports reached him from Callao, where the garrison of fifteen hundred men was on the verge of mutiny. O'Higgins hastened to warn both Torre Tagle and Bolívar of the danger. But Bolívar was ill and Torre Tagle already in secret negotiation with the enemy. At the end of 1823, O'Higgins set sail for Trujillo, and less than a month and a half later, the Callao garrison mutinied and betrayed the fort to the Royalists. Other grave defections followed, those of Torre Tagle and the President of the Congress amongst them. A number of officers were apprehended in the act of conspiracy. One of these was Ramón Novoa, a noted Carrerist whom O'Higgins had already exiled from Chile for his complicity in a plot against his own life. Novoa, now condemned to death by Bolívar, implored the ex-Director to intercede for his life. O'Higgins not only secured his pardon and permission to leave the country, but sent him a generous gift of clothes and money.

O'Higgins' one desire was now to play an active part in Bolívar's campaign. But whilst the Liberator left to organize his force in the sierra, an attack of fever kept O'Higgins prostrate in Trujillo. Only when convalescent did he find a modest opportunity of doing useful service by composing a violent quarrel which had occurred between the Governor of the town and the irascible Captain Guise who had succeeded Cochrane in the command of what was left of the navy. This reconciliation earned O'Higgins a letter of thanks from Bolívar, and a message that, if his health was now good enough, he could count on a post in the army. O'Higgins wrote back eagerly, reminding Bolívar that since he had renounced his rank on leaving Chile and was now only a private citizen, he had no higher ambition than to serve as an ordinary volunteer wherever he could best help to strike a blow in the final campaign against the enemy. To this the Liberator returned a courteous if somewhat vague message to the effect that he would be welcome, since 'a body of Colombian troops operating under your command cannot fail to be victorious.'[1]

On 9 July, 1824, O'Higgins set out to join Bolívar's army. He was accompanied by a small band of friends, including the Irishman John Thomas, with whom he had struck up a friendship on leaving Chile and who was now his confidential secretary and adviser.[2] The route was rough and long. It led across bleak stretches of sandy desert, broken by an occasional fertile valley, and over mountain ranges. After more than a month's hard riding, they reached the plain of Junín, where news reached them that Bolívar had successfully engaged the Royalist cavalry only a few days previously. They pressed on, in the bitter cold, and four days later came up with the Liberator and his staff in Huancayo, where O'Higgins was received with every mark of courtesy and respect. Amongst the officers he found with Bolívar was his old friend and comrade-in-arms Miller who described the meeting in a letter to Paroissien, the English surgeon who had tended O'Higgins' wound after Rancagua—'Just the same honest, kind-hearted, straight-forward, unsuspecting character we always found him to be.'[3]

O'Higgins had supported the fatigues of the campaign remarkably well. 'Despite the tiring marches I have made across burning deserts and icy cordilleras, and indeed over a continuous mountain chain two hundred leagues in length, without a moment's respite, my health is better than ever,' he wrote to his mother, 'and my eagerness to confront the enemy has never been greater.' But these warlike aspirations were not destined to be fulfilled. The post with which Bolívar entrusted him—either because he had but a poor opinion of O'Higgins' talents as a general, or because he was afraid of offending the Chilean government—was but a nominal one. Moreover, the Liberator himself had given up hope of striking the decisive blow against the enemy within the next months. He did not believe that Canterac would venture down from the heights to do battle until the rainy season was over. So Bolívar entrusted the command of the

[1] Vicente Lecuna: *Cartas del Libertador* (Caracas, 1929) Vol. 4, p. 173.

[2] Thomas kept a detailed diary of this journey. See *Diario del General O'Higgins en la campaña de Ayacucho* in *Revista Chilena de Historia y Geografía*, Nos. 23 and 26 1916–1917, Vols. 19–23.

[3] R. A. Humphreys: *Liberation in South America, 1806–27: the career of James Paroissien.* (London, 1952) p. 137.

South America in 1825

army to Sucre and returned to Lima where urgent political tasks awaited him. O'Higgins, loth to give up all hope of seeing action with an army he had taken such pains to join, stayed on for some time before following his example. On 18 December, news reached them both in Lima of Sucre's brilliant victory over the Royalists at Ayacucho. Canterac and La Serna had been taken prisoner and their army totally routed.

The following evening, the Liberator gave a great banquet to celebrate the victory which marked the final triumph of the cause of American independence. In contrast to the bemedalled Colombian, Argentine, and Peruvian generals, O'Higgins appeared in plain civilian dress. His explanation was simple and sincere. 'America, Sir, is now free,' he replied to the Liberator. 'From today, General O'Higgins no longer exists. I am only the private citizen, Bernardo O'Higgins. With Ayacucho, my American mission has ended.'

The home where the private citizen Bernardo O'Higgins was to spend the last eighteen years of his life was a property confiscated from a former Spanish Royalist, the spacious but sadly neglected estate of Montalván, some forty leagues south of the Peruvian capital. It comprised a belt of fertile land, more than a league broad, lying between the picturesque town of Cañete, at the head of the valley of the same name, and the little port of Cerro Azul, on the coast. To the north and south, irrigation canals separated it from neighbouring farms; to the west lay the shores of the Pacific, and to the east the highroad connecting Lima with Arequipa. The house and outbuildings stood back a little from the main road, on the outskirts of Cañete. It was built on the site of an old Indian palace or temple and stood on a raised terrace above a spacious patio to which it was connected by a broad flight of steps built of brick and wood. The date 1788 was engraved above the porch, but the living quarters were more modern. They comprised a single large block; the main entrance hall in the centre, and a broad corridor running the length of the building with other rooms opening off it. In more prosperous days, the ceiling and mouldings had been gilded. Now the walls of the hall were adorned only with two portraits; one of O'Higgins, the other of Bolívar, presented by the Liberator himself.

Montalván was devoted to the production of sugar. In normal times, its anual output of some six thousand *arrobas* and a few barrels of *aguardiente* brought in a modestly comfortable income, but one which now hardly sufficed to cover the repayment of the new owner's debts and his current expenses. The labour force was composed of fifty to sixty negroes; it was not until fourteen years later that O'Higgins had the satisfaction of installing some primitive machinery driven by mules. The out-buildings which housed the slaves were given names commemorating the battles or personalities of past campaigns—San Martín, Bolívar, Junín, Maipo, and others. The management of this estate took up most of its owner's time, and the days went by in tranquil and orderly pattern. By seven in the morning, O'Higgins was up and about his business. He dressed neatly but simply, generally in blue, his frock coat being donned only on Sundays for Mass. True to his resolve, he had put away his soldier's uniform and when, three years later, the head of the Peruvian military college invited him to preside over their annual examinations and parade, the ex-Director of Chile was obliged to refuse because—as he candidly admitted—the moths had been at it and he had no money with which to buy a new one. O'Higgins loved riding—one of his favourite mounts was a gift from Bolívar—and for this he would don a pair of large-rowelled Chilean spurs and a simple *poncho* in preference to the Spanish cloak. His only warlike accoutrement was a short sword or *espadín*, a trophy from the wars.

The evenings were generally passed with his books and papers. O'Higgins was a conscientious correspondent, though writing was never anything to him but a slow and laborious process. Much of his time was spent in the elaboration of various projects which he hoped might one day be of benefit to his beloved Chile. Wines or spirits he seldom touched, but tea was a favourite drink and tobacco his invariable consolation. His love of music was as keen as ever, and he would still amuse himself by playing the accordion which he had treasured in its velvet-lined box throughout a dozen campaigns. On rare occasions he would join the family for a game of *monte* which he would play for low stakes. His friends noticed with a smile that he could invariably be depended upon to back any card opposed to the King.

This calm routine was enlivened by the celebrations of family birthdays, and—most solemn of all—of the Chilean Independence Day on 18 September. In the summer, the whole family would spend a short time at Cerro Azul to sample the beneficial effects of sea-bathing. From time to time, too, there were visits to be paid, chiefly

8

to his neighbour Hipólito Unánue, the distinguished and now elderly savant who had been a friend of his father. Since Montalván lay on the main route from Lima to the south, and Rosita's hospitality was proverbial, guests were not infrequent. But journeys up to Lima were rare and undertaken chiefly when the business of the estate required. A two-storeyed house had been rented in the capital near the main square where Doña Rosita could market the produce of the estate. A few paces away stood a little sweetmeat shop which O'Higgins later gave as a dowry to one of the Araucanian orphans whom his mother had brought up. When this Indian girl grew up and married, O'Higgins became as attached to her little son as he was to herself. 'Every day at lunch time,' his friend José María de la Cruz tells us, 'O'Higgins would stop in front of the shop and clap his hands, at which sound a boy of three or four years of age, the son of this servant, would come running out. He would take him in his arms and at table would seat the child on his left knee.' Cruz adds that he could not but contrast O'Higgins' natural kindliness to children in general with the unaccountable indifference with which he seemed to regard his own natural son, Pedro Demetrio, who occupied an almost menial station beneath the patriarchal roof.[1]

But life at Montalván, for all the simple satisfaction which O'Higgins found in it, was nevertheless still a life of exile. In his heart of hearts there remained the hope that his countrymen would one day call him back—not necessarily to offer him high office, for which he had lost whatever little inclination he once possessed, but to accord him the recognition due to his past services and the full rehabilitation of his honour. The affairs of Chile were never absent for long from his thoughts. Such news as reached him was far from reassuring; everything spoke of increasing anarchy, economic distress, and loss of international prestige. 'Chile has now reached the last depths of national humiliation,' he wrote to San Martín, 'without troops, though still with enemies, with no credit, no funds, no public spirit, no unity, no policy, no judges, no justice, and overwhelmed with every imaginable evil. All moral sense has been lost; decent behaviour is at an end, and laws are not recognized, those passed today being broken tomorrow, for laws mean order and obedience, and that is what they will have none of in Chile...More acts of tyranny have

[1] *M.L. Amunátegui*, in *Revista Chilena de Historia y Geografía*, Vol. 24, No. 28, 1917.

been committed there in the last four years than in the three centuries of Spanish domination.'[1]

Reports from O'Higgins' old friends and supporters in Chile all concurred in painting the gloomiest of pictures. 'Do not be surprised if you see me joining you soon,' Zenteno wrote to him, with a presentiment of his own imminent exile. That restless intriguer, Rodríguez Aldea, characteristically urged him to place himself at the head of the public discontent and return to power. Equally disquieting were the more objective reports on the situation in Chile sent to him by Bolívar, now in Upper Peru. These indicated that Freire's attempt to convoke a congress had been a failure, since Concepción and Coquimbo boycotted it from the start, thus reducing it to the delegates from Santiago. The latter were largely pro-O'Higgins and they hoped to suspend Freire from office and recall their old leader from exile. But Freire, who still had most of the army behind him, countered by dissolving Congress and expelling the pro-O'Higgins politicians.

These events far from discouraged O'Higgins' followers, who now proposed to make direct contact with the exile, convert him to their plans, and return with him to Chile. O'Higgins remained in Montalván, unhappy and perplexed, whilst Rodríguez Aldea redoubled his cajolery from Lima: 'I see that the recovery of Chile is the easiest thing in the world, if we can count on you, but I can also see that even if we were to organize an expeditionary force it would be useless without you at its head. Your presence is worth an army.' Zañartu put the issue more brutally still, warning him that failure to join the conspiracy 'would undo your former eminent services...I must urge you, however reluctantly, to leave your calm and pleasant home, and join the conspirators in Lima.'

O'Higgins was now a prey to the bitterest indecision. Had he not sworn to withdraw for ever from public life? Had he not always set his face against the use of force to overthrow established authority, and how then could he think of putting himself at the head of such an armed coup? Yet the arguments on the other side seemed equally compelling. Had he not abandoned the quiet and wholesome life at Las Canteras to take up arms at the call of the fatherland, and should he not now be prepared to leave Montalván in response to this new summons? His friends had no doubt whatsoever that he should, and their persuasions at length carried the day. Moreover, they had

[1] *Archivo*, Vol. 9, pp. 5–6.

drawn up a plan of action which they were confident could not fail. The plot was to strike first in the island of Chiloé, where the governor was a brother of Pedro Aldunate, one of the Lima conspirators. From Chiloé, the insurgents hoped to raise Valdivia and the south. Aldunate left on his delicate mission, whilst the conspirators waited anxiously for news. When it came, it was only partially favourable. The Governor of Chiloé had indignantly repulsed his brother's advances, accused O'Higgins of disloyalty towards Freire, and refused to have anything to do with the plot. Others however were found to welcome the plan. A *cabildo abierto* was summoned and renounced its adhesion to Freire in favour of supporting O'Higgins. Would the movement spread to other parts of Chile and lead to the overthrow of Freire? O'Higgins, who had returned to Montalván where he was confined to his bed through sickness, was encouraged to think that it might. Zañartu hurried to bring the news to the Liberator, who seemed to favour their cause. But for the moment, there was little that they could do, for they could find no ship to convey them to Chiloé. O'Higgins passed the time by drawing up a proclamation to his countrymen announcing that he was returning from exile to save the country from anarchy and give them an opportunity of electing a new and honest government. He finished by roundly declaring that he only offered his sword, and that he would not consent to resume office if invited to do so.

The days passed and it became clear that the insurrection had proved abortive. Freire was on the point of preparing an expedition against the rebels on Chiloé when a second congress, which he had been compelled to summon in Santiago, removed him from office and elected Blanca Encalada in his stead. This O'Higgins somewhat ingenuously regarded as a development in his favour, for Blanco Encalada had been an old comrade-in-arms and the first commander of the infant Chilean navy. But the new Director showed himself just as determined as Freire to suppress the dissidents. The revolt in Chiloé, and another which had broken out in Osorno, were rapidly brought under control, and a wave of indignation, born of suspicion that Bolívar was scheming to use O'Higgins as a means of dominating Chile, swept over the country. Instead of a friend, Blanco Encalada showed himself a fierce opponent of the ex-Director and demanded that Congress should pass a law branding him guilty of criminal and treasonable activities.

If the course of events in Chile, now sinking into ever greater

anarchy, continued to distress him keenly, they no longer tempted
O'Higgins to offer his sword to restore order. In Santiago, government succeeded government with ineffectual rapidity, revolt followed
revolt, bands of marauders roamed the countryside with impunity,
attempts to introduce a federal system were made and dropped and
even nature seemed bent on deepening the country's economic distress by unleashing disastrous storms and floods during the winter
of 1827. The name of O'Higgins had ceased to recall the glories of
the war of independence; it had become a mere watchword for
warring factions, bandied about without the wish or even the knowledge of the ex-Director. After the outbreak of yet another revolt in
Valdivia, in which the rebels had claimed to be acting in the exile's
name, O'Higgins wrote to the Chilean envoy in Lima disavowing all
complicity and all future pretensions to office; 'I have solemnly
renounced all political power,' he asserted. 'I shall never reassume it
—never—even should the votes of the nation seek to restore me to it.
This I have publicly declared, and I do not go back on my word.' A
letter to the *Mercurio Peruano* publicly reaffirmed the same resolve;
after recalling the retirement of Washington and the famous letter
written to Lafayette from his country retreat on the shores of the
Potomac extolling the simple life of the country in words which so
perfectly expressed his own desires, O'Higgins declared: 'For the
independence of Chile and America I sacrificed my youth, my health,
and my fortune; I wish for nothing further than the satisfaction of
recalling services which were not wholly in vain.'

Twenty-One

The Last Years

IN 1830, AFTER seven years of exile, there came news of developments in Chile which seemed to the exile of Montalván to hold out fresh hopes for the future. The ill-conceived attempt to introduce a federalist system had been succeeded by an equally misguided 'Liberal' régime anxious to push through all manner of hasty reforms which had only driven the federalists and the landed aristocracy to make common cause. Chile was soon rent by civil war, in which the victor proved to be neither the one party nor the other but —as had happened so often in the recent history of the country—the army of the South. This was now under the command of General Prieto, an old comrade-in-arms and intimate friend of O'Higgins. Prieto marched on the capital where he inflicted a crushing defeat on the forces led by Freire, who had sided with the Liberals. Shortly afterwards, O'Higgins had the satisfaction of learning that Prieto had taken over the government and that Freire had fled to Peru.

O'Higgins' hopes rose still higher on receiving the most friendly letters from Prieto which encouraged him to believe that the days of his exile might be drawing to a close. But though Prieto might be head of state, the dominant power in Chile was his minister Portales, a man of iron will and very definite ideas as to the country's future. Portales held that the cause of the prevailing anarchy was the cult of the *caudillo*—the disastrous South American tendency to look at politics in terms of personalities. The nation, he believed, needed instead to develop a respect for the institutions of the new state, and to regard the Law as mightier than any Leader. For this reason Portales resolutely opposed the return of O'Higgins, whose presence in the country could only intensify that partisanship which he bitterly deplored. So great was the Minister's ascendency over the head of state, that Prieto reluctantly concurred and dropped his support of the bill to reinstate the ex-Director in his full rank and military honours which O'Higgins' friends had brought before Congress. This unaccountable coolness on the part of another old comrade-in-arms filled O'Higgins with fresh bitterness.

The victory of Prieto and Portales had brought another influx of Chileans into Peru in search of refuge, or rather, of fresh fields for their intrigues. There were ardent Carrerists amongst them, still bent on pursuing their vendettas with undiminished vehemence. Most violent of all was Carlos Rodríguez, brother of the unfortunate Manuel Rodríguez, who poured out his vituperation in the columns of the Peruvian press. 'Opprobrium eternal to Don Bernardo O'Higgins,' he raved, 'cowardly murderer and public thief, confirmed conspirator, double-faced hypocrite, perpetual blasphemer of the religion of humanity, vile, mean, infamous, perfidious, loathsome, unworthy of all human intercourse, and perpetrator of every conceivable crime.'[1] O'Higgins was goaded into bringing an action against his calumniator in the Peruvian courts, but by the time he had won his case, the turbulent Rodríguez had prudently disappeared.

Freire, too, was now in exile. Some attempts were made to bring about a reconciliation between him and O'Higgins, and though the latter, with his customary warmth of heart, was ready enough to forget old differences, Freire remained adamant in his hostility. He cherished high hopes of returning to Chile and overthrowing his enemies there with the scarcely disguised backing of the Peruvian government. The Liberator had withdrawn from the scene, and power was now in the hands of the wily General Santa Cruz, whose ambition was no less than the establishment of a state as extensive as the old empire of the Incas from whom he claimed descent. Santa Cruz had already gained control of Bolivia and Peru which he formed into a Confederation, with himself as Protector, and was planning to absorb Ecuador. But in Chile he perceived an obstacle to his expansionist designs, as Chile—through the penetrating eyes of Portales—saw in the Confederation a threat to her own independence and a monstrous embodiment of the detested *caudillismo*. Nothing would have been more welcome to Santa Cruz than a change of government in Santiago, and he was only too glad to further Freire's plans by 'selling' him two Peruvian warships which, ostensibly bound for Central America, left Callao for Chile with Freire and his fellow-conspirators in July 1836.

O'Higgins was well aware of these manoeuvres. He had in fact

[1] *Zamudio, op. cit.*, p. 61.

been approached not only by the exiles, but by agents of the Peruvian government anxious to see whether his support could be secured. But his resolve to abstain from all intervention in Chile's internal politics was now unshakable, all the more so as he realized that such conspiracies could only lead to a further deterioration in the relations between Chile and Peru. These were already dangerously strained, and the possibility of open strife between his native and his adopted countries haunted his imagination as the greatest of all possible evils. Though he could see this clearly enough, he was prone to interpret the motives of the chief protagonists with his customary ingenuousness. In the scheming Santa Cruz, who had been careful to cultivate friendly relations with him, he saw nothing but a patriotic, disinterested, and peace-loving statesman, whose only weakness was too great a reliance on imprudent ministers. The scepticism with which Portales received his assurances of the good faith of the Confederation, when O'Higgins wrote to warn Prieto of Freire's conspiracy, may well be imagined.

Freire's schemes ended in ignominious failure. On arrival in Chile, part of his forces deserted him. He was caught, brought before a court-martial, and could count himself lucky to be banished to Australia instead of facing a firing squad. The Chilean government resolved to force a reckoning with the Confederation. So long as the latter existed to promote subversion from abroad and to build up a power capable of dominating the country, there could be no security for Chile. There were old grievances too, dating back to claims against Peru for her share in financing San Martín's expeditionary army and Cochrane's fleet, and other disputes which called for settlement. Though Portales lost his life in a short-lived military revolt, his policy was still pursued. The step which O'Higgins had long dreaded was taken at last. Chile declared war against the Confederation and an expeditionary force was despatched to Peru under Blanco Encalada.

The fortunes of war at first went against the Chileans. Blanco Encalada, caught by vastly superior forces, was obliged to sign a capitulation. This was however repudiated by the Chilean government, who decided to press on with hostilities. A second expedition set sail under the command of General Bulnes, Prieto's nephew, and after a successful engagement at the approaches to Lima, entered the Peruvian capital in triumph at the end of August, 1838. A friendly Peruvian administration was formed which set about recruiting

troops to co-operate with the Chileans against the army of General
Santa Cruz which remained unconquered in the South.

The sight of Chilean troops in the streets of Lima filled O'Higgins
with violently conflicting emotions. Bloodshed between Peruvians
and Chileans seemed to him nothing short of a calamity and a crime
against the sacred cause of American brotherhood, and he bitterly
denounced Prieto for betraying this ideal. How could he, who had
once sent Chilean troops to help the Peruvians gain their mutual
freedom, now witness a Chilean army imposing its will on a sister
nation? Yet the sight of the marching regiments could not but bring
back memories of the heroic days of Rancagua, Chacabuco, and a
hundred other glorious fields. When Bulnes, the Commander-in-
Chief of the Chilean Army, came to salute him he could scarcely
master his emotion.

The occupation of Lima soon proved as empty a triumph as had
San Martín's occupation seventeen years earlier. The populace remained hostile, and the morale and health of the army began to
suffer. Amongst those struck down by sickness was Bulnes' chief-of-
staff, José María de la Cruz, son of an old friend of O'Higgins, who
was nursed back to health at Montalván. In the company of this young
soldier, O'Higgins felt his military ardour revive. If he could not
wish for the victory of one side over the other, the strategic and
tactical problems presented by the campaign excited his liveliest
professional interest. With all the enthusiasm of the old veteran,
O'Higgins would speak of his past battles and explain why he
believed that the Chilean troops, thanks to their more offensive
spirit and the impetus of their attack, must prove victorious in a
pitched battle.

But O'Higgins still clung to the hope that major bloodshed might
be avoided. Bulnes had grown alarmed at the demoralizing effect the
occupation of Lima was having on his troops and decided to evacuate
the city and move to the north. As soon as Santa Cruz reoccupied
Lima O'Higgins sent him a final appeal to stop the war in the
interests of Chilean-Peruvian brotherhood. Santa Cruz, by no means
confident of victory, welcomed this intervention and replied in a
conciliatory letter which O'Higgins at once forwarded to Bulnes.
Both sides then agreed to a parley. Santa Cruz cleverly confined his
proposals for solving the economic and financial points at issue, but
the Chileans insisted on a settlement of the fundamental question—
the withdrawal of Santa Cruz and his forces to Bolivia so that Peru

8*

could freely decide whether it wished to continue in the Confederation. This was something to which Santa Cruz could not consent
without renouncing his grandiose ambitions, and the negotiations
broke down. The issue could only be settled by arms and settled it
was before long by the crushing victory of the Chilean army over
Santa Cruz's forces in the fierce and bloody battle of Yungay, which
spelt the fall of the Protector and the collapse of the Confederation.

Though O'Higgins had done his utmost to prevent the shedding of
blood between Chileans and Peruvians, the news of Yungay stirred
his pride in the victory of his countrymen and raised his hopes that
the war would soon be over and peace restored. But his rejoicing
was clouded by deep personal sorrow. Doña Isabel, whom he loved
more than anyone in the world, had been ailing for some time, and
passed quietly away on 21 April, 1840. Her affection had made up
for the lack of a father's in his childhood, and as a grown man
O'Higgins found in her a companion prepared to share the dangers
and disappointments of his life with unshakable fortitude. Dedication to the cause of Chilean independence had brought poverty and
exile to both of them; but Bernardo had been able to make some
amends for his father's neglect by finding a home for her for six years
in the Governor's palace in Santiago, and though she had died in
exile, by seeing her laid to rest with almost viceregal pomp. The
Chilean army, fresh from its victory at Yungay, bore her to the grave
with full military honours.

If affection for his mother had been the strongest emotion in
O'Higgins' personal life, his intellectual and political outlook was
strangely shaped by the memory of his father. In throwing himself
heart and soul into the struggle against Spain, he had vented his resentment against the injustice which he and his mother had suffered
at the hands of that stern servant of the Crown. But now the hated
bonds of servitude had been broken, and his wrongs avenged. The
symbol of an odious system was eclipsed by the memory of the great
and good statesman whose beneficent labours for Chile would
henceforth be Bernardo's own inspiration. John Thomas, the Irishman who had known and admired Don Ambrosio and was now a
close friend of his son, was always at hand to recall the Viceroy's
achievements and invoke his example. 'You had the misfortune of
being taken away from your father when you were too young to know

him,' he was never tired of reminding Bernardo. 'He was a man of extraordinary gifts, altogether superior both in heart and head. He possessed a capacious and vigorous mind, capable of conceiving and carrying out measures of the most exacting and complicated nature; he had a heart which delighted in doing good to his fellows and which felt profoundly their sufferings and misfortunes...You must always keep the example of your father before your eyes and always endeavour to imitate him.'[1]

O'Higgins had thought more than once of devoting his years of exile to writing a life of Don Ambrosio, or at least of gathering material for such a biography. But literary composition was painful to him and he felt himself unequal to the task. 'I feel deeply ashamed,' he confessed to his cousin Tomás O'Higgins, 'of not having done justice to the memory of my revered father by collecting the edifying material relating to a life so beneficial, so honourable, and so glorious.' Yet though he declined the role of biographer, he liked to see in his own life's work a continuation of the labours of his father and could think of no more useful way of spending his remaining years than to study, and where possible take up again, the many schemes of material improvement which the great Viceroy had left unfinished. 'With the example of my revered father before my eyes,' he wrote to his friend General José María de la Cruz, 'I do not hesitate to say that I should be called unworthy of being his son if I did not continue labouring, so long as I remain alive, for South America, and specially for my native land, for which he toiled so much and which he so greatly benefited. I consider it an indispensable duty to emulate his illustrious example in so far as it lies within my understanding and my powers.'[2]

The schemes with which Bernardo O'Higgins busied himself in the long evenings at Montalván, and which formed the subject of laborious memoranda and letters to a host of correspondents, ranged from Utopian visions to advice on the most practical details of farming. There were proposals for transforming the army into corps of skilled and semi-skilled labour which could be put to good use in peace-time; shrewd suggestions for introducing well-paved threshing floors so as to eliminate impurities in grain deliveries; a project

[1] See *Los Projectos del virrey O'Higgins—Carta de John Thomas a Don Bernardo O'Higgins* in *Revista Chilena de Historia y Geografía* No. 15, Vol. 11, 1914, and *Correspondencia con Don Bernardo O'Higgins, 1825-42 y manuscritos varios,* Archivos Varios, Vol. 566, Archivo Nacional de Santiago.
[2] Quoted by Eyzaguirre, *op. cit.,* p. 460.

to import camels in order to improve communications in the coastal deserts. Most persistent of all was the exile's concern for the vast, unexplored regions stretching from the Araucanian lands to the Straits of Magellan whose neglect was a temptation to foreign powers and a reproach to the civilizing zeal of the Chileans. Don Ambrosio too had been alive to the need to incorporate these remote parts into the life of the community. 'Of his many public services,' his son wrote of him, 'there are none which I have so warmly admired or desired so earnestly to imitate as his incessant endeavours to confer on the primitive indigenous inhabitants of Chile (so absurdly called Indians) the blessings of religion, industry, and civilization...It is truly humiliating that we have let twenty-two years go by since the declaration of our independence without doing anything for love of humanity.'[1]

There were pressing strategic reasons, too, why Chile should make good her claims over the South. Bernardo had read with interest and alarm the narrative of a French Admiral asserting that North Patagonia, the Straits of Magellan, and Tierra del Fuego should be colonized by an European power if they continued to be further neglected. He feared, as Don Ambrosio before him, that a foreign power might indeed use this as an excuse to establish itself in the south of the continent. For a number of years, O'Higgins had exchanged letters with Captain John H. Smith whose ship, the *Cigar*, plied regularly between Peru and England. Smith suggested that the risks to navigation would be greatly reduced if a steam-tug service were to be established and a colony founded in the Straits. O'Higgins took up the scheme with great enthusiasm, urging it repeatedly upon the government in Santiago. The Chilean government at last acted on his advice. The expedition sent to take formal possession of the Straits for Chile and found a settlement there arrived only a few hours before the French warship *Phaeton*, which lingered suspiciously for a time before sailing on to declare a French protectorate over Haiti.

There was one foreign power which figured in all Bernardo O'Higgins' meditations never as a menace but always as the most desirable of allies for his country. 'The whole ambition of O'Higgins was to make of Chile the England of South America,' his friend Casimiro Albano wrote of him. From his Peruvian exile, as in his

[1] See Ricardo Donoso: *Don Bernardo O'Higgins y el Estrecho de Magallanes* in the *Revista Chilena de Historia y Geografía*, Vol. 93, 1942, No. 101.

early days at Las Canteras, the ex-Director never tired of extolling the value of British institutions. He had himself tried with some success to introduce the Lancasterian system as a means of promoting popular education in Chile. Another reform which he advocated was the introduction of trial by jury. He translated a standard work on the subject and suggested that the experiment should be tried out first in Valparaíso where juries could include at least one Englishman or American familiar with the practice. 'The people of England were the first to understand and practice true national freedom,' he wrote to President Prieto, 'and their political principles have been those which have overthrown and will continue to overthrow despotism in all parts of the world.'

To Britain—and in particular, to Ireland—he looked to provide the sort of immigration of which the country most stood in need. His first plan, on leaving Chile, had been to go to Ireland to recruit settlers for Las Canteras—'according to my father's ideas', he wrote to the Peruvian government—and once he had settled in Montalván he was always eager to engage Irishmen to assist him with the work of the estate. Indeed, he would have liked to see Irishmen settling in large numbers in the territory around Trujillo and the Apurimac river, which he regarded as specially suitable, and he kept up a lively correspondence on the subject of Irish immigration with Sir Thomas Hardy, Sir John Doyle, and others. The settlement of the Falkland islands was another project which specially interested him, as he regarded it as the first step towards the colonization and development of the Straits of Magellan.

For these and many other reasons, O'Higgins saw in an alliance with Britain the best guarantee for his country's future. Both were sea-faring nations. Britain would find it useful to make use of Chilean ports, whilst Chile would welcome her friendship as the best deterrent against any attempt by Spain to restore sovereignty over her ex-dominions, and also as a counterweight against any bid for hegemony in the hemisphere by the United States. These reflections were drawn up with the help of John Thomas and embodied in a memorandum entrusted to Captain Coughland of the Royal Navy. The document ends with the vision of a mighty alliance spanning the globe, 'based on truth, justice, religion, and morality,' and 'sustained by the arms, thus irresistible, of England and Chile'.[1]

Perhaps O'Higgins' political sympathies were not uninfluenced by

[1] Eyzaguirre, *op. cit.*, p. 431.

the memories of a youth spent in England where loneliness and exploitation were redeemed by friendships which O'Higgins still recalled with tenderness in the evening of his life. When O'Brien, San Martín's adjutant, was about to return to Europe, O'Higgins asked him to go to Richmond and find out what had become of the Eeles family with whom he had once lived. Some months later, O'Brien wrote to him from Dublin; 'I am sending you the portrait of Miss Charlotte Eeles, your old sweetheart.'[1] But the portrait, if he ever received it, must have brought little consolation, for there came too a letter from the girl's mother saying that the family had fallen upon evil days, Mr Eeles had long been dead, and his daughter had not long survived him. Charlotte never married and had always thought with affection of the young stranger from Chile.

The death of Doña Isabel caused a collapse in her son's health from which he made but a slow and painful recovery. Nothing could console him for the loss of his adored mother, though Rosita was still there to surround him with her bustling care, and Petronila, the Araucanian waif,[2] had grown into a fine-looking woman and the mother of 'a splendid child, the prettiest I have ever seen'. The wounds and hardships of campaigning had taken their toll of his naturally robust constitution. He still hoped that he would be well enough to entertain Bulnes and his fellow officers before they returned to Chile. 'You must have the dining room, the corridors, and the downstairs whitewashed, and patch up the staircase as best you can,' he wrote off to his bailiff. 'Best be prepared in advance and buy three or four turkeys, a dozen hens, and half a dozen young ducks and chickens.' But Montalván had no opportunity of giving the Chilean guests a taste of its hospitality. After a short convalescence, its owner was obliged to return to Lima and remain under the eye of his doctors.

Financial worries, too, added their weight of care and made his

[1] *Archivo Vicuña Mackenna*, Vol. 90, Archivo Nacional de Santiago. Mrs Eeles' letter will be found in *Fondos Varios, Correspondencia dirigida por varias personas, 1817-33*, in the Archivo Nacional.
[2] Some mystery attaches to the origins of Petronila. Gossip had it that she was the illegitimate daughter of either Rosita Riquelme or of O'Higgins. She married José Toribio Pequeño who became joint heir, together with Pedro Demetrio, to the estate of Montalván after the death of Doña Rosita in 1850. Petronila died twenty years later on the way back to Chile, and is referred to in her death certificate as Petronila Riquelme y O'Higgins.

return to Chile the more doubtful. 'I owe six thousand pesos,' he had confided to a friend nearly ten years before, 'and a man of honour never turns his back on his creditors.' Though he had at last been reinstated in his rank of Captain-General, the Chilean Treasury seemed in no hurry to pay his pension, and Doña Rosita was forced to sell the family silver. O'Higgins' one wish was now to return to Chile. Bulnes succeeded Prieto as President of the Republic and wrote to him warmly urging him to come. There were now no obstacles except the poor state of his health and his shortage of funds. 'I do not despair,' he wrote to his friend Captain Smith on 4 February, 1842, 'through the goodness of the Almighty, of living long enough and enjoying good enough health to return to Chile and see a start made on various, if not all, of those measures for its growth and happiness which have constantly occupied my thoughts from the victory of Chacabuco, now twenty-five years ago.'[1] Passages were booked on a vessel due to sail from Callao, proclamations were penned to the Peruvians expressing the exile's undying gratitude for the home they offered him, and to the citizens of Valparaíso—'the cosmopolitan city which knows neither strangers nor foreigners, but only brothers and citizens, no matter where chance may have decided their birth'—who he hoped would soon welcome him. He even bought himself a splendid braided tunic befitting the solemn occasion of his return.

But the day he was due to embark, O'Higgins was laid prostrate with a severe heart attack from which he only just managed to recover. Undaunted, he booked another passage in a ship bound for Chile two months later. Once again, a heart attack prevented embarkation. He was scarcely permitted the labour of writing his letters and memoranda. The hope of again seeing Chile faded from day to day. The dying man faced the future with resignation and fortitude. Despite his clashes with church leaders in his days of office, he had always been a God-fearing man, and the years of exile in Montalván had found him diligent in his reading of the bible and attendance at Mass. Now, when he grew too weak to attend Mass, a small altar was installed in his sick-room.

By the beginning of October, it was clear that the end was near. The lawyer was summoned to draw up his will.[2] The possessions

---

[1] *Revista Chilena de Historia y Geografía*, Vol. 7, No. 11, 1913.
[2] Reproduced in the *Revista Chilena de Historia y Geografía*, Vol. 7, No. 11, 1913, pp. 234–43.

which O'Higgins had to bequeath were not great. He had sacrificed his inheritance in the struggle for national independence, and he now requested the Chilean government to set aside an equivalent sum with which to build an agricultural college in Concepción, a light-house in Valparaíso, and an observatory in Santiago. His half-sister Rosita was declared his general heir; but, in one final and unconscious impulse of emulation of his father, he directed that the estate of Montalván should pass after her death to Pedro Demetrio, the natural son to whom he had shown such strange indifference in his lifetime. On 23 October, 1842, Bernardo O'Higgins, Captain-General and formerly Director Supremo of independent Chile, breathed his last.

The ashes of the exile of Montalván now rest in Chile beneath a monument commemorating the services which he rendered to a tardily grateful country. What should the historian write for his epitaph? That O'Higgins was a man of heroic courage, whose exer-tions were wholly dedicated to the emancipation of his country; that he saw this cause as part of the wider vision of a free and united America, and did his utmost to prevent the nascent forces of nationalism from turning brother against brother; and that just as he showed himself a patriot yet never a chauvinist, so he chose to act as a leader and not as a *caudillo*. That he had the rare honesty to recognize his country's greatness and well-being as not inseparable from his own greatness and well-being as its undisputed ruler. He laid down office when he still retained what his old rival Carrera had once described as the Presidency of the Bayonets. This voluntary relinquishing of office that the popular will might express itself through constitutional processes, though the ruler still had the will to power and the means to enforce it, has been all too rare in the classic lands of the *pronunciamento* and the military dictatorship. Less rare, indeed, in Chile than elsewhere. In the famous Letter from Jamaica in which Simón Bolívar surveyed the prospects of the republics then struggling to be born, Chile was singled out as 'destined, by the nature of its location, by the simple and virtuous character of its people, and by the example of its neighbours, the proud republicans of Arauco, to enjoy the bless-ings that flow from the just and gentle laws of a republic'. 'If any American republic is to endure, I am inclined to believe it will be Chile,' concluded the Liberator. 'In a word, it is possible for Chile to be free.' No man, by his practice and precept, did more than Bernardo O'Higgins to make that noble prophecy come true.

Glossary

Acequia	Irrigation canal or ditch
Asesor	Civilian advisor to a governor or general
Auditor de guerra	Jurist attached to the staff of a general and responsible for legal duties
Audiencia	High Court of Justice
Bando de gobierno	Proclamation of laws and rules of conduct issued by a new governor on assuming office
Cabildo	Town Council
Cabildo abierto	Meeting of the Town Council enlarged by the inclusion of other prominent citizens
Cacique	Indian chief
Casucha	Small and roughly built house or shelter
Cecina	Dried meat
Captain-General	A royal governor independent of a viceroy and directly responsible to the Spanish Crown; also indicates the rank of Commander-in-Chief
Consulado	Merchant guild established by royal charter to perform the functions of a chamber of commerce and certain administrative and judicial duties; the building where this body meets
Caudillo	Leader or political 'boss'
Cédula	Royal decree or warrant
Chasquis	Indian messengers or carriers. Originally couriers used to transmit the Incas' commands
Charqui	Meat cut up into thin strips and preserved by being dried in the sun
Chirimoya	(*Annona cherimolia*) Juicy tropical fruit with delicious flavour
Chueca	Ball game resembling hockey played by the Araucanians
Cortes Generales	The Spanish Parliament
Creole	One born of European descent in Spanish America
Congrio	Conger-eel
	Sort of mackerel; white sea bass
Cuadra	Block of buildings or rectangular area

	comprising the subdivisions of a Spanish town
Cordillera	Mountain range; used particularly of the Andes
Encomienda	Originally a grant of Indians 'entrusted' to a conquistador or settler; by extension, the landed estate worked by such Indians
Espadín	Short sword
Flota	The fleet sailing regularly in armed convoy to convey bullion from the Indies to Spain, and Spanish goods to the Indies
Fresquero	Vendor of refreshing drinks
Gringo	Foreigner, often used to denote one of Anglo-Saxon origin
Hacienda	Country estate
Huaso	Chilean cowboy or herdsman
Inquilino	Tenant; generally used to denote labourers on a Chilean estate
	Administrative district on the French model which superseded the traditional Spanish jurisdictions in the late eighteenth century
Intendente	Governor of such a district
Junta	Board or committee
Junta de gobierno	Body of this nature vested with powers of government
Juicio de residencia	Enquiry conducted into an official's conduct of affairs, generally at the end of his tenure of office
Manto	Mantle of black silk reaching to the waist and worn over the head and shoulders in such a way as to let only one eye be seen
Maestre de campo	Commanding officer, generally of a frontier region
Matucho	Devil; epithet applied to Spaniards by Creoles
Mestizo	Half-breed; one of mixed Indian and Spanish descent
Monte	Game of chance, played with a pack of 45 cards
Palta	Avocado pear
Pampa	The Argentine plain or prairie
Pejerrey	King fish
Plaza	Town or village square
Poncho	Blanket with a slit down the middle which allows it to be worn over the head like a cloak
Real	Small coin worth the eighth part of a *peso*
Residencia	See *juicio de residencia*
Ruca	Araucanian hut or wigwam
Saya	Long, pleated skirt
Sierra	Mountain range; the uplands of Equador, Peru, and Bolivia

Tertulia	Circle of friends who meet together regularly and generally in the same place
Vecinos	Householders; residents of a Spanish town possessing traditional rights and status

Bibliographical Note

BERNARDO O'HIGGINS is the subject of an extensive literature in Spanish. This is surveyed most fully in José Zamudio's *Fuentes bibliográficas para el estudio de la vida y de la época de Bernardo O'Higgins* published in the *Boletín de la Academia de Historia* (Santiago de Chile, Nos 25, 26, and 27, 1943; 29 and 30, 1944; and 31 and 32, 1945) and more briefly in R. A. Lord's *Contribution toward a bibliography on the O'Higgins family in America* in the *Hispanic American Historical Review* (Vol 12, No 1, 1932, pp 107–143).

The basic documents for a study of O'Higgins' life and times will be found in the monumental *Archivo de don Bernardo O'Higgins*, which began publication in Santiago in 1946 and now comprises more than twenty volumes. From this rich quarry, which supersedes earlier but still useful compilations such as Ernesto de la Cruz: *Epistolario de don Bernardo O'Higgins*, (2 Vols, Santiago, 1916,) the present account, and most of the documents quoted, have been taken. Another valuable source is the *Collección de Historiadores y de Documentos relativos a la Independencia de Chile*, now running to nearly forty volumes. For the general background of the independence period I have drawn primarily on the notable histories of Diego Bárros Arana; *Historia General de Chile*, (16 Vols, Santiago, 1884 –1902), and Francisco A. Encina: *Historia de Chile*, (20 Vols, Santiago, 1940–52). Many valuable contributions to the subject are to be found in the pages of the *Revista Chilena de Historia y Geografía*, the *Boletín de la Academia de Historia*, and *Historia*, published by the Catholic University of Chile.

The narratives of British travellers and participants in the wars of independence, many of whom knew O'Higgins personally, are also indispensable and fascinating reading. Outstanding amongst these books are Thomas Cochrane, Earl of Dundonald: *Narrative of*

Services in the Liberation of Chili, Peru and Brazil (2 Vols, London, 1859); John Miller: *Memoirs of General Miller, in the Service of the Republic of Peru* (2 Vols, London, 1828); Maria Graham: *Journal of a Residence in Chile during the year 1822* (London, 1824); Captain Basil Hall: *Extracts from a Journal written on the coasts of Chile, Peru, and Mexico in the years 1820, 1821, and 1822* (2 Vols, Edinburgh, 1824); Alexander Caldcleugh: *Travels in South America during the years 1819, 1820, and 1821* (2 Vols, London, 1825); Thomas Sutcliffe: *Sixteen years in Chile and Peru, 1832–39* (London, 1841); and Samuel Haigh: *Sketches of Buenos Ayres, Chile, and Peru* (2 Vols, London, 1825).

Of the biographies of Bernardo O'Higgins, those by Benjamín Vicuña Mackenna, *El Ostracismo del General don Bernardo O'Higgins*, (Valparaíso, 1860) and *Vida del Capitán General de Chile, don Bernardo O'Higgins* (Santiago, 1882) are still valuable if somewhat too hagiographical for modern taste. Of recent biographies, the scholarly and readable works by Jaime Eyzaguirre: *O'Higgins* (Santiago, 1946) and E. Orrego Vicuña: *O'Higgins, Vida y Tiempo* (Santiago, 1946) are particularly good. For an adverse view of O'Higgins, one cannot do better than consult the apologies for his rival, José Miguel Carrera, such as Eulogio Rojas Merry: *El General Carrera en Chile* (Santiago, 1951) and Julio Alimparte: *Carrera y Freire, fundadores de la República* (Santiago, 1963). A valuable new survey of the whole period will be found in S. Collier, *Ideas and Politics of Chilean Independence* (C.U.P., 1967) which unfortunately appeared too late to be consulted in the preparation of the present work.

For the life of Bernardo's father, the standard work is Ricardo Donoso: *El Marqués de Osorno, don Ambrosio O'Higgins* (Santiago, 1941).

Index